Cold War and Counterrevolution

Also by Richard J. Walton

The Remnants of Power: The Tragic Last Years of Adlai Stevenson

America and the Cold War

Beyond Diplomacy

The United States and Latin America

RICHARD J. WALTON

Cold War and Counterrevolution

THE FOREIGN POLICY OF

JOHN F. KENNEDY

The Viking Press / NEW YORK

Again, for Richard and Catherine

Acknowledgments

Atheneum Publishers: From *John F. Kennedy, President* by Hugh Sidey. Copyright © 1963, 1964 by Hugh Sidey. Reprinted by permission of Atheneum Publishers.

Doubleday and Company, Inc.: From *To Move a Nation,* by Roger Hilsman, Copyright © 1964, 1967 by Roger Hilsman. From *Anatomy of a Crisis,* by Bernard B. Fall. Copyright © 1969 by Dorothy Fall as Executrix of the Estate of Bernard B. Fall. Both reprinted by permission of Doubleday and Company, Inc.

Harper & Row, Publishers: From *Kennedy* by Theodore C. Sorensen. Copyright © 1965 by Theodore C. Sorensen. By permission of Harper & Row, Publishers.

Houghton Mifflin Company and André Deutsch Limited: From *A Thousand Days* by Arthur M. Schlesinger, Jr. Copyright © 1965 by Arthur M. Schlesinger, Jr. Reprinted by permission of the publishers.

W. W. Norton & Company, Inc.: From *Thirteen Days, A Memoir of the Cuban Missile Crisis,* by Robert F. Kennedy. Copyright © 1969 by W. W. Norton & Company, Inc. Copyright © 1968 by McCall Corporation. Reprinted by permission.

Contents

Cold War and Counterrevolution

His untimely and violent death will affect the judgment of historians, and the danger is that it will relegate his greatness to legend. Even though he was himself almost a legendary figure in life, Kennedy was a constant critic of the myth. It would be an ironic twist of fate if his martyrdom should now make a myth of the mortal man.[1]

—THEODORE SORENSEN

CHAPTER ONE

The Beginning

Sorensen is right. It is time and past time to look at the mortal man, the Kennedy of life, not the Kennedy of legend. The legend is real, for John Fitzgerald Kennedy "seemed, in his own person, to embody all the hopes and aspiration of this new world that is struggling to emerge—to rise, Phoenix-like, from the ashes of the old."[2] Real too was the terrible grief felt not only in our land but in all others, even those we often term our enemies. The legend materialized spontaneously. It was inevitable, given the events of that terrible November day in Dallas. But beyond that, Kennedy was the stuff of which myths are made: young, handsome, heroic, with a style, grace, and vitality that most applauded and many envied. If personal specifications had been designed for the ideal postwar President, Kennedy would have fitted them. The circumstances and the man were right for myth-making, and with them came the myth-makers. Sorensen, despite his words, was one, and so was Arthur Schlesinger and so were the others. No doubt they meant to write the record as honestly as they knew how, but each must have recognized, even if only subconsciously, that he was establishing not only Kennedy's place in history but his own. They could not know what future claim they might have, but the feeling may have been inescapable that their place in history depended on his. Yet if self-justification is human, and thus almost inevitable, it would be unfair to say that this was the primary motive for books

3

often lyrical, frequently reverential, sometimes even rhapsodic. These men, intelligent and gifted all, believed what they wrote. Not only were they entirely dedicated to Kennedy but they shared his values, his attitudes, his assumptions. With minor differences, they saw the world as he did; thus they wrote as friends, colleagues, admirers, not as historians. Their accounts are indispensable, but they are biased. It is essential, if the mortal Kennedy is to survive the mythic Kennedy, to examine these same events with other eyes.

That, in the field of foreign policy, is the purpose of this book. I concentrate on foreign policy because Kennedy did. As Sorensen wrote, "Foreign affairs had always interested him far more than domestic. They occupied far more of his time and energy as President." [3] And Roger Hilsman wrote, "Certainly, he thought foreign affairs were central to his concern. He used to say that a domestic failure could hurt the country, but a failure in foreign affairs could kill it." [4]

Kennedy's admirers have written that he was free of the sterile dogmas of the Cold War, that he brought a fresh approach, a new understanding of a complex world to the exercise of American foreign policy. They see him as the representative of a new generation that understood the yearnings of the underdeveloped nations of the world for rapid and substantial change as the unimaginative Eisenhower could not and the inflexible Dulles would not. This Kennedy can be seen in the inaugural address, when he asked of "those nations who would make themselves our adversary . . . that both sides begin anew the quest for peace, before the dark powers of destruction unleashed by science engulf all humanity in planned or accidental self-destruction. . . .

"Let both sides seek to invoke the wonders of science instead of its terrors. Together let us explore the stars, conquer the deserts, eradicate disease, tap the ocean depths and encourage the arts and commerce."

This is the Kennedy the world prefers to remember, but is that the Kennedy who was President? Or was there an ambivalent Kennedy, one who sometimes spoke the conciliatory words of peace but at other times invoked the harsh words of the Cold War? This ambivalence was demonstrated in his words on the Capitol steps when he also said of "those nations who would make themselves our adversary" that "we dare not tempt them with weakness. For only when our arms are sufficient beyond doubt can we be certain beyond doubt that they will never be employed." And later he went on to say, in the rhetorical style that marked most of his formal statements, "In the long history of the world, only a few generations have been granted the role of defending freedom in its hour of maximum danger. I do not shrink from this responsibility—I welcome it." If one hand held out the olive branch, the other brandished the sword.

Which tendency would dominate, or would the two continuously contend, with first one, then the other dominant? It was clear which the Soviet Union intended to encourage. The suspicious will argue that it was merely a tactical gambit, but at 4 p.m. on Inauguration Day a friendly message from Nikita Khrushchev and Leonid Brezhnev was delivered to the White House. After congratulating Kennedy, the two Soviet leaders expressed

> . . . the hope that by our own joint efforts we shall succeed in achieving a fundamental improvement in relations between our countries and a normalization of the whole international situation. We are convinced that, step by step, it will be possible to remove existing suspicion and distrust and cultivate seeds of friendship and practical cooperation between our peoples. On its side, the Soviet Government is always ready to support any good undertakings in this direction and to do everything in its power in order that durable peace may be established in the world, so that all nations may live in friendship and without enmity.[5]

Kennedy replied in routine formal language. A few days later the Russians gave substance to their words by informing Kennedy that they would release the two survivors of a six-man RB-47 reconnaissance plane shot down by the Russians over the sea near Murmansk on July 1 the year before. As Pierre Salinger, Kennedy's press secretary, wrote, the release of Captains Freeman B. Olmstead and John R. McCone was "an obvious gesture of friendship toward the new President, and was to signal, if only briefly, a hopeful new atmosphere in our relations with the Kremlin."[6] Kennedy in his first press conference, on January 25, declared that "this action of the Soviet government removes a serious obstacle to improvement of Soviet–American relations."

For the moment it appeared that Kennedy had responded to the Soviet gestures of word and deed. The moment was brief. It was ended by John Kennedy less than a week after the release of the RB-47 fliers. On January 30 the President stepped before a joint session of Congress to deliver his first State of the Union message. This was not John Kennedy the conciliator but John Kennedy the Cold Warrior. He chilled the Congress and the nation with a bleak assessment of the world situation that went beyond even the alarms of John Foster Dulles. He told the Congress that he spoke "in an hour of national peril" and he declared that it was "by no means certain" that the nation could endure. And in the kind of language normally reserved for moments of mortal danger, Kennedy declared:

> No man entering upon this office, regardless of his party, regardless of his previous service in Washington, could fail to be staggered upon learning—even in this brief ten-day period—the harsh enormity of the trials through which we must pass in the next four years. Each day the crises multiply. Each day their solution grows more difficult. Each day we draw nearer the hour of maximum danger, as weapons spread and hostile forces grow stronger. I feel I must inform the Congress that our analyses over the last ten days make it clear that—in each of the principal areas of crisis—the tide of events has been running out and time has not been our friend.

The President left no doubt who, in his view, was to blame.

> Our greatest challenge is still the world that lies beyond the Cold War—but the first great obstacle is still our relations with the Soviet Union and Communist China. We must never be lulled into believing that either power has yielded its ambitions for world domination—ambitions which they forcefully restated only a short time ago. On the contrary, our task is to convince them that aggression and subversion will not be profitable routes to pursue these ends.[7]

This was the young President who was supposed to be free of the tired and sterile ideologies of the Cold War. This revived crusade was not to be merely a rhetorical campaign such as Dulles's. Kennedy told the men and women who would have to provide the funds of the urgent need for "a Free World force so powerful as to make any aggression clearly futile." As a first step—and Kennedy made it clear there would be others—to make American arms "sufficient beyond doubt," he said immediate measures would be taken to increase airlift capacity, to speed the Polaris submarine-building program, and to "accelerate our entire missile program."

This was only two weeks after President Eisenhower had warned in his famous farewell address of the dangers of the military-industrial complex. Kennedy was in effect accusing the lifelong soldier of not providing sufficient strength to protect American national security. As we shall see, in less than six months Kennedy was to ask for—and get—nearly $6 billion in additional defense appropriations—this despite intelligence studies already beginning to demonstrate that there was no "missile gap," criticism of which had been one of Kennedy's major campaign charges. And successive studies reduced, rather than increased, estimates of Soviet strength.

The probable dangerous consequences of such a military buildup were many, but one is immediately apparent. Whenever the United States has attempted a giant leap forward in the arms race, the Soviet Union has responded in kind, feeling, as surely the United States would feel in similar circumstances, that it had no choice. This immutable law of the postwar arms race must have been obvious to the Kennedy administration. First the United States spends a fortune that could be put to better use; then the Soviet Union spends a fortune that it can afford even less. Both sides are poorer in money spent and needs unmet, yet neither is relatively any stronger, and international tensions have been increased. One can always hope that the other side, for whatever reason, will decide not to respond, but Kennedy could have had no such hope. In December 1960 Walt W. Rostow and Jerome B. Wiesner, who were soon to hold high posts in the Kennedy administration, were among the Americans at informal disarmament talks in Moscow. They met with V.V. Kuznetsov, one of Andrei Gromyko's top aides in the Soviet Foreign Office. He expressed concern over Kennedy's emphasis on the "missile gap" and asserted that the Russians could not be expected to stand still if Kennedy went in for massive rearmament. Rostow, Schlesinger writes, "replied that any Kennedy rearmament would be designed to improve the stability of the deterrent, and that the Soviet Union should recognize this as in the higher interests of peace" [8] Although Kuznetsov as a communist could hardly have been a stranger to Orwellian logic, he could not accept the premise that weaker was stronger.

Kennedy began a swift and massive military buildup nonetheless —despite Kuznetsov's specific warning, despite the fact that the times were comparatively tranquil, despite Khrushchev's gestures of goodwill, despite Eisenhower's warning, and despite the administration's increasing realization that the Soviet Union was much weaker than the United States. This was no sudden, uncharacteristic, and temporary turnabout in Kennedy policy. Though middle-aged liberals may find it difficult to remember, as I did until I sought out the record, Kennedy's campaign had been dominated by a hard-line, get-tough attack on communism. Perhaps we did not remember because we did not really listen. We were all so eager for Kennedy to defeat the despised Nixon that we just assumed that what he said was acceptable. Kennedy was a liberal, wasn't he? Well, almost a liberal. He had inherited Stevenson's mantle, liberals such as Schlesinger and Galbraith and Bowles were flocking to his banner—and writing his speeches. But what many of us did not realize was that by far the biggest group of liberals in the Kennedy camp was composed of hard-line anti-communists, more elegant, less dogmatic than the McCarthy-Nixon-Mundt hawks, to be sure, but hawks nonetheless. Blinded by our passion to defeat Nixon, we did not really listen to Kennedy.

But to understand the man who became President and to understand what he did, particularly in the first two years of his administration, it is necessary to re-examine what he said during the 1960 campaign. For Kennedy, much more than most politicians, practiced in power what he preached in its pursuit. There is no shortage of hawkish statements in Kennedy's earlier Congressional years, but those perhaps could be attributed to his father's influence, his Catholicism, or his constituency. But the following are some of the statements in the weeks preceding the election—and they are not isolated or atypical—of the man who was to bring a new look to American foreign policy.

On August 24, 1960, at Alexandria, Virginia, Kennedy said:

. . . We standing here tonight cannot, with certainty, make a judgment of our times or the last five years or the last decade.

But I think there is a great danger that history will make a judgment that these were the days when the tide began to run out for the United States. These were the times when the communist tide began to pour in. These were the times when people began not to worry about what they thought in Washington, but only to wonder what they thought in Moscow and Peking. I run for the office of the Presidency not because I think it is an easy job in soft times. I think it is going to be the most difficult and hazardous year in our country's history. This is a time of danger. . . .

During the past eight years that he [Nixon] has presided over the National Security Council, never in all that time in our country's history has our strength declined more rapidly than it has during the comparable period, in terms of defensive strength and retaliatory capacity, in terms of our alliances, in terms of our scientific effort, and our national reputation.[9]

Nixon did not really preside over the National Security Council, but Kennedy made the attack in this way because he did not dare make it against Eisenhower, who had been responsible for national policy. And such an attack, had it been made by Nixon instead of against him, would have caused outraged liberal cries of a campaign of fear and dissension.

On September 20 at Washington, Kennedy called for a swift military buildup of nuclear and conventional arms. "Only then can we get Mr. Khrushchev and the Chinese communists to talk about disarmament, because having the second best defensive hand in the 1960s will be like having the second best poker hand." [10] The speech was not only marked by this glib and superficial remark but contained a brief passage—almost funny now—that raised campaign hyperbole to new heights. "But there is very little time. The enemy is lean and hungry and the United States is the only strong sentinel at the gate."

On September 23 Kennedy outdid himself, perhaps influenced by the place, the Mormon Tabernacle in Salt Lake City.

The enemy is the communist system itself—implacable, insatiable, unceasing in its drive for world domination. For this is not a struggle for the supremacy of arms alone—it is also a struggle for supremacy between two conflicting ideologies: Freedom under God versus ruthless, godless tyranny.[11]

It is possible to dismiss these statements as attempts, however dubious, to outflank Nixon on the right or, in the most extreme cases, to make a calculated political appeal to a particular audience. Yet there is a consistency to them—and those quoted are only a small sampling—and it is observable fact that Kennedy's words and deeds after his inauguration indicate that they represented his deep convictions.

It must be made clear that his was not the kind of free-swinging anti-communism of which Joe McCarthy would have approved. It was tough, to be sure, but cool. As President, Kennedy slapped down, quickly and hard, any attempts to revive a latter-day McCarthyism. As Sorensen justly points out:

> The young Congressman who voted for the McCarran Internal Security Act, and who was—by his own admission—insufficiently sensitive to the ruin of reputations by McCarthyism, became the President who awarded the Enrico Fermi prize to the much-abused J. Robert Oppenheimer, pardoned communist leader Junius Scales, halted the postal interception of communist propaganda, welcomed the controversial Linus Pauling into the White House, and appointed to his administration several of McCarthy's favorite targets.[12]

Yet, although Kennedy often spoke of the aspirations of the Third World with a sincerity that demonstrated a great divergence from the neutrality-is-immoral concept of John Foster Dulles, when it came to communism itself, Kennedy was no less moralistic. Where Dulles was generally content with rhetoric, Kennedy embarked, as we shall see, on an anti-communist crusade much more dangerous than any policy Eisenhower ever permitted. It reached its fearsome climax in the Cuban missile crisis, which seemed to sober Kennedy and his inner circle. From crusade, Kennedy shifted in his last months to a selective détente, this last marked by his enduring speech at American University—one that Khrushchev later told Averell Harriman was "the greatest speech by any American President since Roosevelt." [13]

The capital city, somnolent in the Eisenhower years, had suddenly come alive. The air had been stale and oppressive; now fresh winds were blowing. There was the excitement which comes from the injection of new men and new ideas, the release of energy which occurs when men of ideas have a chance to put them into practice.[1]

— ARTHUR SCHLESINGER

CHAPTER TWO

The First Crisis

It was an exciting time. Even such medium-grade civil servants as I felt the excitement that swirled through the city. At last something was going to happen. It all seemed good. The Alliance for Progress was in its short, and very public, gestation period. The Kennedy administration moved swiftly and effectively to win the friendship of the new African nations by a dramatic reversal of the Eisenhower policy on the Portuguese colony of Angola. Adlai Stevenson in the UN Security Council voted for a resolution that would have established a subcommittee to investigate the situation in Angola, where Portugal was trying to put down an African rebellion. The resolution was defeated by the Council—only the three Afro–Asian sponsors, the United States, and the USSR voting for it—but there was a wave of jubilation in the UN. The new American administration had lived up to its promise and had voted with the Afro–Asians. Kennedy put pressure on Chiang Kai-shek to remove Nationalist troops still left in Burma from the war. And, again at the UN, Stevenson rode to the rescue of Secretary General Dag Hammarskjöld, whom the Russians had bitterly attacked in the Security Council as responsible for the death of Patrice Lumumba in the Congo.

More important decisions were made less publicly, decisions that were to adversely affect the course of American history for more than a decade. The massive military buildup was being planned, as was the invasion of Cuba at the Bay of Pigs. But what most preoccupied Kennedy in the first two months was Laos. He established a special task force on that subject and told it he wanted daily reports. The Laos "mess," Eisenhower told Kennedy the day before the inauguration, was the most difficult situation he was bequeathing to his successor. "You might have to go in there and fight it out." [2]

Kennedy did not want to go in there and fight it out, but the Eisenhower mess was bad and bewildering. Any detailed account of it would trap the reader—and the writer—in a bizarre Byzantine tangle of plots and counterplots, bloodthirsty communiqués and bloodless battles, incompetence and corruption. (Were it not for their tragic consequences, the United States' attempts to Americanize placid, peaceful, exotic Laos would have made marvelous costume comic opera.) But a brief account is necessary for any understanding of Kennedy's decisions. [3]

When the Indochina war ended in 1954, Dulles decided that Laos must not be permitted to fall to the communists, so he took it under the wing of his newly formed South East Asia Treaty Organization (SEATO). That was only the beginning. The United States then decided to make Laos a bulwark of anti-communism with a strong little army of 25,000 men trained and supplied by Americans. After two or three years of incredible blundering by the United States, it became obvious to pro-Western Prince Souvanna Phouma that his country could be saved from communism only if it had a militarily neutral government. After endless negotiations, both complex and comic, with a number of unstable factions and with the much more stable pro-communist Pathet Lao (led by his tough and competent half-brother, Prince Souphanouvong), Souvanna Phouma finally put together a coalition government. Then with extraordinary diplomacy he went to Peking and Hanoi and got their approval for the government that, although formally neutralist, was pro-Western. Returning to Laos in November 1957, he capped his achievement by getting the Pathet Lao to agree to muster out most of its army and integrate what little remained into the Royal Laotian Army.

When you consider that this was all done on the doorsteps of China and North Vietnam, this delicate balancing act should have occasioned hurrahs in Washington. But no, Souvanna Phouma's triumph was brusquely dismissed, the CIA and the State Department (sometimes supporting contending factions) barged in, toppled the coalition, and in four years totted up these achievements: wasted most of a half billion dollars in aid, so corrupted the army that it usually turned tail and fled as soon as (and sometimes before) a shot was fired, pushed China and Russia into supporting the Pathet Lao so it grew powerful enough to conquer most of Laos, caused Hanoi to discard the restraints imposed by its agreement with Souvanna Phouma, and began a chain of misery for the Laotian people that has no end in sight.[4]

Although most American press coverage during these years was grossly incompetent, there was some limited knowledge outside the executive branch of what was really happening. In June 1959, when the House Committee on Government Operations reported on the situation in Laos, it found that ". . . *U.S. support of a 25,000-man army [and] of the entire military budget . . . is, in fact, based on a political determination, made by the Department of State contrary to the recommendations of the Joint Chiefs of Staff.* In Laos, the only country in the world where the United States supports the military budget 100 per cent, military judgments have been disregarded."[5] The United States military has never been reluctant to build up anti-communist armies all over the world, but it believed it unrealistic to establish an army on such unpromising ground, where the nation presumably threatened did not spend a penny for its own defense.

After Souvanna Phouma was displaced in 1958, the political pendulum swung back and forth without much real change. But for the right-wing, pro-American government in power, the nationwide legislative elections set for April 24, 1960, seemed like too good a bet to overlook. The government more or less openly made thorough preparations to rig the elections. It succeeded. In one Pathet Lao stronghold, for instance, the Pathet Lao candidate got four votes while his opponent piled up 18,189.[6] In another district the government nominee got 2000 more votes than there were voters. Not a single Pathet Lao or even neutralist candidate had won a seat of the fifty-nine at stake.

While this no doubt pleased Washington, it did not please Prince Souphanouvong, who had been arrested nearly a year before. He had been, along with fourteen Pathet Lao associates, a model prisoner in a camp on the outskirts of Vientiane. Reportedly they tended a little garden, did some physical exercise, read the newspapers and their mail, and talked with their guards. They must have been fairly good talkers, for when they escaped, on the night of May 23, they took most of their guards, an elite police force, with them.

Once again it seemed that civil war would come to the peace-loving Laotians, but the pro-American government had some confidence. Not only had the Pathet Lao forces voluntarily been dispersed, but the government had a crack paratroop battalion commanded by a tough French- and American-trained soldier, Captain Kong-Lê. For a couple of months not much happened. In the heavy rainy season the Pathet Lao had done some fighting but not much. However, in early August Kong-Lê and some of his staff officers of the Second Lao Paratroop Battalion got their American and French advisers to go through a tactical exercise: how to hold and defend a major city. The young Laotian officers suggested that it would be more realistic if they chose Vientiane for their exercise. Their Western advisers were pleased with their students' enterprise, and they went through the defense of Vientiane step by step.

At 3 a.m. on August 9 the paratroopers struck Vientiane and by 7 a.m. had control of the city. The captain of a lower-class ethnic minority had completely fooled his own government and its French and American advisers. And he carried out his stunning attack with a sophistication that merits examination. Each of his soldiers wore medal-fashion around his neck a tiny transistor radio provided by American aid. It was tuned to Radio Vientiane, one of the first places occupied. From there the officers directed their men from target to target.

This young product of American Special Forces training went on the radio immediately and called on Laotians "to quit killing other Laotians." He demanded a "policy of genuine neutrality" and, most shocking of all, he attacked "a great power" which was infiltrating "every organization in the country. Even my own battalion," said Kong-Lê, "has ten Americans attached to it, whom the government has allowed to infiltrate us."

Kong-Lê's motivation for the coup was made more evident a few days later, when he declared:

> What leads us to carry out this revolution is our desire to stop the bloody civil war; eliminate grasping public servants [and] military commanders . . . whose property amounts to much more than their monthly salaries can afford; and chase away foreign armed forces as soon as possible. . . . It is the Americans who have bought government officials and army commanders, and caused war and dissension in our country. . . . All Laotians must remain wide awake and not allow themselves to be led like ignoramuses. We must help each other drive those sellers of the Fatherland out of the country as soon as possible. Only then can our country live in peace.[7]

While Kennedy and Nixon were flailing away at each other in the United States, the situation in Laos developed in characteristic confusion. Kong-Lê hastily formed a forty-man Provisional Executive Committee which included not only left-wingers but Prince Souvanna Phouma. The prince announced the following day that his name had been used without his permission and proceeded to call into session the Laotian National Assembly. (In the latest switch of hats he had become its president.) Premier Somsanith was in the royal capital, Luangprabang, and the pro-American General Phoumi Nosavan fled to his stronghold in the south, Savannakhet.

Although the National Assembly was dominated by right-wing, pro-American legislators, they had no real support, and in less than three hours the pro-American government was "voted" out of office, the legislators perhaps influenced by the hundreds of battle-dressed paratroopers with tanks and armored cars ringing the assembly building.

Souvanna Phouma again tried to put together the kind of neutralist coalition the Americans had wrecked two years earlier. But now the newly organized Pathet Lao was stronger, less willing to negotiate, and it was doubtful that Peking and Hanoi would be as cooperative as they had been. And there were still the Americans to contend with. Washington's hand had lost none of its skill. Although the Kong-Lê–Souvanna Phouma regime was more or less recognized, American aid shifted to General Phoumi.

This, then, was the picture. Kong-Lê and Souvanna Phouma had the administrative capital but out in the countryside the Pathet Lao was grabbing land, making particular gains in the north. While harassed in this manner by his half-brother, Souvanna Phouma was also embarrassed by General Phoumi. For security reasons most of the Laotian Army supplies were in the south, where Phoumi could control them, and he was preparing an offensive against the government. Souvanna Phouma had the bulk of the Laotian aircraft, but his forces suffered from a severe shortage of fuel and food supplies, while thousands of tons of American aid meant for Laos piled up in Bangkok warehouses. To complicate things, Marshal Sarit Thanarat of Thailand, a supporter of the United States and General Phoumi, imposed a blockade against both the Pathet Lao and the government.

On September 18 there was the extraordinary spectacle of a mortar and machine-gun barrage against Vientiane from the Thai side of the Mekong River. That is, an American-supported faction was attacking, with American weapons, an American-supported government. The tragicomedy developed further when General Phoumi began his campaign upriver against Vientiane. On September 22 his tank-supported force of 1200 men ran into a few hundred of Kong-Lê's paratroops. In the finest tradition of the American-trained, American-financed Royal Laotian Army, Phoumi's army simply fled, leaving the paratroopers a windfall of brand-new American weapons. This encounter raises the fundamental question about United States intervention in Indochina: why do "our" guys so often run and "their" guys almost always fight?

Thus, by the end of September the chaos was complete, and a three-cornered civil war was in progress. What was Washington doing to sort out the mess for which it was largely to blame? It did not know what to do. Laos and Washington were like two mirrors, each reflecting the confusion of the other. On September 25, General Williston B. Palmer, director of the Pentagon's military-assistance program, who happened to be in Bangkok, declared that United States aid to Laos would be "slowed down" until the situation became clearer. A week later, in Manila, he amplified his statement and said all military aid to Laos was "suspended." But the Voice of America, the official United States radio, broadcast to the Far East that press reports had "misrepresented General Palmer's intentions and misinterpreted United States policy." The United States Embassy in Vientiane then reported that "American aid not only had *not* been suspended but was in fact being used to pay both the Laotian troops under control of the Laotian government recognized by Washington and those which, under the command of General Phoumi, were in active rebellion against that government—surely one of the most unusual instances of United States aid distribution." [8] Further clarification came on October 7, when Prime Minister Souvanna Phouma reported that his government was receiving neither military nor financial aid from the United States. With this the State Department turned around and admitted that it had stopped aid to Laos.

While these clarifications proliferated, the Prime Minister continued his efforts on behalf of a coalition, neutralist government, efforts encouraged by Great Britain, co-chairman of the 1954 Geneva Conference, which ended the Indochina war, and by France, which still had responsibilities in Laos under the 1954 agreement. But neither had much influence in Washington. Neither had the American Embassy and the middle echelons of the State Department, both of which vigorously advocated neutrality. At the higher levels of the Eisenhower administration, despite Dulles's death, the old rigidities persisted.

Christian A. Herter, Dulles's successor, decided that something had to be done, but what he did could not have been worse. He sent to Vientiane to talk with Souvanna Phouma none other than Assistant Secretary J. Graham Parsons, who, as Ambassador to Laos, had been chiefly responsible for destroying the Prime Minister's earlier coalition government. Even apart from that, the two men despised each other. The auguries were not good, and it was hardly surprising that Parsons did not succeed in getting Souvanna Phouma to alter his position.

Students of political irony will be interested to note that while Parsons was trying to recruit Souvanna Phouma, a Soviet ambassador had arrived in the country for the first time. Just at the time that Souvanna Phouma and Parsons were making the final break, Laos accredited its first Soviet Ambassador, Alexander Abramov, who promptly offered economic aid that the Prime Minister said he was "very happy" to accept. He had little choice, since Vientiane was desperately in need of supplies. The United States responded by resuming the payment of the salaries of both the government and the right-wing rebel forces.

Then General Phoumi—acting, it is generally agreed, with the encouragement of the CIA—pulled off a coup in the royal capital, Luangprabang, thus gaining for his side the person of the King. This was on November 12, after Kennedy had been elected. Phoumi's forces, strengthened with additional American equipment and American advisers, began to move toward Vientiane. Kong-Lê's paratroopers began digging trenches outside Vientiane and rolled into place new artillery and heavy mortars airlifted in by the Soviet Union. The Pathet Lao guerrilla leader turned up in Vientiane in full American battle dress. Souvanna Phouma at this extreme stage evidently found his position untenable, so he resigned and went into exile.

On December 13 General Phoumi began the three-day battle for Vientiane, which left the city a shambles. Bernard Fall, whose dispatches from Indochina were by far the best, wrote bitterly of the American press:

> Here also, the reporting in the American press differed widely from that of its British and French counterparts. While the former reported mainly the military aspects of the fighting, the latter emphasized the needless human suffering that had been caused by it: The fact that *five hundred* civilian casualties had been inflicted while the contending armed forces lost but a handful of dead, the fact that the armored vehicles of Phoumi (Kong-Lê had no armor) literally used defenseless civilians in the streets for target practice, that the French military hospital (one of whose two doctors went back on duty three days after having been operated on for appendicitis because of the overflow of Laotian wounded) had been the object of particularly vicious machine-gun fire in spite of the fact that its location was perfectly well known and that it flew a large Red Cross flag—all that went unreported in the United States.[9]

The polarization was now complete. The United States had succeeded in pushing into the communist camp Laotians who actually wanted a pro-Western government but who had been spurned by Washington and then attacked by forces advised, equipped, and financed by the United States.

This was the "mess" in Laos that Kennedy inherited. He was

hardly to be blamed for not immediately knowing what to do. Schlesinger writes that Kennedy thought Laos not "worthy of engaging the attention of great powers," that attempts to make it a pro-Western bastion had been absurd. "But he knew that the matter was not that simple any longer. For the effort had been made, American prestige was deeply involved and extrication would not be easy." [10] In his first press conference, on January 25, Kennedy said that he was "anxious that there be established in Laos a peaceful country—an independent country not dominated by either side but concerned with the life of the people within the country. . . . And the United States is using its influence to see if that independent country, peaceful country, uncommitted country, can be established under the present very difficult circumstances."

It may well be, as his admirers have written, that Kennedy quickly recognized that a neutral Laos was the only rational goal. Yet for a while he continued the discredited Eisenhower policy. In early February, Phoumi was allowed to open another campaign. The Pentagon assured the President that the Plaine des Jarres could be swiftly recaptured from the joint Kong-Lê–Pathet Lao forces. This prediction was as realistic as most predictions the American armed forces have made about Indochina. Before long the Royal Laotian Army again turned tail, again covering its rear with a barrage of communiqués about bloody fighting. Then the pro-American government in Vientiane resorted to an old trick, declaring that Laos had been invaded by communist forces—variously North Vietnamese, Chinese, and Russian. Whereas once the American press had swallowed such stories whole, now they were promptly dismissed as nonsense. Vientiane tried fabricating in press releases victories it didn't even try to win on the battlefield. But any hope that Kennedy might have had that Phoumi's forces could win or even stabilize the situation must have vanished on March 7, when Kong-Lê struck hard at the royalist lines and the American-trained, American-supplied regulars fled in panic.

Kennedy needed a new plan. Frantic planning went on behind the scenes, and urgent talks were held in various capitals. In his March 15 news conference, Kennedy again advocated a "genuinely independent and neutral Laos, which is the master of its own fate." But now he tried to blame the Pathet Lao, the neutralists, and their Russian supporters for the troubles: "However, recent attacks by rebel forces indicate that a small minority backed by personnel and supplies from outside is seeking to prevent the establishment of a neutral and independent country. We are determined to support the government and people of Laos in resisting this attempt." Because the American people, and even the American press, knew so little about the actual circumstances in Laos, it was easy for the President thus to distort the facts. The current series of military engagements had been started by General Phoumi. Even if his successful anti-neutralist coup had taken place while Eisenhower was still in office, the renewed drive against Kong-Lê and the Pathet Lao had been allowed to start under Kennedy with the new administration's approval. Kong-Lê had accepted Soviet military aid because his opponents were even more handsomely supplied by the Americans. The Kong-Lê–Pathet Lao advances were the inevitable consequence of Phoumi's incompetent, irresolute attacks. In short, the whole disastrous chain of events begun under Eisenhower had been allowed to continue under Kennedy.

However the administration's public statements departed from the facts, privately those facts had to be dealt with. The American position in Laos was on the verge of collapse. (Not only did Kennedy have to face the clamor of opposing views on Laos; he was in these same crowded days moving toward a decision on the Bay of Pigs, discussing plans for a rapid military buildup, coping with the chaos in the Congo, plus dealing with the untold number of major and minor decisions to be made by the young, activist administration.) According to the insiders, the administration considered a wide range of possibilities on Laos, from doing nothing, to sending a small, symbolic contingent of troops to pressure the Russians to accept a neutralist government, all the way to sending 60,000 troops complete with air cover, with the use of nuclear weapons not excluded. Kennedy quickly rejected doing nothing. To do nothing "would shake the faith of every small nation we were pledged to protect," particularly South Vietnam and Thailand. Kennedy, like Eisenhower, could see the dominoes falling. But his crucial concern was this: "We cannot and will not accept any visible humiliation over Laos." [11] Several times during his administration Kennedy expressed this fear of losing face—not, perhaps, the best basis for foreign policy. Often, as we shall see, appearances were more important to him than reality. It seemed never to occur to Kennedy and his advisers that whenever the Laotians were left to themselves they worked out some sort of accommodation based on national realities, however wondrous strange their methods might seem in Washington. Nor is it easy to imagine, as a result of American inaction, any more "costly" embarrassment in Indochina than what overtook Kennedy and his successors despite his initiatives in Laos.

Kennedy decided that the communists would agree to a neutral Laos only if he demonstrated that any other course might be dangerous. At his televised March 23 press conference a somber Kennedy stood before three maps of Laos showing Pathet Lao advances. His language was grim.

> If there is to be a peaceful solution, there must be a cessation of the present armed attacks by externally supported communists. If these attacks do not stop, those who support a truly neutral Laos will have to consider their response. The shape of the necessary response will, of course, be carefully considered, not only here in Washington, but in the SEATO conference with our allies, which begins next Monday.
>
> SEATO—the Southeast Asia Treaty Organization—was organized in 1954, with strong leadership from our last administration, and all members of SEATO have undertaken special treaty responsibilities towards an aggression in Laos.
>
> No one should doubt our resolution on this point.

Roger Hilsman, one of Kennedy's top advisers on Laos, later wrote bluntly, "The implication was war." [12] Hilsman was, no doubt, overstating the case. More likely, Kennedy hoped that tough talk would avoid the necessity for tough action. But his press conference merits closer examination, for it throws considerable light on Kennedy's policy in all Southeast Asia and on the way successive American governments have discussed Indochina in the past decade.

In the first place, Kennedy engaged in the rewriting of history. He said in his opening statement that Laos "contained contending factions, but in its first years real progress was made towards a unified and neutral status. But the efforts of a communist-dominated group to destroy this neutrality never ceased." The facts are quite the contrary. It was the United States that attempted to use Laos as a pawn in the Cold War and it was the United States that on several occasions sabotaged a neutralist government.

Kennedy went on to say, "In the last half of 1960 a series of sudden maneuvers occurred and the communists and their supporters turned to a new and greatly intensified military effort to take over." Again, as we have seen, this is not so. It was General Phoumi who, under both Eisenhower and Kennedy, attempted to take over, triggering the successful counterattacks by the combined neutralist and Pathet Lao forces. And the President spoke of "externally supported warfare that creates the present grave problem," as if Russian military supplies had not been accepted by the Souvanna Phouma government only because American supplies had been cut off. And, of course, Russian supplies had been arriving for only a few months, whereas American military supplies and payments, to the amount of some $200 million, had been pouring into Laos since 1954. Total American aid to Laos had been over $300 million, the highest per-capita aid to any country in the world. This lack of candor, to give them the benefit of what little doubt there may be, has characterized public presidential statements on Indochina for at least a decade.

Though Kennedy was less than scrupulous about the facts in this press conference, there is no reason to doubt the genuineness of his statement that he wanted "to make it clear to the American people and to all of the world that all we want in Laos is peace, not war; a truly neutral government, not a Cold War pawn; a settlement concluded at the conference table and not on the battlefield." And in an oblique way he acknowledged that there might have been some doubt about the depth of Washington's commitment to neutrality: "And if in the past there has been any possible ground for misunderstanding of our desire for a truly neutral Laos, there should be none now."

Yet Kennedy's concern for peace followed the customary postwar American course, based on the old conviction that the communists prepared for peace only if the United States prepared for war. A couple of days after the press conference, Kennedy flew down to Key West for an urgently arranged meeting with Prime Minister Harold Macmillan, who was vacationing in the Caribbean. Macmillan, who had the gravest doubts of the success of any Western military intervention in Laos, reluctantly agreed to send a token contingent of British troops to the Mekong should it prove necessary. De Gaulle gave a flat no to a similar request.

From Washington orders went out to make the customary moves on the military chessboard. Troops were alerted on Okinawa, the Seventh Fleet moved closer, 500 Marines with helicopters landed in Thailand across the Mekong from Vientiane. In Bangkok, at the SEATO meeting, Secretary of State Dean Rusk got pledges of troops from Thailand, the Philippines, and Pakistan, although French opposition prevented any positive response by SEATO itself.

On April 1, Nikita Khrushchev announced that he was ready to accept, in principle, Britain's earlier suggestion that another Geneva Conference be called, this one to establish a neutral Laos. Again Kennedy's admirers have asserted that the President's resolution, his skillful balancing of military and diplomatic factors, induced Khrushchev to agree to a conference. This accords with the doctrine that communist reasonableness is almost invariably the result of American resolution. But it seems a dubious assumption that Moscow, Peking, and Hanoi *never* adopt a rational course for reasons of their own. This has been a terrible flaw in American foreign-policy-making since the end of World War II. Washington has seen the world only with its own eyes; it has seldom attempted to see through the eyes of its adversaries or even of its allies. Perhaps seized by ideological fervor, it has seldom seemed to consider trying to understand why other governments do what they do, to understand that other governments, friendly or otherwise, have their own reasons for action and that these reasons do not necessarily have anything to do with the United States. Washington has become ethnocentric and sees the whole world as an extension of itself—inevitably to respond even to a pinprick at the most remote extremity. It has come to see the United States not as one nation among many, however significant, but as *the* nation whose burdens and responsibilities and commitments can never be relinquished. No doubt Kennedy's posture was an influence on Khrushchev's acceptance of the idea of another Geneva Conference. Or maybe Khrushchev simply did not see any point in getting involved over Laos, particularly when he believed, as he told Ambassador Llewellyn Thompson, "Why take risks over Laos? It will fall into our laps like a ripe apple." [13] Or maybe Khrushchev did not think that Laos was all that important.

But agreement in Washington and Moscow was one thing; agreement on the scene was another.

Kennedy was upset that Khrushchev had not succeeded in imposing a cease-fire on the neutralist–Pathet Lao forces. Perhaps he should have known from his own experience that events in Laos did not always swiftly respond to decisions made in distant capitals. Maybe Khrushchev was in no hurry for a cease-fire while the Pathet Lao was doing so well. Perhaps he had to consult with Peking and Hanoi. Most likely, however, events in Laos had developed their own momentum.

While all the geopolitical maneuvering was going on in various capitals, American officials in Laos decided on a carefully planned and executed counterattack. This time, to make sure nothing went wrong, American advisers accompanied the royal troops. The counterattack began on April 5. By April 14 the government troops were in full retreat. It was obvious now why the Kennedy administration was insisting on a cease-fire as a first step in the resolution of the Laos war. If the fighting continued much longer, virtually all Laos would be in the hands of the neutralist–Pathet Lao forces before the conference convened.

For a few days Kennedy's attention was necessarily diverted by the fiasco developing at the Bay of Pigs. But events in Laos allowed him no time to brood over that smarting defeat. To prove that the American failure to ensure the success of a Bay of Pigs landing was not caused by weakness of will, Kennedy tried to demonstrate anew American resolution by ordering United States advisers in Laos to doff their civilian clothes (which had fooled no one) and put on their uniforms. This they did on April 20, and four days later Kong-Lê captured his first uniformed Americans, a captain and three sergeants. They had been abandoned by Royal Laotian troops when the Pathet Lao suddenly overran the important town of Vang Vieng.

On April 27, according to Schlesinger, the National Security Council held "a long and confused session. Walt Rostow has told me that it was the worst White House meeting he attended in the entire Kennedy administration." [14] There was some sentiment from the Laos task force for a limited intervention if a cease-fire were not soon achieved, but the military now suggested that the 60,000 troops it had recommended earlier would not be enough.

Although, according to accounts of the meeting, the Pentagon's plans seemed sketchy and poorly considered, the current recommendation seemed to be at least 140,000 men armed with tactical nuclear weapons. There was even some talk about perhaps being forced to nuclear-bomb Hanoi and even Peking.

It was after the Bay of Pigs, however, and Kennedy was not so willing to accept so-called expert advice. By chance, on that very day he saw General Douglas MacArthur, who strongly recommended against sending troops to the mainland of Asia. American allies were dragging their heels, and even the most anti-communist members of Congress were not ready to advocate sending United States troops to Laos. Nor would it be easy for Kennedy to justify to the American people sending troops to fight communism halfway around the world when he would not send them ninety miles to fight communism in Cuba.

Even so, Kennedy was still considering military intervention of some sort when, on May 1, representatives of the warring sides in Laos negotiated a cease-fire. It went into effect on May 3, and on May 11 the newly revived International Control Commission of the 1954 Geneva Conference reported general observance. Finally, on May 16, after a couple of days of procedural wrangling, the conference began what were to be endless sessions. Whatever Kennedy's motives and however little his diplomatic and military moves had contributed to that end, the President had moved a significant step away from the Eisenhower administration's discredited and wholly unsuccessful attempts to make the pacific and remote Laotians soldiers in the anti-communist crusade.

This move was not entirely popular at home, and many in politics and the press were bitter in their criticism. Joseph Alsop, a close friend of the President, began to establish his incontestable claim to the eminence of "superhawk" by calling Kennedy's action nothing less than the recognition of defeat. The Kennedys have never been keen on defeat, and attacks from such natural allies as Alsop must have pained the President. One can only speculate how much such attacks influenced his thinking on the even more crucial question of Vietnam.

Although for most of the rest of Kennedy's administration Laos remained on the back burner, it did have moments when it reasserted its claim to presidential attention. Both Russia and the

United States were having difficulty with their client factions in Laos, exemplifying, to use Roger Hilsman's words, what the United States was to learn even more tragically in Vietnam, "that it is sometimes difficult, most great powers discover, to avoid becoming the satellite of one's 'satellites.' " [15]

The Geneva talks were recessed while Kennedy and Khrushchev held their historic meeting in Vienna in early June. Although the minutes of those two days of talks have yet to be made public, the conversations can be pretty well reconstructed from the accounts of those close to Kennedy. It is clear the Khrushchev simply was not very interested in Laos and preferred to discuss Germany and the general question of "wars of national liberation." However, Kennedy pressed him on Laos. He said he hoped they could agree on Laos. Even though it had no strategic importance to either side, the United States had treaty commitments. Nonetheless, the United States wanted to reduce its involvement in Laos.

Khrushchev responded that the Soviets had no desire to assume responsibilities in remote areas and pointed out that Russia was in Laos only at the request of Souvanna Phouma. He referred to Souvanna as the legitimate leader of Laos, whereas the United States had recognized the right-wing regime that had forced him into exile. Khrushchev also took issue with the concept of American commitments. He said that America was so rich and powerful that it claimed rights for itself that it denied to others. He told Kennedy that if the United States really wanted to normalize the world situation and avoid confrontations, it must renounce its claims to special rights.

Kennedy conceded that United States policy in Laos might not always have been wise, but he said that American commitments had been made before he was President. In any case, whatever had happened was in the past. The task now was for both sides to reduce their commitments and get a truly neutral, independent Laos. Khrushchev was not quite ready to let Kennedy off the hook. He expressed doubt that all the American commitments were a legacy. He pointed out that Kennedy had put United States military advisers into uniform and had alerted American forces in Asia. Nonetheless he said that the Soviet Union would exert every effort to establish a genuinely neutral government. He suggested, with characteristic earthy humor, that he and Kennedy should lock up their foreign ministers together until they came up with a solution. Khrushchev also agreed to make observance of the shaky cease-fire a matter of priority. This, according to all published accounts, was the only firm agreement reached at Vienna. Although Kennedy and Khrushchev obviously found themselves in deep disagreement on other questions, the dialogue on this issue was reasonable. Indeed, Khrushchev, who had most of the political and strategic cards in his hand, was downright conciliatory.

With the Kennedy–Khrushchev talks over, the Geneva talks resumed. Since Laos was being discussed, naturally the talks were chaotic. The princely heads of the three factions—Pathet Lao, neutralist, and right-wing—were forever stalking out of the conference, their sensibilities offended by something or other. And there were discussions of theological subtlety about gradations of neutrality. It was an international conference largely because the United States had wanted it one, but the basic problems could be solved only by the Laotians themselves. They seemed in no hurry.

Finally, in mid-September, while most of Washington was preoccupied with the "Berlin crisis," an impatient Averell Harriman flew to Laos. He saw Souvanna Phouma, who was still eager for a settlement; the King, Savang Vathana, who, although he tried to remain aloof from day-to-day politics, had great influence; and General Phoumi and his princely supporter, Boun Oum. Harriman did not attempt to hide his impatience. Perhaps his visit was responsible; in any event the three factions announced on October 8, 1961, that they had agreed that Souvanna should head a new provisional coalition government. This was to have sixteen members, four each from the Pathet Lao and the right wing, and eight neutralist supporters of Souvanna. Again Souvanna succeeded in putting together a coalition government. But there was a big difference.

Almost to the day, the Laotian crisis was exactly where it had begun four years earlier on November 2, 1957, when Souvanna Phouma had formed his first coalition regime, which included two Pathet Lao leaders.

There were a few far-ranging differences, however. Instead of two communists in Cabinet positions, there would be four now; instead of having to deal with 1500 poorly armed Pathet Lao fighters, there were close to 10,000 now, well-armed with new Soviet weapons; instead of being neutral without ties to a communist country, Laos now had diplomatic relations with almost all of them; in addition to assistance rendered by American and French technicians, it was now to receive aid from several Soviet bloc countries (including Red China and North Vietnam); and instead of being able to count on either the "umbrella clause" of SEATO or the as yet unchallenged readiness of the West to support it, Laos was now completely isolated from effective help when it needed it most. Finally, in spite of the enormous sums of money which it had received from the United States, it is today as poor as ever and covered with the searing scars of corruption, chaos, and civil war.[16]

It can hardly be surprising that there was also a big difference between agreeing to a coalition government and implementing the agreement. As in the past, the main difficulty was caused by General Phoumi. He stalled on reaching agreement on who was to be in the coalition government, hoping the United States could be lured to support him in another military attack on the government. But it was no longer J. Graham Parsons who was handling things for the United States; it was the aged but redoubtable Harriman, the rich former Governor of New York, whose record of sustained high-level government service may well be unequaled in American history. Sporadic negotiations continued through the fall of 1961 and then collapsed because Phoumi wanted the posts of minister of defense and interior for himself. It was obvious, of course, that the Pathet Lao would not for a moment consent to let such crucial posts go to its arch enemy; they could go only to neutralists.

When Phoumi persisted in his intransigence, Harriman got fed up.[17] He persuaded Kennedy to cut off in February 1962 the money used to pay Phoumi's troops. Then Harriman plunged into the bureaucratic baronies in Washington and, in an epic struggle, again with Kennedy's support, insisted that every United States agency in Laos replace every American who was a personal friend of Phoumi. But by early 1962 Phoumi still had not succumbed to American pressure. This was an instance—and they have multiplied in the past decade—in which Washington wondered with considerable puzzlement how an obscure political figure in an obscure country, both totally dependent on American support, could defy the United States. It is not an easy puzzle to solve, but perhaps such figures concluded that the Americans had nowhere else to turn without departing from the goals that had caused them to make these choices in the first place.

Kennedy had to face another problem: the cease-fire was becoming unstuck. Whether the Pathet Lao was also becoming impatient with Phoumi's stalling or whether it was making a calculated attempt at significant new military gains is difficult to know without access to Pathet Lao councils. Whatever the reason, in early May 1962 Pathet Lao forces, accompanied by North Vietnamese troops, hit the town of Nam Tha. Tucked in the northwest corner of Laos, Nam Tha had become of increasing interest to the Pathet Lao. For the first months of 1962 it had been in a chicken-and-egg situation, with Phoumi gradually increasing the strength of his forces as the Pathet Lao increased its, with the Pathet Lao's surrounding forces probing Phoumi's defenses and Phoumi responding with further reinforcements, including much of his artillery, against the counsel of his American military advisers, who feared that the other side was planning another Dienbienphu. But Phoumi refused to pull out. The battle for Nam Tha, where Phoumi now had 5000 of his best troops, began on May 2 with some fire against part of the defense perimeter. On May 3 the Pathet Lao captured an airfield twenty-five miles distant, the last one held by the royalists in the north. On May 4 an outpost was captured. At 3 a.m. May 6 the Pathet Lao and North Vietnamese launched a full-scale attack. Within six hours the town had fallen, the twelve American advisers had evacuated by helicopter, while Phoumi's troops fled in panic toward the Mekong River and Thailand. No Pathet Lao movements immediately followed the capture of Nam Tha. This is the way Roger Hilsman has reported that the Kennedy administration analyzed the situation:

> . . . The attack had been a large-scale probe, a major although still-limited violation of the cease-fire, designed both to discredit Phoumi and his forces and to test American determination. Unless the United States responded promptly and effectively, the communist side would be encouraged to step up their military effort. . . . It was the Laos crisis of 1961 all over again—only worse.[18]

These words are characteristic of the Kennedy administration, indeed of every American administration since World War II.

They demonstrate a tendency to see events in apocalyptic terms, as fateful testings of American resolve that might have terrible consequences unless the United States responds with unmistakable but measured firmness. These words also demonstrate the American conviction that Washington can, without any genuine attempt at understanding an adversary, unerringly read his mind. It may be, of course, that "the other side," to use Dean Rusk's term, was engaged in a stern test of American resolve. If so, where did the command come from? Moscow? Peking? Hanoi? Why was the Pathet Lao concerned with such cosmic geo-politico-military matters? Perhaps, given Laos's turbulent and often unfathomable history, the assault was purely a local matter in response to some immediate concern with internal politics. There is no firm proof for the latter conclusion, but neither is there for the former, yet Washington has seldom considered a simple explanation when there is a more complex one available that better suits the world of strategic concepts, scenarios, games theory, and the mighty struggle of opposing forces.

Anyway, the awesome decision-making wheels began to move again: the White House, State, the Pentagon, the CIA. Again the fateful questions: Send troops? If so, how many? Where should we make our stand? Should we try to get allies to come in with us? Should we bomb North Vietnam? Will the Chinese come in? What should trigger American intervention? Position papers flew about, and there seemed to be the real possibility that the United States might intervene in a nation of no strategic importance on the side of a faction that had demonstrated yet again that it had no capacity to fight. But perhaps all this bureaucratic activity was necessary to make credible the concrete steps Kennedy did take. On May 12 the United States announced that the Seventh Fleet was steaming toward the Gulf of Siam, and on May 15 word came that troops were being sent to Thailand. In subsequent days the Pathet Lao said it was ready to resume talks, although the difficulty in the talks had come more from Phoumi than from the Pathet Lao. On May 25 Khrushchev chimed in with a statement that the Soviet Union "continued" to support the establishment of a neutral Laos, although he asserted that the American troop landings in Thailand had "hindered" a settlement. That same day Souvanna Phouma, who was forever flying back and forth, said he would return to Laos for further talks, but he set a deadline of June 15 for agreement on his coalition government. By now the starch had gone out of Phoumi; the combination of Harriman's pressure and the chastening defeat at Nam Tha was too much for him. So finally, on June 11, Souvanna again announced that agreement on a coalition government of national union had been reached. This agreement on the scene was rapidly translated into an international agreement, signed at Geneva on July 23. Kennedy's biographers have attributed this achievement to the President's display of force. That may well be so. On the other hand, it may have been just a result of the normal tortuous course of events in Laos. Neither conclusion is susceptible of proof.

The Laos agreement was an untidy one, but it at least eliminated Laos as a major point of international contention. The North Vietnamese never did remove all their troops as they were supposed to do, retaining some to protect and maintain the "Ho Chi Minh trail" to South Vietnam. On the other hand,

> Harriman, especially, felt strongly that the United States should comply with both the letter and the spirit of the agreements in every detail, that its record should be absolutely clean. Our military advisers should be withdrawn promptly, and thereafter there should be no violation of any kind by the United States, neither "black" reconnaissance flights to confirm whether the North Vietnamese had actually withdrawn nor cloak-and-dagger hanky-panky. . . . If the Geneva agreements and the political solution failed in Laos, he wanted it to be the communist side that had to pay the political cost. . . . If the communists broke the agreements and the United States had to intervene with force, he wanted to make sure we had all the international political support we could get.[19]

In writing that Kennedy decided to go along with Harriman, Hilsman clearly implies that the United States during the rest of the Kennedy administration scrupulously observed the 1962 Geneva agreements. However, on June 7, 1970, Dr. John A. Hannah, director of the Agency for International Development, said on a radio news program that the Kennedy administration *in 1962* decided to use AID as a cover for CIA operations in Laos.[20] Although it is possible that Hilsman was not aware of this, as Assistant Secretary of State for the Far East, it is unlikely. It may be that, since such information was classified, Hilsman did not feel at liberty to disclose it. This seems to be one instance of several in which Kennedy's biographers covered up information that later became known. It is impossible to guess how many other instances have not yet come to light. In the present case, it is one thing to argue that communist violation of the 1962 agreements justified American violation; it is quite another to make the clear implication that the Kennedy administration observed the agreements in every detail.

Left somewhat more to themselves—although outside interference never ended and later increased, climaxed by the American–South Vietnamese invasion of 1971—the Laotians in 1963 began to work out their own affairs. Again the natural balance began to assert itself, and when the Pathet Lao tried to make use of Kong-Lê, as the rightists had earlier, he pulled away from them. He was even, during the rest of the year, able to withstand direct military attacks by the North-Vietnamese-augmented Pathet Lao. Thus he again wound up a neutralist, which he would have been all along if the Americans under Eisenhower and, to a lesser degree, Kennedy had not pushed him into the arms of the communists. The bickering continued among the three factions, there was a limited amount of fighting, but the agreements more or less held during the final months of Kennedy's life. Although even Kennedy's admirers are reluctant to say of Laos that it was anything more than "a victory—of sorts," they do assert that it was a valuable contribution to Kennedy's development. Schlesinger wrote that "in retrospect the Laos crisis of 1961 seems in some ways a dress rehearsal for the Cuban missile crisis of 1962." And Hilsman wrote: "But in retrospect, it seems obvious that for President Kennedy, Laos was not so much a lesson as the crucible for the strategic concept that armed him for as great a test as any American President has yet faced—the Cuban missile crisis of 1962."[21]

Another judgment might be that Kennedy left Laos somewhat better off than he found it, not because he was unwilling to intervene but because he had concluded that intervention would demand too high a price. This, I believe, is the most revealing conclusion to be drawn about the Laos situation. Kennedy was willing to intervene directly and said on a number of occasions privately, as his intimates have written, that he might well have intervened in 1961 if the Bay of Pigs, coming right at the time of decision, had not caused him to doubt the success of such intervention. This, as we shall see in discussing the Bay of Pigs, the little-known case of British Guiana, and Vietnam, demonstrates his conviction, one that he shared with other Presidents going back to Teddy Roosevelt and, even further, to James Polk, that the United States has the unique right to intervene by force of arms in the domestic affairs of other sovereign states.

It was a bold plan, the kind that appealed to the Kennedy spirit. This kind of action, the Kennedy brothers felt, fitted the New Frontier. It was full of chance, certainly, but it was audacious, glamorous and new. It was irresistible.[1]

—HUGH SIDEY

CHAPTER THREE

The Bay of Pigs

The invasion of Cuba at the Bay of Pigs in April 1961 came as a terrible, numbing shock to many Kennedy supporters the world over. It seemed wholly out of character for the John F. Kennedy who, liberals had convinced themselves, was in the tradition of Franklin D. Roosevelt and Adlai E. Stevenson. But, once again, liberals simply had not listened to Kennedy's own words. Here again we must consider Kennedy's ambivalence. The evidence leaves no doubt that he was an anti-communist crusader. Any such crusade necessarily operates on two planes: against Russia and/or China and against communism in the underdeveloped nations. The first, obviously, is dangerous. A direct conflict with Russia, being most dangerous, has been avoided for a quarter-century, although in the Cuban missile crisis it came perilously close. Korea proved that direct conflict with China could also be costly, so that too has been avoided ever since. But it has been possible to carry on the anti-communist crusade in Latin America and Asia, even if at high cost, without engaging the two communist giants directly. While Kennedy carried on his crusade on both planes, he went much further in the developing nations, again excepting the Cuban missile crisis, where the two planes intersected.

Now there is absolutely no reason to doubt the genuineness of Kennedy's sympathy for the aspirations of the peoples of the Third World. He understood both the passionate desire and the need for substantial and rapid change. He genuinely supported the idea of a democratic left. He knew that governments arising from

34

these circumstances might be uncomfortable for the United States
to live with, and he was fully prepared to accept that. But Kennedy, like virtually the entire American foreign-policy establishment in the past quarter-century, did not understand revolution.
(A fuller discussion of this follows when we consider his revealing
controversy on the matter with Khrushchev at Vienna.) However
sympathetic he was to the need for change, whenever he saw communism in a developing nation, he saw red. This was the case
with Castro and Cuba.

Two years before his election, on December 15, 1958, in
Puerto Rico, Kennedy said:

> I realize that it will always be a cardinal tenet of American foreign
> policy not to intervene in the internal affairs of other nations—and
> this is particularly true in Latin America. I realize that we cannot
> force out any duly constituted government, however repugnant its
> methods or views may be—particularly when we have no guarantee
> that its successors in the long run will be a real improvement. . . .
> But an announced policy of nonintervention becomes a sham when
> it is turned off and on to suit our own purposes.[2]

But then he appears to have contradicted the words he had just
spoken: "For there is little question that should any Latin country
be driven by repression into the arms of the communists, our attitude on nonintervention would change overnight." A principle is a
principle, "a cardinal tenet," until we decide to violate it. His ambivalence toward Cuba had another aspect, too. In a statement in
his *Strategy of Peace,* dated January 1, 1960, Kennedy wrote:
"Whether Castro would have taken a more rational course after
his victory had the United States Government not backed the dictator Batista so long and so uncritically, and had it given the fiery
young rebel a warmer welcome in his hour of triumph, especially
on his trip to this country, we cannot be sure." [3] This seems to
imply a certain sympathy, but contrast that statement to one made
in a press conference on April 23, 1963: "I think it is unfortunate
that [Castro] was permitted to assume control in the 1950s, and
perhaps it would have been easier to take an action then than it is
now." On one hand Eisenhower should have been friendlier, and
on the other, Eisenhower should have prevented Castro's taking
power.

Even a cursory examination of Kennedy's pre-election words suffices to predict how this ambivalence would be resolved. A Bay of Pigs attitude had been explicit in his own words during the campaign. Liberals simply hadn't paid attention. On September 2, at Portland, Maine, Kennedy elaborated on what seemed to be a Latin American "domino theory."

> I think he [Castro] should be condemned. I think he is a source of maximum danger. I think the big task of the next administration is going to be to contain this revolution in Cuba, itself, and not have it spread through Latin America. We did make progress to a degree, though not satisfactory, however, in my opinion, and a constant struggle is going to go on if we are going to isolate this communist conspiracy in Cuba.[4]

On September 21 at Nashville, Tennessee, Kennedy declared:

> I am not satisfied to see a communist satellite ninety miles off the coast of Florida, eight minutes by jet. Those who say they will stand up to Khrushchev have not demonstrated ability to stand up to Mr. Castro.

On October 6 at Cincinnati, Ohio:

> But Castro is not just another Latin American dictator—a petty tyrant bent merely on personal power and gain. His ambitions extend far beyond his own shores. He has transformed the island of Cuba into a hostile and militant communist satellite—a base from which to carry communist infiltration and subversion throughout the Americas. With guidance, support and arms from Moscow and Peiping, he has made anti-Americanism a sign of loyalty and anti-communism a punishable crime—confiscated over a billion dollars' worth of American property—threatened the existence of our naval base at Guantanamo—and rattled red rockets at the United States, which can hardly close its eyes to a potential enemy missile or submarine base only ninety miles from our shores.

In two more statements, quoted below, Kennedy seemed to be advocating a Bay of Pigs type of operation. At Johnstown, Pennsylvania, October 15:

> What can a new administration do to end this drift?
> 1. The first thing we have to do is let the Cuban people know our determination that they will someday again be free. We did not

make clear to the Cubans our devotion to freedom during the brutal regime of the Batista dictatorship—and we are not making our position any clearer under the Castro dictatorship. We have no Cuban Voice of America broadcasts in Spanish at all, and only one hour a day in Spanish beamed in general to all Latin America. We must promptly initiate a major broadcast program for Cuba in particular, and more for Latin America in general.

2. *Secondly, we must end the harassment, which this government has carried on, of liberty-loving anti-Castro forces in Cuba and other lands. While we cannot violate international law, we must recognize that these exiles and rebels represent the real voice of Cuba, and should not be constantly handicapped by our Immigration and Justice Department authorities.* [Emphasis added.]

3. Third, we must let Mr. Castro know that we do not intend to be pushed around any longer and in particular do not intend to be pushed out of our naval base at Guantanamo, or denied fair compensation for American property he has seized.

4. Fourth, we must let Mr. Khrushchev know that we are permitting no expansion of his foothold in our hemisphere—and that the Organization of American States will be given real strength and stature to resist any further communist penetration by whatever means are necessary.

5. Fifth, and finally, we must strengthen the cause of freedom throughout all Latin America, creating an atmosphere where liberty will flourish, and where Cuban communism will be resisted, isolated, and left to die on the vine.

Five days later, the Kennedy campaign organization released this statement:

The next administration will have to do much better than Mr. Nixon has done, if it intends to wage a serious offensive against communism on our very doorstep.

First, we will have to work with the Organization of American States and our European allies in order to promote collective action against communism in the Caribbean. For, unless we secure the cooperation of our allies, Mr. Castro will be able to trade at will with the free world, rendering our own partial embargo futile. Despite this pressing need for joint action, the Republicans have completely failed to enlist the cooperation of our allies. And the reason is plain. For under the Republican leadership our prestige has fallen so low that our Latin American allies are no longer willing to follow our leadership in the fight against communism in this hemisphere.

Second, we must consider more stringent economic sanctions—

such as the seizing of all Cuban assets in this country to be used to pay off some of the vast sums which Cuba still owes us. Of course Cuban assets in this country—which were an estimated $200 million in June—have declined drastically in the last months as the Republicans have let this potential opportunity slip away. We should also consider measures to prevent goods from being shipped to Castro via a third country.

Third, we must attempt to strengthen the non-Batista democratic anti-Castro forces in exile, and in Cuba itself, who offer eventual hope of overthrowing Castro. Thus far these fighters for freedom have had virtually no support from our Government. [Emphasis added.]

Fourth, and most important—we must immediately act to prevent communism from taking over other countries in Latin America—by removing the conditions under which communism thrives.

Kennedy was calling for "a serious offensive" against Castro. Although he later said that he was not aware of the exiles' invasion being planned by the Eisenhower administration, Nixon evidently thought he had learned of the plans from a CIA briefing and was taking unfair advantage of the knowledge to score campaign points against him. It is instructive to see what Nixon said about Cuba the following day, during the fourth and final television debate with his opponent:

I think that Senator Kennedy's policies and recommendations for the handling of the Castro regime are probably the most dangerously irresponsible recommendations that he's made during the course of this campaign. In effect, what Senator Kennedy recommends is that the United States Government should give help to the exiles and to those within Cuba who opposed the Castro regime, provided that they are anti-Batista.

Now let's just see what this means. We have five treaties with Latin America, including the one setting up the Organization of American States in Bogota in 1948, in which we've agreed not to intervene in the internal affairs of any other American country, and they as well have agreed to do likewise.

The Charter of the United Nations, its preamble, Article I and Article II also provide that there shall be no intervention by one nation in the internal affairs of another. Now I don't know what Senator Kennedy suggests when he says that we should help those who oppose the Castro regime both in Cuba and without. But I do know this, that if we were to follow that recommendation that we would lose all of our friends in Latin America, we would probably be condemned in the United Nations, and we would not accomplish our objective. I know something else. It would be an open invitation for Mr. Khrushchev to come in, to come into Latin America and to engage us in what would be a civil war and possibly even worse than that.

Whatever Nixon's reasons for making that statement, and however hypocritical it was, it was a telling indictment of the Bay of Pigs adventure. Note particularly the final sentence: "It would be an open invitation for Mr. Khrushchev to come in . . ." It was, in fact, the Bay of Pigs fiasco that brought Khrushchev into Cuba and precipitated the Cuban missile crisis. But we are anticipating our story.

Seventeen days before Kennedy took office, the outgoing administration broke off diplomatic relations with Cuba. During the previous two years hostility had developed between the new Castro government and the Eisenhower administration, each side blaming the other. The Castro government, unlike earlier revolutionary regimes, had clearly decided to reduce drastically Cuba's economic dependence on the United States. As Castro increasingly expropriated American-owned firms, with terms of repayment that the United States regarded as unsatisfactory, Eisenhower began to take economic reprisals, particularly cutting the quota of Cuban sugar that was sold to the United States at a higher-than-world-market price. At the same time Cuba began moving economically and politically toward the Soviet Union and the East European countries. How much of this was deliberate choice and how much was encouraged by the increasing political and economic difficulties with the United States is difficult to say. Perhaps varying degrees of responsibility resided in Washington and Havana; perhaps the course of the Cuban revolution made hostility inevitable. It would take an entire book to discuss the deteriorating relations between the United States and Cuba during Castro's first two years in power. Suffice it to say that on the eve of Kennedy's inauguration the hostility was deep and bitter. When Castro suddenly demanded that the United States Embassy be reduced to just eleven members in forty-eight hours—some have suggested that Castro ad-libbed this demand in one of his epic speeches—Eisenhower responded by breaking off diplomatic relations on January 3. Granted that Castro's demand was childish, one wonders whether it was a worse offense than the exiles' invasion even then being planned by the CIA.

Normally an incoming administration might be distressed that so important an action as breaking diplomatic relations had been made in the waning days of the outgoing administration. But since Kennedy had already decided on a hard-line approach to Castro, the break was probably an advantage, in effect giving advance approval to the steps he contemplated. The intellectual justification for his hostility to Castro was well expressed by Arthur Schlesinger: "Yet, despite the jostling for position between communists and *Fidelistas*, the year 1959 saw the clear commitment of Castro's revolution to the establishment of a Marxist dictatorship in Cuba and the service of Soviet foreign policy in the world—a commitment so incompatible with the expressed purpose of the revolution as surely to justify the word betrayal." [5]

So fine a historian as Schlesinger should have known that revolutions develop their own dynamics, that it is almost impossible to predict with any precision what course they will take. Given the depth of Castro's legitimate grievances against the United States and the degree of the United States' quite predictable (but not very imaginative) response, and given the fact that the communists for economic and political reasons abroad and for organizational reasons at home were the only ones to whom Castro could turn, it was inevitable that he embrace them. But as Schlesinger must have recognized, Castro was hardly a puppet of the Soviet Union and was often nearly as much of an embarrassment to Moscow as he was to Washington. If there was a "betrayal" by Castro, it was of the revolution that the Kennedy administration thought should have taken place, not of the revolution that did take place. In any case, Cuba was, and is, fully entitled to have any kind of government it wants, even communist. Furthermore, as the confrontation developed, it was difficult for anyone but an American chauvinist to confuse the roles of David and Goliath.

Although his admirers have always lauded Kennedy for his lack of dogma, for his cool, unshakable pragmatism, his preoccupation with Castro constituted a concern so deep "as surely to justify the word" obsession. Throughout his presidency, as during his campaign, Kennedy spoke as if Castro were the aggressor, when it was plain for all the world to see that it was the United States that was undertaking a military, political, and economic offensive against a Cuba that had pitifully few weapons with which to respond. About all that Castro had was the idea of revolution—but that already existed all through the hemisphere, and, as events proved, Castro's revolution was not itself exportable. It did, however, serve as an inspiration to revolutionaries throughout Latin America, but then so did the philosophy of the American Revolution. The elephant confronted the mouse, and even the elephant's nominal allies in Latin America derived enormous if concealed pleasure from Castro's success—to shift the metaphor—in twisting Uncle Sam's beard.

It did not take long for Kennedy's "serious offensive" against Castro to take shape. At his first news conference, on January 25, 1961, he was asked if the United States planned to resume diplomatic relations with Cuba. Speaking first about the Castro revolution, Kennedy said:

> What we are of course concerned about is when these movements are seized by external forces and directed not to improving the welfare of the people involved but towards imposing an ideology which is alien to this hemisphere. That is a matter of concern particularly when that intervention takes the form of military support which threatens the security and the peace of the Western Hemisphere. . . .
>
> So in answer to your question we have no plan at present to resume diplomatic relations with Cuba, because of the factors involved in that island.

There was, of course, no evidence then, nor has any come to light since, that Castro's revolution was "seized by external forces." Beyond question, then and to the time of this writing, Castro and his revolutionary colleagues, not the Kremlin, have been the masters in Havana. Nor can there be any serious question that the purpose of the revolution, however much it has floundered, was to improve the welfare of the Cuban people. Communism was a means adopted after the revolution to achieve the ends of the revolution, most likely because it was the only means available. And it was hypocrisy of a staggering dimension to speak of "military support which threatens the security and the peace of the Western Hemisphere" when even then plans were afoot to invade Cuba. This was just the beginning of an exercise in Orwellian logic and language.

On February 15, in another press conference, Kennedy said his administration was considering further economic steps, especially curbing Cuban imports to the United States. (Eisenhower had earlier banned United States exports to Cuba.) And Kennedy put public pressure on a liquor company not to go through with a $12-million purchase of Cuban molasses: "On the molasses there is some question as to under what conditions we could intervene in that transaction, but, of course, it has been my hope that that transaction would not be consummated. I am not convinced that we are totally without resources and we are considering what steps we could take to consider that particular transaction." Also in February, Arthur Schlesinger of the White House staff, and George McGovern, then director of the new Food for Peace program, toured Latin America to find out, among other things, what direct steps the Organization of American States was prepared to take against Castro. On the last day of March, Kennedy cut the Cuban sugar quota to zero.

These were important steps, but infinitely more important was what was brewing in secret—or perhaps semi-secret would be a better word. So much has been written about the Bay of Pigs (Schlesinger's account is particularly detailed, and horrifying) that there is no need to go into great detail here. Kennedy was informed of the plans shortly after his election and on November 29, 1960, he had received a detailed briefing from Allen Dulles, brother of John Foster Dulles, who was head of the CIA.

Kennedy listened carefully and told Dulles to go ahead with the planning, but he made it clear that he would make his mind up later.

It could be argued that this decision was not very important, was merely tentative, that Kennedy could hardly be expected to know how powerful was the effect of bureaucratic momentum. But the inescapable fact remains that Kennedy with that decision demonstrated that he was prepared to violate the territorial integrity of a sovereign state, that he was prepared to violate a "cardinal tenet" of international law, including a number of specific American commitments, not to intervene in the domestic affairs of hemisphere states. If he were not, he would have scotched the plan right then and there, despite any fears that to do so would make him appear to be "soft" within the government national security apparatus, despite any fears that his decision would leak out to the public, making him appear less tough on Castro than Eisenhower.

When the chance did come after inauguration for review and consideration, there was virtually no opposition to the plan within the Kennedy administration. The Pentagon and the CIA, both with the reputation of being supremely pragmatic, thought the plan would work. Rusk, in his Delphic way, seemed to approve of it. Schlesinger, however, wrote a memo to Kennedy saying that, above all, "this would be your first dramatic foreign policy decision. At one stroke you would dissipate all the extraordinary goodwill which has been rising toward the new administration through the world. It would fix a malevolent image of the new administration in the minds of millions." [6] But even Schlesinger, who has sometimes seemed to regard himself as something of a moralist, did not oppose the Bay of Pigs for the simple reason that it was wrong. The only one strenuously to do that was Senator J. William Fulbright, whom Kennedy had informed of the plan. Fulbright said, "To give this activity even covert support is of a piece with the hypocrisy and cynicism for which the United States is constantly denouncing the Soviet Union in the United Nations and elsewhere. This point will not be lost on the rest of the world— nor on our own consciences. . . . The Castro regime is a thorn in the flesh; but it is not a dagger in the heart." [7]

Yet throughout March the planning went ahead. Chester Bowles, then Under Secretary of State, was against it but did not press his views, and Kennedy did not solicit them. Edward R. Murrow, the great broadcaster, then head of USIA, was also against it but was not fully informed of or involved in the plans. Adlai Stevenson at the UN learned about it too late to say any more than that he thought it was a bad idea. Indeed, he knew so little about it that he found himself in the humiliating position of lying at the UN when he declared Cuban defectors were bombing Castro forces and not United States pilots in United States planes.

Llewellyn Thompson reported from Moscow that Khrushchev was increasingly preoccupied with Cuba, and Schlesinger has written that Kennedy seemed increasingly skeptical of the plan. "Had one senior adviser opposed the adventure, I believe that Kennedy would have cancelled it." [8] That may be so, but there is reason to doubt it. In a private White House meeting with Dean Acheson shortly before the landing Kennedy discussed the plan. If any man in postwar American government is entitled to the designation "super-anti-communist" it is Acheson, the chief architect of Truman's Cold War policies in Europe. Yet he was flatly against the proposal. This is how Acheson recalled the meeting on April 27, 1964, in an interview recorded for the Oral History section of the John F. Kennedy Library:

> I was very much alarmed about the thing, and said I hoped he wasn't serious about it. He said, "I don't know if I'm serious or not, but this is the proposal and I've been thinking about it and it is serious—in that sense, I've not made up my mind but I'm giving it very serious thought." I remember saying that I did not think it was necessary to call in Price, Waterhouse [the famous public accountants] to discover that 1500 Cubans weren't as good as 25,000 Cubans. It seemed to me that this was a disastrous idea. We talked about it for a little bit and then I went off. I really dismissed it from my mind because it seemed like such a wild idea. While I was in Europe the Bay of Pigs came off and this really shattered the Europeans. They had tremendously high expectations of the new administration, and when this thing happened they just fell miles down with a crash.[9]

From Acheson's account, it is difficult to escape the conclusion that Kennedy *wanted* to go ahead with the Bay of Pigs. Not only did he reject the advice of Acheson and Fulbright, but he knew that Castro was forewarned. "I can't believe what I'm reading," he said to Pierre Salinger a week before the invasion. "Castro doesn't need agents over here. All he has to do is read our newspapers. It's all laid out for him." [10]

This was typical Kennedy. Although no President has ever been more successful in cultivating the working newsmen—he genuinely enjoyed their company—no President has become more outraged when the press reported something he did not want the public to know. He seemed genuinely to feel that it was the obligation of the press not to embarrass him, that to do so was an act of betrayal. Yet few Presidents in history have had such a favora-

ble press. On the Bay of Pigs he certainly could have no complaint.[11] The story of the training of exiles in Guatemala had been
kicking around since mid-November 1960, when *The Nation* raised
the question. Copies of *The Nation* piece were sent to *The New York
Times* and other news organizations in New York. Yet the story
was deliberately not picked up. Eventually *The Times* and other
news media began to circle warily around the story, printing bits
and pieces of it, but nothing explicitly about an invasion. After
a while Miami newspapermen—the major concentration of Cuban
exiles was in that city—got most of the story. Finally, just a few
days before the invasion, Tad Szulc, a splendid correspondent, got
the whole story, but *The New York Times,* at Kennedy's request,
deleted references to a forthcoming invasion from it. The *New
Republic* killed a similar story at Kennedy's request. Kennedy and
The Times were both later to regret that the story had not been
published; it might have prevented the fiasco. Yet while many of
the news media were aware that something involving Cuban exiles
was going on in the Caribbean, the press dismissed as nonsense
Cuba's charges at the United Nations and elsewhere that the
United States was planning an invasion. Kennedy certainly could
have no complaint about the press. It was the American people who
should have complained.

In any case, it should have been obvious to any sensible man
who was informed of it that the plan was doomed from the beginning. All questions of morality or international law aside, how
could Kennedy have expected 1400 poorly trained men without
adequate air cover or naval support successfully to invade a land
defended by well-motivated, well-trained, and well-armed men
who vastly outnumbered the invaders? The affair shows gross incompetence of an astounding magnitude. The President, obsessed
with secrecy, did not even employ the services of those in the government who knew the most about Cuba, the Cuban specialists in
the State Department. The officer-in-charge of Cuban affairs at
State was Robert A. Hurwitch. In an Oral History interview for
the Kennedy Library, he said on April 24, 1964, that he knew
nothing of the Bay of Pigs plans nor, to the best of his knowledge,
did his immediate superiors, the Director and Deputy Director of
Caribbean and Mexican Affairs.

Therefore, there was in my judgment, a divorce between the people who had daily, or minute by minute, had access to information, to what was going on, and the people who were making plans and policy decisions. This divorce is one which has cost us, as history has shown. . . .

The general impression the Embassy gave us was that there were areas of disaffection, that Castro had lost a considerable amount of support. . . . But the Embassy, as I recall, never indicated that, even to the extent that they were aware of an organized underground, indicated that Castro's hold on the country was really shaky or in jeopardy.[12]

Although Allen Dulles, in conferences with the President and other planners at the White House, gave the impression that a wide uprising could be expected, he had never asked his own people in the CIA to investigate that point further and, as we see, the State Department was not asked either. Also, Kennedy had just read in the *New York Herald Tribune* a first-hand report from Cuba that Castro had the support of his people. Yet such an uprising was regarded as crucial to the success of the invasion.

Five days before the invasion, on April 12, Kennedy was asked this question at a press conference:

Mr. President, has a decision been reached on how far this country will go in helping an anti-Castro uprising or invasion of Cuba?

THE PRESIDENT. First, I want to say that there will not be, under any conditions, an intervention in Cuba by the United States Armed Forces. This Government will do everything it possibly can, I think it can meet its responsibilities, to make sure that there are no Americans involved in any actions inside Cuba. . . .

The basic issue in Cuba is not one between the United States and Cuba. It is between the Cubans themselves. I intend to see that we adhere to that principle and as I understand it this administration's attitude is so understood by the anti-Castro exiles from Cuba in this country.

The fact that Kennedy lied is of little moment compared to the disastrous chain of events he had already set in motion. The Bay of Pigs was bad enough in itself, but worse, it led directly to the brink of nuclear war in the Cuban missile crisis a year and a half later.

On April 10, two days before Kennedy's press conference, the

Cuban exiles were on their way by truck from Guatemala to Puerto Cabezas in Nicaragua. On April 13 they began to board American ships and on April 14 they got the specific invasion plan. On April 17 the brave Cuban exiles hit the beach at the Bay of Pigs. The fact that they went there eagerly is no defense against the fact that they were sent to death and captivity by an American administration whose primary motive was not a concern for the people of Cuba but the fear that Castro represented a diplomatic and political threat to United States hegemony in Latin America. The landing was botched from the start; not only had the invasion been poorly planned and executed, but Castro's military forces responded with a skill and vigor that the CIA had not thought possible. Within a few hours it became evident that it would soon meet the doom that had been decreed for it from the beginning. For those killed, wounded, and captured, that was enough. But for the world as a whole there was a grim but as yet unclear foretelling of what was to come. Khrushchev sent an angry diplomatic note pledging "all necessary assistance to Castro." Eighteen months later Kennedy would learn what that assistance was.

The dimensions of the disaster are well delineated by Schlesinger. Everything went wrong. Even as the disaster was taking place, the Kennedy administration tried to maintain its innocence. On Monday morning, April 17, although it was still too early to know exactly what was happening on those once lonely beaches, the Washington press knew that some sort of an invasion was under way in Cuba. Dean Rusk held a press conference. He told the newsmen: "The American people are entitled to know whether we are intervening in Cuba or intend to do so in the future. The answer to that question is no. What happens in Cuba is for the Cuban people to decide."

By Tuesday bad news began to flood into the White House. By Wednesday it was just about over. Brave men had been sacrificed by Kennedy on a mission that should never have been undertaken. They were killed, wounded, and captured because of Kennedy's determination to overthrow Castro by direct military intervention in the domestic affairs of a sovereign state. Kennedy was obsessed by Castro. That certainly seems suggested by his campaign speeches and by the Bay of Pigs. Further support is given this view by Senator George Smathers of Florida, a close friend of the

President. On March 31, 1964, in an Oral History recording for the Kennedy Library, he said:

> I don't know whether he brought it up or I brought it up. We had further conversation of assassination of Fidel Castro, what would be the reaction, how would the people react, would the people be gratified. I'm sure he had his own ideas about it, but he was picking my brain on this particular question as I had heard many times he picked the brain of others. And on those occasions he would very rarely express his own view because he wanted to know what the other man's view was before he made up his mind—or maybe he had his mind already made up. He knew if he expressed a contrary view, a lot of people couldn't help but be a bit tempered in their statements if they knew the President held a contrary view. As I recollect, he was just throwing out a great barrage of questions— he was certain it could be accomplished—I remember that—it would be no problem.
>
> But the question was whether or not it would accomplish that which he wanted it to, whether or not the reaction throughout South America would be good or bad. And I talked with him about it and, frankly, at this particular time I felt, and I later on learned that he did, that I wasn't so much for the idea of assassination, particularly when it could be pinned on the United States.[13]

Too much should not be made of this, for it might have been idle conversation, yet the fact remains that Kennedy was sufficiently preoccupied with Castro to carry on such a conversation. What an irony.

Whatever the basis for the decision to invade Cuba, whether it was a cool, pragmatic, nonideological decision or the product of an overpowering preoccupation, the invasion was collapsing even as Kennedy answered Khrushchev's note, the day after. The tone of his reply was nothing less than snippy, as if it were Khrushchev and not Kennedy who was engaged in counterrevolution:

> You are under a serious misapprehension in regard to events in Cuba. For months there has been evident and growing resistance to the Castro dictatorship. . . . It cannot be suprising that, as resistance within Cuba grows, refugees have been using whatever means are available to return and support their countrymen in the continuing struggle for freedom. Where people are denied the right of choice, resource to such struggle is the only means of achieving their liberties.

I have previously stated, and I repeat now, that the United States intends no military intervention in Cuba. In the event of any military intervention by an outside force we will immediately honor our obligations under the inter-American system to protect this hemisphere against external aggression. While refraining from military intervention in Cuba, the people of the United States do not conceal their admiration for Cuban patriots who wish to see a democratic system in an independent Cuba. The United States can take no action to stifle the spirit of liberty. . . .

I believe, Mr. Chairman, that you should recognize that free peoples in all parts of the world do not accept the claim of historic inevitability for the communist revolution. What your government believes is its own business; what it does in the world is the world's business. The great revolution in the history of man, past, present and future, is the revolution of those determined to be free.[14]

This was a use of the language of revolution to justify counter-revolution. Nor did the utter failure of the landings, obvious to the whole world within a couple of days of his note to Khrushchev, do much to chasten President Kennedy. His biographers have written that Kennedy faced failure manfully, taking all the blame himself, even though he had been given bad advice, even though he had little choice in the matter given the fact that the operation was already in the works and that he was so new in office. It is true that Kennedy shouldered the blame, but why not? The blame was his. Yet the experience seems not to have chastened him in any way. On April 20, he discussed Cuba before the American Society of Newspaper Editors.[15] First, he refused to admit American responsibility:

. . . I have emphasized before that this was a struggle of Cuban patriots against a Cuban dictator. While we could not be expected to hide our sympathies, we made it repeatedly clear that the armed forces of this country would not intervene in any way.

Any unilateral American intervention, in the absence of an external attack upon ourselves or an ally, would have been contrary to our traditions and to our international obligations.

This is quite an extraordinary statement. Not only was the invasion planned by the United States, but the United States recruited, paid, and trained the exile force. To say that "the armed forces of this country would not intervene in any way" stretches the truth beyond the breaking point. The exiles used American military equipment. They were trained by American military men, whether or not they wore uniforms. The warplanes were American, flown by Americans. The frogmen who were the first on the beach were American. American ships carried the invaders, and American naval units accompanied them. Americans were killed in the operation. To claim that America did not intervene was to lie and be caught in the lie. Further, Kennedy must have surprised many Latin Americans when he claimed that unilateral intervention "would have been contrary to our traditions." "Contrary . . . to our international obligations," to be sure, but hardly to our traditions, as Kennedy knew: Cuba and Colombia and Panama and the Dominican Republic and Haiti and Nicaragua and Guatemala and Mexico.

Then the President said:

> But let the record show that our restraint is not inexhaustible. Should it ever appear that the inter-American doctrine of non-interference merely conceals or excuses a policy of nonaction—if the nations of this hemisphere should fail to meet their commitments against outside communist penetration—then I want it clearly understood that this Government will not hesitate in meeting its primary obligations which are to the security of our Nation.

Kennedy did not apologize; rather he issued threats. And he reiterated his amendment to the Monroe Doctrine: that Latin American nations were free to choose their own governments, but only as long as they were not communist. Then the President went on to say that if the United States should ever use military force in the hemisphere, "we do not intend to be lectured on 'intervention' by those whose character was stamped for all time on the bloody streets of Budapest." Kennedy was knocking down straw men. Russia, of course, was supremely hypocritical in decrying intervention, but, as Kennedy well knew, the significant outcry over the Bay of Pigs came not from the communist bloc but from pro-American, pro-Kennedy countries the world over. Most significant were the protests from American liberals who had provided the heart, soul, and much of the muscle for Kennedy's own political successes. While it is true that most Americans rallied behind the President—Kennedy was incredulous when the polls showed that something like 80 per cent supported him—vigorous dissent appeared on the campuses, an avant-garde of the swelling forces that were to bedevil Lyndon Johnson on the Dominican Republic and Vietnam and finally drive him from office.

But while what Kennedy said about Cuba was important, more important was how he moved from the particular to the general. It must be remembered that Kennedy was at this time grappling with the difficult problem of Laos, beginning to give serious thought to Vietnam, in the early stages of a vast military buildup, and only a month and a half from his crucial meeting with Khrushchev. His final paragraphs on that April day were a righteous call to arms in the anti-communist crusade, beyond anything said by John Foster Dulles. Implicit in these paragraphs were the Berlin crisis, the Cuban missile crisis, and, most fatefully, the endless, debilitating, and divisive entanglement in Vietnam. So important are these words to an understanding of Kennedy's foreign policy, so explicit are they, that they should be read directly and not filtered through the prejudices of this author.

First, it is clear that the forces of communism are not to be underestimated, in Cuba or anywhere in the world. The advantages of a police state—its use of mass terror and arrests to prevent the spread of free dissent—cannot be overlooked by those who expect the fall of every fanatic tyrant. If the self-discipline of the free cannot match the iron discipline of the mailed fist—in economic, political, scientific and all the other kinds of struggles as well as the military—then the peril to freedom will continue to rise.

Secondly, it is clear that this Nation, in concert with all the free nations of this hemisphere, must take an ever closer and more realistic look at the menace of external communist intervention and domination in Cuba. The American people are not complacent about Iron Curtain tanks and planes less than 90 miles from their shore. But a nation of Cuba's size is less a threat to our survival than it is a base for subverting the survival of other free nations throughout the hemisphere. It is not primarily our interest or our security but theirs which is now, today, in the greater peril. It is for their sake as well as our own that we must show our will.

The evidence is clear—and the hour is late. We and our Latin friends will have to face the fact that we cannot postpone any longer the real issue of survival of freedom in this hemisphere itself. On that issue, unlike perhaps some others, there can be no middle ground. Together we must build a hemisphere where freedom can flourish; and where any free nation under outside attack of any kind can be assured that all of our resources stand ready to respond to any request for assistance.

Third, and finally, it is clearer than ever that we face a relentless struggle in every corner of the globe that goes far beyond the clash of armies or even nuclear armaments. The armies are there, and in large number. The nuclear armaments are there. But they serve primarily as the shield behind which subversion, infiltration, and a host of other tactics steadily advance, picking off vulnerable areas one by one in situations which do not permit our own armed intervention.

Power is the hallmark of this offensive—power and discipline and deceit. The legitimate discontent of yearning people is exploited. The legitimate trappings of self-determination are employed. But once in power, all talk of discontent is repressed, all self-determination disappears, and the promise of a revolution of hope is betrayed, as in Cuba, into a reign of terror. Those who on instruction staged automatic "riots" in the streets of free nations over the efforts of a small group of young Cubans to regain their freedom should recall the long rollcall of refugees who cannot now go back—to Hungary, to North Korea, to North Vietnam, to East Germany, or to Poland, or to any of the other lands from which a steady stream of refugees pours forth, in eloquent testimony to the cruel oppression now holding sway in their homeland.

We dare not fail to see the insidious nature of this new and deeper struggle. We dare not fail to grasp the new concepts, the new tools, the new sense of urgency we will need to combat it—whether in Cuba or South Vietnam. And we dare not fail to realize that this struggle is taking place every day, without fanfare, in thousands of villages and markets—day and night—and in classrooms all over the globe.

The message of Cuba, of Laos, of the rising din of communist voices in Asia and Latin America—these messages are all the same. The complacent, the self-indulgent, the soft societies are about to be swept away with the debris of history. Only the strong, only the industrious, only the determined, only the courageous, only the visionary who determine the real nature of our struggle can possibly survive.

No greater task faces this country or this administration. No other challenge is more deserving of our every effort and energy. Too long we have fixed our eyes on traditional military needs, on armies prepared to cross borders, on missiles poised for flight. Now it should be clear that this is no longer enough—that security may be lost piece by piece, country by country, without the firing of a single missile or the crossing of a single border.

We intend to profit from this lesson. We intend to re-examine and reorient our forces of all kinds—our tactics and our institutions here in this community. We intend to intensify our efforts for a struggle in many ways more difficult than war, where disappointment will often accompany us.

For I am convinced that we in this country and in the free world possess the necessary resources, and the skill, and the added strength that comes from a belief in the freedom of man. And I am equally convinced that history will record the fact that the bitter struggle reached its climax in the late 1950s and the early 1960s. Let me then make clear as the President of the United States that I am determined upon our system's survival and success, regardless of the cost and regardless of the peril!

A manifesto for counterrevolution. Kennedy, after the humiliation of the Bay of Pigs, looked and saw around him a hostile and threatening world. The Visigoths were at the gate. There was only one solution: gird for a long struggle and take the offensive. But this was *not* the world as it existed in 1961; it was a construct of fact, fear, and fantasy. The pragmatist was basing his decisions on the Book of Revelation according to Dean Acheson and John Foster Dulles. The question was not whether some communist societies were odious. Many were, and are. Yet is it not possible that threats from outside the communist world—whether real or imagined—increase the rigidity of totalitarian rule? Nor was the question whether or not some new nations would go communist. Some no doubt would. Yet was it not—and is it not—the question for Washington policy-makers to determine the threat to American national security in the *foreign policy* of other nations, not in their method of governance? And is it not likely that a simplistic vision of communism as an evil force will make more difficult the cool assessment of facts essential to a rational foreign policy? Kennedy's speech to the newspaper editors seems to indicate not a cool assessment of the facts, but rather an alarmist, dogmatic view of the world, with perhaps a touch of *machismo*.

(The author is neither qualified for nor disposed to a psychoanalytic evaluation of Kennedy, but *machismo,* that assertion of masculinity usually attributed to Latin Americans but so applicable to

North Americans as well, certainly seems a characteristic of John Kennedy and his brothers. What more normal time for such an assertion of masculinity than after a humiliating defeat at the Bay of Pigs and after being charged with throwing in the towel on Laos? "His campaign pledges to aid anti-Castro rebels had not forced his hand, as some suspected, but he did feel his disapproval of the plan would be a show of weakness inconsistent with his general stance." [16])

One cannot help noting that Arthur Schlesinger seemed to approve of Kennedy's extraordinary speech. In the reverential language not untypical of Kennedy's biographers, Schlesinger wrote:

> He moved now with sure instinct and remarkable dexterity, showing, as he had shown nearly twenty years earlier in the Solomons, the strength to accept disaster, omit recrimination and pitch in to bring the situation back. . . . The President's concern was to head off any outcry within the United States for violent retaliation [for what?] against Castro, to reassure the democratic world about the prudence of Washington and at the same time to dissuade the communists from regarding restraint as evidence of weakness. . . . The speech to the editors offered the opportunity to explain the policy of restraint and to divert the demand for action against Castro into a general strengthening of American purpose. [17]

Retaliation? Restraint? Curious words from one normally so precise. Or perhaps Schlesinger saw Castro as Goliath in David's clothing.

Kennedy's speech before the newspaper editors was not his only extraordinary performance in the aftermath of the Bay of Pigs. At a news conference the next day he declined to discuss Cuba, but a week after he spoke to a meeting of newspaper publishers. [18] Kennedy spoke of the need for a free press. He said the government should not "withhold from the press and the public the facts they deserve to know." He said he did not want the government to cover up its mistakes or attempt to stifle dissent. He said he welcomed controversy, criticism, and debate, that he recognized the government's "obligation to provide you with the fullest possible information outside the narrowest limits of national security—and we intend to do it." Nonetheless, his speech clearly calls on the press to join the crusade against communism. The following long passage is the heart of his message:

. . . I do ask every publisher, every editor, and every newsman in the nation to re-examine his own standards, and to recognize the nature of our country's peril. In time of war, the government and the press have customarily joined in an effort, based largely on self-discipline, to prevent unauthorized disclosures to the enemy. In time of "clear and present danger," the courts have held that even the privileged rights of the First Amendment must yield to the public's need for national security.

Today no war has been declared—and however fierce the struggle may be, it may never be declared in the traditional fashion. Our way of life is under attack. Those who make themselves our enemy are advancing around the globe. The survival of our friends is in danger. And yet no war has been declared, no borders have been crossed by marching troops, no missiles have been fired.

If the press is awaiting a declaration of war before it imposes the self-discipline of combat conditions, then I can only say that no war ever posed a greater threat to our security. If you are awaiting a finding of "clear and present danger," then I can only say that the danger has never been more clear and its presence has never been more imminent.

It requires a change in outlook, a change in tactics, a change in missions—by the government, by the people, by every businessman or labor leader, and by every newspaper. For we are opposed around the world by a monolithic and ruthless conspiracy that relies primarily on covert means for expanding its sphere of influence— on infiltration instead of invasion, on subversion instead of elections, on intimidation instead of free choice, on guerrillas by night instead of armies by day. It is a system which has conscripted vast human and material resources into the building of a tightly knit, highly efficient machine that combines military, diplomatic, intelligence, economic, scientific and political operations.

Its preparations are concealed, not published. Its mistakes are buried, not headlined. Its dissenters are silenced, not praised. No expenditure is questioned, no rumor is printed, no secret is revealed. It conducts the Cold War, in short, with a wartime discipline no democracy would ever hope or wish to match.

Nevertheless, every democracy recognizes the necessary restraints of national security—and the question remains whether those restraints need to be more strictly observed if we are to oppose this kind of attack as well as outright invasion. For the facts of the matter are that this nation's foes have openly boasted of acquiring through our newspapers information they would otherwise hire agents to acquire through theft, bribery or espionage; that details of

this nation's covert preparations to counter the enemy's covert operations have been available to every newspaper reader, friend and foe
alike; that the size, the strength, the location and the nature of our
forces and weapons, and our plans and strategy for their use, have
all been pinpointed in the press and other news media to a degree
sufficient to satisfy any foreign power; and that, in at least one case,
the publication of details concerning a secret mechanism whereby
satellites were followed required its alteration at the expense of considerable time and money.

The newspapers which printed these stories were loyal, patriotic,
responsible and well-meaning. Had we been engaged in open warfare, they undoubtedly would not have published such items. But in
the absence of open warfare, they recognized only the tests of jour-
nalism and not the tests of national security. And my question tonight is whether additional tests should not now be adopted.

That question is for you alone to answer. No public official
should answer it for you. No governmental plan should impose its
restraints against your will. But I would be failing in my duty to the
Nation, in considering all of the responsibilities that we now bear
and all of the means at hand to meet those responsibilities, if I did
not commend this problem to your attention, and urge its thoughtful consideration.

On many earlier occasions, I have said—and your newspapers
have constantly said—that these are times that appeal to every citizen's sense of sacrifice and self-discipline. They call out to every citizen to weigh his rights and comforts against his obligations to the
common good. I cannot now believe that those citizens who serve
in the newspaper business consider themselves exempt from that appeal.

I have no intention of establishing a new Office of War Information to govern the flow of news. I am not suggesting any new forms
of censorship or new types of security classifications. I have no easy
answer to the dilemma I have posed, and would not seek to impose
it if I had one. But I am asking the members of the newspaper pro-
fession and their industry in this country to re-examine their own
responsibilities, to consider the degree and nature of the present
danger, and to heed the duty of self-restraint which that danger imposes upon us all.

Every newspaper now asks itself, with respect to every story: "Is
it news?" All I suggest is that you add the question: "Is it in the national interest?" And I hope that every group in America—unions
and businessmen and public officials at every level—will ask the

same question of their endeavors, and subject their actions to the same exacting test.

And should the press of America consider and recommend the voluntary assumption of specific new steps, I can assure you that we will cooperate whole-heartedly with those recommendations.

Perhaps there will be no recommendations. Perhaps there is no answer to the dilemma faced by a free and open society in a cold and secret war. In times of peace, any discussion of this subject, and any action that results, are both painful and without precedent. But this is a time of peace and peril which knows no precedent in history.

Kennedy was asking the press to waive voluntarily a substantial proportion of its rights. If one agrees with his assessment of the world in early 1961, his request, although unprecedented, may not seem unreasonable. But if one does not see a world irreconcilably divided, does not see democracy locked in mortal combat with communism, does not see the enemy at the gate, then his speech must be seen as a wholly unwarranted attempt to intimidate the press. The irony, of course, is that the American press has almost always behaved in the postwar years just as Kennedy wished— avoiding any searching examination of American foreign policy and the basic assumptions that underlie it. Had it acted otherwise, over the Bay of Pigs and on other issues, the national interest would have been better served. The national interest is too important a matter to be left solely to the government, particularly when governments throughout all history have demonstrated how little they can be trusted with it.

Now, more than a decade later, what can finally be said about the Bay of Pigs? Even his greatest admirers—Schlesinger, Sorensen, Hilsman, and Salinger—readily concede that it was a disaster and that Kennedy was ultimately responsible, although they try to qualify his responsibility somewhat. Yet they try to make the case that it was not all that much of a disaster and that, whatever its dimensions, it was soon forgotten, leaving behind no irreparable damage to the Kennedy administration. Whereas in a parliamentary system the incident would probably have caused the government to fall, it is true, albeit incredible, that the Bay of Pigs strengthened Kennedy at home rather than weakened him. It is also true that internationally the fiasco was soon forgotten, such was the President's enormous personal appeal and so deep was the urge to believe that a new age had dawned in America.

The main thrust of the argument given by Kennedy's admirers is that the Bay of Pigs taught him an invaluable lesson. Roger Hilsman put it this way: ". . . it was through this comparatively small disaster, though disaster it clearly was, that President Kennedy learned the lessons that enabled him to avoid a much greater, nuclear disaster a year and a half later by managing the Cuban missile crisis with such a sure and steady hand. If so, the price may have been cheap." [19] Sorensen wrote: "In later months he would be grateful that he had learned so many major lessons— resulting in basic changes in personnel, policy and procedures—at so relatively small and temporary a cost." [20] The most elegant apologia, as usual, came from Arthur Schlesinger:

> The impact of the failure shook up the national security machinery. It taught every adviser something about the President, the other advisers, himself and his own department. It was a horribly expensive lesson, but it was well-learned. In later months the President's father would tell him that in its perverse way, the Bay of Pigs was not a misfortune but a benefit. I doubt whether the President ever fully believed this; the thought of the men of the Brigade suffering in Cuban prisons prevented easy consolation. But no one can doubt that failure in Cuba in 1961 contributed to success in Cuba in 1962.[21]

A plausible explanation—until it is more closely examined. One can only wonder what Kennedy and his advisers— McNamara, Rusk, Bundy, Rostow, *et al.*—learned from this adventure in counterrevolution, for they were soon to plunge into intervention in Vietnam and into the frightening Berlin crisis, and these same advisers after Kennedy's death counseled Lyndon Johnson when he intervened in the Dominican Republic and when he extended the escalation in Vietnam.

Although it seemed a transient episode during Kennedy's administration, the Bay of Pigs was profoundly revealing. It demonstrated that Kennedy, like his predecessors, like his society, was excessively preoccupied with communism, that he was an interventionist prepared to violate national sovereignty in an attempt to strike it down. It demonstrated that Kennedy lacked prudence, an essential quality in the nuclear age. Although it has long been fashionable to scorn Eisenhower as lethargic and a bumbler, it is difficult to believe that he would have approved the Bay of Pigs. Even though planning was begun in his administration, Eisenhower was a careful man, and even if he had been prepared to entertain the plan in principle, he almost certainly would have dismissed it as absurd in practice. But even if the planning had not been an exercise in gross incompetence, even if it had not demonstrated a profound ignorance of revolution, even if it had not revealed a political attitude that would lead to more dangerous adventures, even if it had not led directly to the Cuban missile crisis, the Bay of Pigs would have still left an indelible stain on Kennedy's record. It was wrong.

In three years Kennedy's buildup of the most powerful military force in human history—the largest and swiftest buildup
in this country's peacetime history, at a cost of some $17 bil-
lion in additional appropriations—provided him, as he put it,
with a versatile arsenal "ranging from the most massive deter-
rents to the most subtle influences." [1]

—THEODORE SORENSEN

CHAPTER FOUR

The Military Buildup

The establishment of "the most powerful military force in human
history" is often cited as one of John Kennedy's great achievements. But perhaps another view is possible. Perhaps it can be
argued that this extraordinary buildup contributed massively to
the growth of the military-industrial complex that Eisenhower
warned against just three days before Kennedy's inauguration.
That it represented a diversion of resources, material, intellectual,
and even spiritual, that contributed to the domestic upheavals
soon to come. That it increased world tensions. That it demonstrated Kennedy's tendency to see the world's problems in military, not political terms. That it provided the wherewithal which
led inevitably to Vietnam.

It has often been said that Kennedy not only strengthened the
military establishment but put it, under his and Robert McNamara's direction, more firmly than ever under civilian control.
Kennedy may well have believed that he did, yet that too must be
questioned. Adam Yarmolinsky was one of those close to Kennedy during the election campaign and after, serving as Deputy
Assistant Secretary of Defense for International Security Affairs.
As it did so many others, the Vietnam war caused Yarmolinsky to
re-evaluate things. This is what he believes now:

> The influence of the military establishment on domestic politics
> or the domestic economy may be functions of its budget or size or

power, but its influence on foreign policy depends on an altogether different variable—the extent to which civilians in the executive branch, in Congress and among the public bear in mind or forget General Marshall's maxim that political problems, if thought about in military terms, become military problems.[2]

Civilian control versus military control is a distinction without a difference if the civilians think the same way the military does. During his presidential campaign Kennedy time and time again declared that United States military forces, both conventional and nuclear, had to be strengthened. Indeed, the "missile gap" that he said had been allowed to develop during the Eisenhower administration was one of his principal themes. On October 13, in one of the television debates with Vice President Nixon, Kennedy said:

> Well, I think we should strengthen our conventional forces. And we should attempt in January, February, and March of next year to increase the airlift capacity of our conventional forces. Then I believe that we should move full time on our missile production, particularly on Minuteman and on Polaris. It may be a long period but we must get started immediately.

This Kennedy proceeded to do almost from the moment he moved into the White House. At first glance it might seem that he showed a consistency other elected candidates should emulate, but remember that Kennedy the candidate genuinely believed that there was a missile gap, genuinely believed—minus a normal discount for campaign oratory—that communist armed strength was growing while the United States grew relatively weaker. But as soon as Kennedy and his top officials examined Pentagon and CIA intelligence reports, they learned that the contrary was true. Not only was the United States vastly stronger, but its superiority was growing steadily, for the Soviet Union had reduced its military spending and was not making a major effort even in the area of intercontinental ballistic missiles, the one area in which it had a momentary technological superiority. Although it is foolish to attempt to read Khrushchev's mind, one likely reason for his outrage over the U-2 flights (which became public knowledge when one was shot down over Russia in early 1960) was the fact that Washington knew from these overflights how few nuclear missiles he had emplaced, thus rendering futile any attempt by Khrushchev to use his missile "superiority" as a force in international power politics. Ironically, then, Kennedy's campaign theme served Khrushchev's purpose, not for Washington, which knew Russia's weakness, but for the rest of the world, which might have been impressed by Khrushchev's boasting.

Needless to say, much of the relevant material on nuclear and other weaponry is classified, but enough has emerged to make it absolutely certain that America's military superiority was overwhelming and that Kennedy knew it from his first days in office. The field of nuclear deterrent is arcane indeed, more suitable for theological disputation than for ordinary discourse. To discuss this aspect of Kennedy's military policy would require a separate book, but a certain limited amount must be said, even for the purposes of this study. In brief, a nation is said to have a "first-strike capability" if its nuclear strength is such and is so targeted that it can attack another nation with such overwhelming power that it need not fear a significant counterattack. This not only is awesomely expensive but frightens the other nation into developing a similar capability if it can, initiating a higher order of arms competition. Thus both sides live in constant fear of sudden, overpowering attack. Consequently, in recent years both the United States and the Soviet Union have settled for a "second-strike capability," that is to say, each has deliberately restricted its nuclear attacking power. Nonetheless, each has enough nuclear strength—in hardened sites, hidden away ashore or wandering, almost impossible to detect, beneath the seas in submarines—so that, even if the other side strikes first, it will be able to respond with a nuclear salvo aimed at big cities that would take an unacceptable toll, thus "deterring" an initial attack. This deterrent strategy can also give rise to an arms race—and has done so—but it is not so expensive or so terrifying as a first-strike arms race.

By the time Kennedy took office the Eisenhower administration had almost achieved a first-strike capability, not so much through deliberate policy as by willy-nilly increasing the defense budget because of anti-communist fervor.[3] The United States nuclear stockpile was estimated at about 30,000 megatons or the equivalent of about 10 tons of TNT for every living person. And, according to the Defense Department, the United States nuclear delivery vehicles, strategic and tactical, numbered "in the tens of thousands." "This included over a hundred missiles of intercontinental and intermediate range, eighty Polaris missiles, 1700 intercontinental bombers, 300 nuclear-armed carrier-borne aircraft with megaton warheads and nearly 1000 supersonic land-based fighters with nuclear warheads." [4]

Compare this to Russian might in 1962. The estimate was 50 intercontinental missiles, 150 intercontinental bombers, and 400 intermediate-range missiles aimed at United States overseas and NATO bases. The Soviet Union's only advantage was that its ICBMs could carry heavier payloads, but that was overwhelmed many times over by American numerical superiority in delivery vehicles. The United States delivery vehicles were stationed, for the most part, in Europe, the Middle East, and Asia, close to the Soviet Union, while the Soviet missiles were stationed on Russian soil, distant from the United States. If Soviet men were anything like their American counterparts, they must have been terribly concerned, and this concern must have grown by quantum jumps as Kennedy during his first six months kept announcing further steps in the buildup.

In his inaugural address Kennedy declared, "Only when our arms are sufficient beyond doubt can we be certain without doubt that they will never be employed." This statement raises several issues. The first is the subtle one of tone. It sounded then, and still sounds, like tough talk, a new variation on the theme so often sounded in the Truman and Eisenhower administrations, "peace through strength." This has a nice ring to it at first hearing, but what it means is obvious: we're going to be so much stronger than the other guy that he won't dare step out of line. Equally obviously, it is an invitation to an arms race, for what great power would dare to ignore such a challenge? But in any event, history has disproved the validity of the entire statement. American arms were "sufficient beyond doubt" when Kennedy took office, but this sufficiency did not make it certain that arms would not be used. They were used increasingly in Vietnam, and their use was made possible only by the increased sufficiency. This is a crucial point.

Before considering it, however, it is necessary to examine the first few months of the Kennedy administration, when the military buildup swung into high gear. Even before Kennedy took office the United States had a more than three-to-one advantage in missiles and a more than ten-to-one advantage in intercontinental bombers. During 1960 the United States intelligence community had *cut* by 70 per cent its estimate of Soviet missile strength. By June 1961 the estimate was down to 15 per cent of the original figure, and by September it was down to only 3.5 per cent.[5] Certainly there was never a disposition for United States intelligence to underestimate Soviet strength, so these figures should be seen as maximum.

On February 6 Secretary of Defense McNamara held a background briefing for reporters. He was new to the subtleties of the art in which government officials speak without attribution, a practice newsmen favor because they can get stories that otherwise might not be available. (It also gives officials a chance to manipulate the news without having to take responsibility for the stories.) In this case there was no contest between the experienced reporters and the inexperienced McNamara. He disclosed that there was no missile gap, confirming what outgoing President Eisenhower had said just the month before. The unattributed story, needless to say, was given front-page treatment, and such was its magnitude that its source soon emerged.[6] The next day Pierre Salinger, Kennedy's press secretary, said with the President's approval that McNamara was "absolutely wrong." The President and his Secretary of Defense held a quick huddle, and on February 8, in a press conference, Kennedy toned down his criticism. In answer to a direct question as to whether there was a missile gap, Kennedy took refuge by exercising a customary governmental gambit, saying that a study of military preparedness was under way and that it was "premature to reach a judgment as to whether there is a gap or not a gap."

It is perhaps understandable that Kennedy fudged. It was still early in the administration and the course had not yet been determined. And no politician likes to admit that one of his fundamental campaign charges was entirely wrong, even if it was made in good faith. What was important was not what Kennedy said in early February, even if he dissembled, but what he decided to do in the following months. The decision was not long in coming. Kennedy had decided on "the largest and swiftest buildup in this country's peacetime history." This was consistent not only with his campaign but with his decision to go ahead with the Bay of Pigs invasion.

The obvious question is: Why did Kennedy decide on such a massive buildup? There is no obvious answer. A careful examination of his public statements encounters much stirring rhetoric but little that is more specific than this passage from his State of the Union message on January 30: "First, we must strengthen our military tools. We are moving into a period of uncertain risk and great commitment in which both the military and diplomatic possibilities require a Free World force so powerful as to make any aggression clearly futile."

This and similar statements are puzzling. Obviously, any determination of America's military posture must attempt to take into account the Soviet Union's intentions and capabilities. While it is impossible to be certain of the Kremlin's intentions, it is nonetheless true that Khrushchev directed very friendly words toward Kennedy after his election and at his inauguration. Further, he gave substance to his words by releasing the RB-47 fliers. It is also true that during the last months of Harry Truman's administration and all during the Eisenhower years, particularly after Stalin's death in 1953, the Russians had signaled in many ways on many occasions that they wanted better relations with the United States. While it may have been true, as Dulles and the Cold Warriors generally argued, that these signals were just attempts to get the West to drop its guard, little endeavor was made to determine, by undertaking serious talks, just how sincere—or insincere—the Russians were. The possibility of peaceful intentions was real enough not to be dismissed out of hand. But even though Kennedy was of the conventional school of thought which maintains that Russian intentions can never be trusted, he knew that the Soviet Union was much too weak to be a serious threat in any direct confrontation and thus would not be likely to seek one.

Therefore it is necessary to seek elsewhere for an explanation. First to be dismissed is the possibility that Kennedy was a warmonger. There is absolutely no reason to doubt his commitment to peace. No responsible student of the Kennedy years could suggest that he intended to use the increased might in an outright military offensive. A more likely possibility is that he had the politician's need to redeem his campaign pledges and prove his campaign charges. But that could have been done with two or three hundred million dollars and some suitable rhetoric. The most likely possibility seems to be that Kennedy intended to end the Cold War by scoring a victory, that by a combination of unchallengeable military and economic strength, backed with cool and unshakable resolve, he would force the Soviet Union, short of war, short of humiliation, to accept a Pax Americana. Kennedy was much too intelligent to believe that this would be a neat and tidy resolution; he recognized that there would be constant tugging and hauling and maneuvering, but hoped that in broad outline the Soviet Union would tacitly settle for stability and the considerable prerogatives accruing to even a number-two power. This view would seem to be consistent with Kennedy's anti-communism and that of his closest advisers, and consistent with his demonstrable *machismo* and activism. He was determined to be a President who went down in history as a doer of great deeds. What greater deed than to end the Cold War with victory—not a narrow, nationalistic victory, but one that would benefit not only the Free World (suitably capitalized) but the peoples of the communist countries and the Third World as well? It would be the logical culmination of a democratic but messianic streak that runs all through American history, personified in earlier eras by Polk and Teddy Roosevelt and Woodrow Wilson.

This, of course, is only speculation. Others have argued that Kennedy was the victim, willing or otherwise, of the military-industrial complex, or that he did not want to risk public confrontation with the Joint Chiefs of Staff, who, despite their powerful adherents in Congress, had never dared to oppose Kennedy's five-star predecessor. A Naval Reserve lieutenant (j.g.) might be reluctant to engage in a public tug-of-war with generals and admirals. These and other factors may all have had their influence. Yet it may be better to put aside speculation and return to the facts, in the hope that candid memoirs by Dean Rusk or Robert McNamara or others high in Kennedy's counsel will be more specific on this point than what has been written thus far.

The facts are clear. In those crowded early weeks, while facing also difficult decisions on Laos, Cuba, and the Congo, while coming to grips with a whole range of domestic problems, Kennedy made his basic decision, one that changed the course of American history. With his knowledge that the Soviet Union was—in relative terms—weak, he could have moved toward détente with Russia, for even without further buildup, he held all the high cards. But he chose instead, for whatever reason, to launch a mighty offensive against communism, one that would turn the tide that, in his campaign speeches, he saw unfavorable to the "Free World." Such an offensive, even though Kennedy was confident it could be conducted short of war, required military superiority even greater than that the United States already possessed.

When, in three installments, he presented his needs to Congress, they added up to about $6 billion more than President Eisenhower had requested, in a budget which he had insisted was fully adequate. Kennedy, in effect, had invited the Pentagon to pull out the shopping lists Eisenhower had made them put back in the drawer. Now, a case can be made that Eisenhower had relied too heavily on "massive" nuclear retaliatory power and had allowed conventional armed strength to languish, thus inviting "brushfire" wars dangerous to American interests yet too limited to justify the use of nuclear weapons. However, a better case can be made that having the ability to intervene in a brushfire war increases the likelihood that the United States will intervene. Nonetheless, for the sake of argument, let it be agreed that while the intelligence data demonstrated America's vast superiority in strategic weapons, its conventional strength was limited. Yet of the $2.4 billion requested by Kennedy on March 28 in his first installment, $1.8 billion was for additional spending on existing strategic programs, about two-thirds of it for the Polaris program and other large sums for the Minuteman and Skybolt missile systems. Only about one-third of the entire request went for conventional forces. While the great increase in strategic-weapon spending must have alarmed the Kremlin, it was Kennedy's concern with local wars involving conventional forces that was to have the greatest long-term consequences. It is worth noting Kennedy's words:

> The Free World's security can be endangered not only by a nuclear attack, but also by being slowly nibbled away at the periphery, regardless of our strategic power, by forces of subversion, infiltration, intimidation, indirect or non-overt aggression, internal rev-

olution, diplomatic blackmail, guerrilla warfare or a series of limited wars.

Whereas Kennedy saw the strategic competition with the Soviet Union and "wars of national liberation" as two battlefronts of the same struggle, they were and are substantially distinct, although sometimes related. It was the inability to make this distinction that was Kennedy's terrible failure, one that was tragically compounded by Lyndon Johnson.

For the moment, however, let us concentrate on the strategic buildup. Kennedy, in this revealing statement, ducked the essential question of justification for his extraordinary requests by saying blandly:

> It would not be appropriate at this time or in this message to either boast of our strength or dwell upon our needs. It is sufficient to say that the budgetary recommendations which follow, together with other policy, organizational and related changes and studies now under way administratively, are designed to provide for an increased strength, flexibility and control in our defense establishment. . . .

In short, Kennedy was telling Congress, which as an equal branch of government had the constitutional authority "to raise and support armies, . . . to provide and maintain a navy," not to ask any questions. And Congress didn't. Regarding the "missile gap," about which he had promised to speak, the President said only, "It has been publicly acknowledged for several years that this nation has not led the world in missile strength." In effect: because I kept repeating for several years that there is a missile gap, it is "publicly acknowledged" that there is a missile gap, although, as I have learned since taking office, there never was a missile gap. However, "it would not be appropriate at this time or in this message" to admit it.

It is difficult to find any publicly stated recognition by members of the Kennedy administration of the obvious fact that the military increases were bound to have repercussions in the Kremlin, that they would affect the relations between the new administration and the Soviet Union, that they might trigger undesirable diplomatic, political, or military responses. Perhaps Kennedy was confident that the United States was so strong that the Soviet Union would not dare to do anything unpleasant, although a student of postwar history such as Kennedy should have recognized that the Russians, even when they were defenseless before the short-lived American atomic monopoly, refused to be intimidated (much to the consternation of a succession of United States officials). Prudent, yes; overawed, no.

One final thing has to be said about Kennedy's message of March 28, one that points up a great difficulty in coming to a judgment about him. Often, on many issues, Kennedy gave first-rate speeches, and so persuasive was his public personality, so eager were Americans to feel their faith in him justified, that he was often judged on his words rather than on his deeds. For instance, in this March 28 statement he said, "The basic problems facing the world today are not susceptible to a military solution. Neither our strategy nor our psychology as a nation—and certainly not our economy—must become dependent upon the permanent maintenance of a large military establishment." One wants to cheer such words, but unfortunately they were uttered just three weeks before the Bay of Pigs invasion was launched and they were embedded in a request for actions that directly contradicted these words. How often, when espousing a hard line, he acted in complete accordance with his words; and how often (but not always), when being conciliatory, he did just the opposite.

It was up to Secretary of Defense McNamara to carry out the new military policy and, simultaneously, somehow to establish mastery over the conglomeration of feuding baronies and duchies that was the Defense Department. An extraordinary man, McNamara was equal to the first task and as equal to the second as any mortal man could be. It soon became clear to Washington-watchers that McNamara was, as Sorensen put it, the "star" of the Cabinet and, as Robert Kennedy wrote, the man regarded by President Kennedy "as the most valuable public servant in the administration and the government." [7] McNamara was the master of that new art which was to dominate the decade: technocracy, the inevitable successor to bureaucracy. The conventional view of his emergence was well put by William E. Leuchtenburg in *The American Review*:

. . . McNamara has asserted the authority of the civilian Secretary of Defense over the entire military establishment. In an era when

Americans are growingly alarmed by the rise of the "garrison state," McNamara's achievement may well stand out as the most important development of the Kennedy era.[8]

McNamara and his "Whiz Kids" from corporate management confronted the bewildered generals and admirals with a dazzling and mysterious array of programing, planning, and budgetary techniques that successfully challenged the heretofore almost unchallenged expertise of the career military men. For a few years, these new techniques, supported by a massive use of computers, even offered some hope that the leaders of government would at last gain control of the enormous and complex apparatus of government. But that hope petered out late in the Johnson administration, at about the same time as did the hope for victory in Vietnam which, to so large an extent, had been based on these managerial miracles.

Thus it is not surprising that Kennedy invited his Secretary of Defense to participate in decisions that were primarily the concern of other agencies: on civil defense, space, intelligence, paramilitary operations, foreign aid, and foreign policy in general. The danger in this development has in retrospect become clear:

> Regardless of the individual avowals and commitments of the principal officers of the new industrial machine, it is necessarily the case that the increased competence of this organization contributes to the competence of the parent body—the Department of Defense. This competence is a war-making capability. Hence, the very efficiency and success of the new industrial management, unavoidably and regardless of intent, enhances the war-making capability of the government of the United States. As the war-making department accumulates diverse resources and planning capability, it is able to offer the President blueprint-stage options for responding to all manner of problem situations—while other government agencies look (and are) unready, understaffed and under-equipped. This increases the likelihood of resources to "solutions" based on military power.[9]

Perhaps the most valuable contribution in Roger Hilsman's valuable *To Move a Nation* is his frequent pointing out of how often—as he knew from participation in important decisions—the Defense Department dominated the discussion of matters that should have been directed by the State Department, and how Kennedy, although he often reflected aloud that State was not as strong as he would like it to be, acquiesced in this. By now a great deal has been written about how Defense, because of its greater resources and its inherent disposition to see things in concrete, specific terms, was often able during the Kennedy and Johnson years—and is still, no doubt—to prepare concise, concrete position papers more likely to appeal to busy Presidents than the necessarily more discursive, speculative papers from the State Department. Indeed, this emphasizes another of Kennedy's basic flaws. He wanted concise, concrete presentations and admired the "hard-nosed realists," as they liked to consider themselves, who could provide them, being impatient with expansive, idealistic types such as Adlai Stevenson and Chester Bowles. This confusion of brevity with wisdom was nothing less than tragic, for the proposals of the "realists" who operated on Kennedy's wavelength— McNamara, McGeorge Bundy, W. W. Rostow—led to the Bay of Pigs, to the brink in the missile crisis, to the involvement in Vietnam. In every one of these momentous questions the "idealists" were more realistic than the "realists." Therefore, even if Kennedy and his advisers genuinely believed that they were establishing civilian dominance over the military, it was a distinction without a difference, for these particular civilians were no different beneath their Brooks Brothers suits from the military beneath their uniforms.

As the Kennedy administration moved toward the next installment of its request for escalating military spending, it was, of course, dealing with many other matters as well. Besides the whole range of domestic problems, we have seen how in these first months Kennedy had to take decisions of historic importance on Laos and Cuba, in both of which crises came to a head in April. Also the Alliance for Progress was undergoing its birth pangs, as was the Peace Corps. The foreign-aid bill was being prepared, and the United States was getting ready for talks at Geneva on disarmament and nuclear testing. Then there was the Congo, where the situation was seldom better than chaotic; and underlying all else were relations between the United States and the Soviet Union. In February, Kennedy had instructed Ambassador Llewellyn Thompson to invite Khrushchev to a summit meeting at some mutually convenient site. While waiting for the answer, Kennedy also had to find time to consider a foreign problem with somewhat lower priority than some of the others, but one that would eventually become the most difficult, most divisive problem of the 1960s, Vietnam. On May 5 Kennedy announced at a news conference that Vice President Johnson would head a fact-finding mission to Southeast Asia and that the administration was considering the possibility of sending troops to Vietnam. And a week later Kennedy got the word that Khrushchev had agreed to private talks in Vienna.

On May 25, less than two weeks before he was to meet Khrushchev at Vienna, Kennedy went in person before Congress with the second installment of his military requests. Although the amount of money was not so great this time, the message was wider in scope than that of two months before. Kennedy asked for $160 million to improve the Army's ability to respond quickly with conventional weapons to conventional or unconventional military situations, to increase counterinsurgency forces, and to expand the Marine Corps. He also asked for an additional $2.4 million for the U.S. Information Agency, and an additional $285 million on top of the $1.6 billion he had already requested for the Military Assistance Program. He spoke of the need for an active civil-defense program that would provide fallout shelters for millions of people. He put the program under the Secretary of Defense and said it would cost "more than triple the pending budget requests; and they will increase sharply in subsequent years." Kennedy also included three paragraphs on disarmament in which he said, "I cannot end this discussion of defense and armaments without emphasizing our strongest hope: the creation of an orderly world where disarmament will be possible. Our arms do not prepare for war—they are efforts to discourage and resist the adventures of others that would end in war." And he said he would send to Congress a measure establishing a strengthened and enlarged Disarmament Agency. However, even Kennedy's admirers concede that, particularly early in his term, he regarded disarmament as unrealistic, a pious hope.

Again, in this speech we see rhetoric that seems to indicate a realistic assessment of the world. Speaking of nations in a revolutionary situation, he said:

We would be badly mistaken to consider their problems in military terms alone. For no amount of arms and armies can help stabilize those governments which are unable or unwilling to achieve social and economic reform and development. Military pacts cannot help nations whose social injustice and economic chaos invite insurgency and penetration and subversion. The most skillful counterguerrilla efforts cannot succeed where the local population is too caught up in its own misery to be concerned about the advance of communism.

This would seem to be an irrefutable argument against getting involved in South Vietnam—but that was what the Kennedy administration was about to do. Again and again, and it must be reiterated to the point of tedium, Kennedy would make a perceptive observation and then act in directly contrary fashion: Kennedy the pragmatist versus Kennedy the ideologue. Here, in this speech of May 1961, both were present but, as usual, it was the crusader who triumphed.

. . . the adversaries of freedom plan to consolidate their territory —to exploit, to control, and finally to destroy the hopes of the world's newest nations; and they have ambition to do it before the end of this decade. It is a contest of will and purpose as well as force and violence—a battle for minds and souls as well as lives and territory. And in that contest, we cannot stand aside.

We stand, as we have always stood from our earliest beginnings, for the independence and equality of all nations. This nation was born of revolution and raised in freedom. And we do not intend to leave an open road for despotism.

Again the call to arms; again that expression of mission that has resounded all through American history, making the world safe for democracy—a noble slogan, but one with the fateful implication that a self-righteous America must set the world straight.

It is not surprising that this was the occasion on which President Kennedy declared, "I believe that this nation should commit itself to achieving the goal, before this decade is out, of landing a man on the moon and returning him safely to earth." Many have written that this challenge was issued not out of an abiding interest in space flight, not with thoughtful concern for the human risks and financial burdens and priorities involved, but out of a sense of wounded national pride that Russia was first in space. Although the space race was not, in the mundane sense at least, a matter of foreign policy, Kennedy saw it as a major factor in the mighty struggle between the two great powers. This interpretation is supported by his opening words in the passage on space. He refers to the first manned space flight, by Soviet cosmonaut Yuri A. Gagarin, who orbited the earth on April 12, 1961, and the first American flight (suborbital), by Alan B. Shepard, Jr., on May 5.

> Finally, if we are to win the battle that is now going on around the world between freedom and tyranny, the dramatic achievements in space which occurred in recent weeks should have made clear to us all, as did the Sputnik in 1957, the impact of this adventure on the minds of men everywhere, who are attempting to make a determination of which road they should take.

Kennedy was determined to win the contest on earth and in the skies, and soon he would journey to Vienna to meet in person his adversary, Nikita S. Khrushchev. From that confrontation would come the third, and largest, installment of Kennedy's military buildup. And from it too would come the Berlin crisis. They must be considered together.

The President, in his pre-Vienna studies and in his talks with Adenauer in Washington and De Gaulle in Paris, recognized more clearly than ever that West Berlin was the touchstone of American honor and resolve, and that Khrushchev was certain to use it to test Allied unity and resistance.[1]

— THEODORE SORENSEN

The Berlin crisis of 1961 represented a further step beyond Laos in the education of the President in the controlled employment of force for the service of peace. One never knows, of course, what would have happened if Kennedy had ordered full mobilization or if he had rushed straight to negotiation; but either extreme might well have invited Soviet miscalculation and ended in war. Instead he applied power and diplomacy in a combination and sequence which enabled him to guard the vital interests of the West and hold off the holocaust.[2]

— ARTHUR SCHLESINGER

The modern state, among other things, is an engine of propaganda, alternately manufacturing crises and claiming to be the only instrument which can effectively deal with them.[3]

—CHRISTOPHER LASCH

CHAPTER FIVE

Vienna and Berlin

John Kennedy and Nikita Khrushchev met in Vienna on June 3 and 4, 1961. It was, as the Kennedy admirers have written, a historic meeting, but not necessarily for the reasons they suggest. The conventional view has been that Vienna, part cordial feeling-out, part courteous but tough confrontation, was most significant as the trigger for the tense and dangerous Berlin crisis of that summer.

75

Vienna did lead to Berlin, but it was Kennedy, not Khrushchev, who forced the issue, and since the Berlin crisis, although real, was largely fabricated in Washington, Vienna was more occasion than cause. Vienna was more important for Vietnam than it was for Berlin, for in these candid talks with Khrushchev, Kennedy revealed to a greater degree than on any other occasion his profound and critical misunderstanding of revolution and communism. His admirers have always talked about Kennedy's capacity to learn from experience. Here was an important chance to learn, and he flunked it.

Again we must go back to Kennedy the candidate. As early as December 9, 1959, in an interview with John Fischer of *Harper's,* Kennedy spoke of the possibility of war over Berlin:

> If we took the view which some Englishmen took, that Prague or the Sudetendeutsch were not worth a war in '38—if we took that view about Berlin, my judgment is that the West Berliners would pass into the communist orbit, and our position in West Germany and our relations with West Germany would receive a fatal blow. With West Germany neutralized, all Western Europe would soon be neutralized, and it would be a decisive victory for the Soviet Union. For us to think that what the central struggle is about is just Berlin would be a great mistake. They're fighting for New York and Paris when they struggle over Berlin. Therefore, I think we would have to make it cold—and mean it—that we would fight.[4]

Kennedy, then, saw Berlin not only as important in itself but as the key to the Western position in Europe. And even before he took office he was expecting trouble there. On October 7, in one of his television debates with Vice President Nixon, Kennedy declared:

> Now, the next President of the United States, in his first year is going to be confronted with a very serious question on our defense of Berlin. Our commitment to Berlin. There's going to be a test of our nerve and our will. There's going to be a test of our strength and because we're going to move in '61 and '62, partly because we have not maintained our strength with sufficient vigor in the last years. I believe that before we meet that crisis that the next President of the United States should send a message to Congress asking for revitalization of our military strength because come spring or

late in the winter, we're going to be face to face with the most serious Berlin crisis since 1949 or '50.

On October 13, in the third debate, Kennedy returned to Berlin:

> I have stated on many occasions that the United States must
> meet its commitment on Berlin. It is a commitment that we have to
> meet if we're going to protect the security of Western Europe. And,
> therefore, on this question, I don't think that there is any doubt in
> the mind of any American. I hope there is not any doubt in the
> mind of any member of the community of West Berlin. I am sure
> there isn't any doubt in the mind of the Russians. We will meet our
> commitments to maintain the freedom and independence of West
> Berlin.

Some might see this as a laudable expression of national resolve, but in retrospect it seems more like a self-fulfilling
prophecy. A giant step toward that fulfillment was taken in March
1961, when Kennedy asked Dean Acheson to undertake an inten-
sive study of the problems of NATO and Germany. Joseph Alsop,
once the press agent for General Claire Chennault and his Flying
Tigers, was delighted. Hawks of a feather flock together. But Walter Lippmann, who had been warning of the dangers of the Cold
War since its beginning, was alarmed. Both knew, as did Kennedy,
what to expect of such a study: "Be tough, don't give up an inch,
the communists respect only force, they're out to test your man-
hood." That was the result and that was the line Acheson pushed
when Harold Macmillan and his Foreign Secretary, Lord Home,
came to Washington in early April. With his magnificent arrogance, and to the horror of the British, Acheson spoke blandly of
sending an American division over the *Autobahn* to West Berlin
if any trouble should develop. The British thought such a position
was negative and tried to discuss the political aspects, saying that
the inevitable diplomatic talks on Berlin could not be entered
without a Western position. And Britain suggested that after sixteen years the right of conquest in West Berlin was growing thin.
Acheson was, of course, equal to that, suggesting that it was Western power that was growing thin. With the support of the State
Department representative, he suggested that since the West had
nothing to gain from talks about Germany and Berlin, such talks

should be avoided. Kennedy said little during this conversation but evidently agreed. This was the genesis of the Berlin crisis. While Khrushchev had reiterated his call for a peace conference and treaty, Kennedy was deciding to avoid talks.

The British were not the only participants in the meeting to be horrified. Among the Americans so to respond was Adlai Stevenson, whom Acheson treated, whenever they could not avoid meeting, with faintly concealed scorn. Later Stevenson said, "Maybe Dean is right, but his position [the need for a military showdown] should be the conclusion of a process of investigation, not the beginning. He starts at a point which we should not reach until we have explored and exhausted all the alternatives." [5]

When Kennedy went to Vienna, he had pretty much decided to avoid making an American commitment to subsequent talks on Berlin. Not only that, but he carried to Austria the burden of the history of his administration, however brief: Kennedy had sent the Cuban exiles off to the Bay of Pigs, he had flexed his military muscle over Laos, he had twice asked Congress for funds for a massive military buildup (with more, obviously, to come), and in the week and a half after the Bay of Pigs fiasco he had made two hostile and alarmist anti-communist speeches. It is unlikely that Khrushchev regarded these as gestures of conciliation.

Although the minutes of the Kennedy–Khrushchev talks have not been made public, enough has emerged, largely from Kennedy's admirers, to give a pretty clear account of what happened. Both men were well prepared. Khrushchev knew of Kennedy's major speeches and messages and also obscure Congressional debates in which he had engaged in earlier years. As noted earlier, the two men had little difficulty in agreeing on Laos, although Khrushchev could not resist chiding Kennedy for doing some sword-rattling in April and May. And Khrushchev told Kennedy that the American military buildup was putting pressure on him to increase Russian preparedness. He recognized, he said, that both of them were under pressure from scientists and military men to resume nuclear testing. "But we will wait for you to resume testing and, if you do, we will." [6] However, only a few months later Russia began a series of massive tests that alarmed most of the world and angered Kennedy, but perhaps the swift-moving events just then getting in motion caused Khrushchev to change his mind, possibly under the pressure of his military men.

According to Sorensen, Kennedy's major thesis articulated at Vienna about relations between the two superpowers was that they should avoid situations in which their vital interests were committed in a direct confrontation from which neither nation could back down. This, of course, makes sense. But confrontation is possible in two ways: it is also possible indirectly in a country such as Vietnam. Whereas Kennedy saw the problem of developing countries as another aspect of the same struggle, Khrushchev saw it as a separate question. I shall examine this matter more fully in the discussion of Vietnam.

For the moment let us concentrate on the direct confrontation over Berlin. Khrushchev insisted that the situation in Berlin and Germany could not be permitted to continue, that if the West would not reach a peace treaty on the basis of two Germanys, he would sign a separate treaty with East Germany by the end of 1961. Western rights in West Berlin resulting from the German surrender in 1945 would no longer exist, and any further arrangements would have to be made with the East German government. Khrushchev did not insist that West Germany withdraw from NATO; he did not even insist that the Western powers recognize East Germany, just that they sign a peace treaty recognizing the reality of two Germanys and making a long-range settlement on Berlin.

Kennedy thanked Khrushchev for being so frank, but he said that this was not merely a legal matter; it was of primary and vital concern to American security. The United States was not in Berlin by sufferance; it had fought its way there and its presence was a matter of contract among the United States, Britain, France, and the Soviet Union. If the United States allowed itself to be expelled, American pledges and commitments all around the world would be regarded as mere scraps of paper. If the United States abandoned West Berlin, it would mean the abandonment of Western Europe, and the United States had already proved in two world wars that it regarded Western Europe as essential to its security. If Khrushchev agreed that world power was now roughly in balance, he should understand that the United States could not accept anything that would significantly change the balance of power.

Khrushchev objected that Kennedy did not understand him. All he wanted to do was lessen tension in the most dangerous place in the world. A peace treaty would not change borders; it would merely regularize them. Berlin had no military significance, he said, and after a treaty West Berlin could be a "free city" and have ties with and be accessible to any countries it chose, guaranteed by the United States and the Soviet Union, jointly or through the United Nations. But if Kennedy insisted on occupation rights after Russia and East Germany signed a treaty, and if the East German borders were violated, force would be met with force. "I want peace," said Khrushchev, "but if you want war, that is your problem." Kennedy said, "It is you, and not I, who wants to force a change." [7] But Khrushchev insisted that if there were no peace conference he would unilaterally sign a treaty with East Germany by December, pointing out that the United States had not permitted Russia to sign the Japanese peace treaty. As they parted, Kennedy said, "It will be a cold winter."

Many chroniclers of the Kennedy administration have written as if Khrushchev were responsible for the Berlin crisis. There is good reason to dispute this. In the first place, it *was* 1961, sixteen years after the end of World War II, long past time for a German peace treaty. Half a generation had passed, and the West was still relying on the surrender agreement to keep its military forces in West Berlin, contrary to both logic and the expectation in 1945 that a peace treaty would follow within a reasonable time. Berlin was deep within East Germany, and West Berlin was serving as an escape hatch for thousands of East Germany's most talented young people, who were traveling to East Berlin and then crossing to West Berlin, where they sought political asylum. Although one unreservedly and entirely sympathizes with those East Germans who were "voting with their feet," as Western propagandists happily put it, they obviously presented a serious problem to East Germany and Russia. It was foolish for Britain, France, and the United States to pretend that East Germany did not exist as a separate state. However unfortunate, it did exist. Further, one wonders why the United States over the years staked so much on Berlin. It is true that Stalin's reckless blockade in 1948 inevitably increased the American commitment to West Berlin, but that commitment seemed to increase in intensity thereafter to the extent that West Germany had something of a veto power over American policy.

Even if Kennedy was not prepared to make the concessions that would be inevitable in any full-scale peace conference, he could have avoided the alarming war talk on both sides simply by agreeing to talk things over. He did not have to agree to a peace conference, merely to talks about a peace conference or even talks about talks about a peace conference. In 1958 Khrushchev had blustered in similar fashion but had settled for inconclusive talks. Indeed, later in 1961 when Kennedy did finally agree to talks, the Berlin crisis—which had the nation fearing the possibility of war and caused the ugly bomb-shelter scare—vanished as if by magic. Let there be no mistake: I believe that the Berlin crisis, with all the dangerous consequences we shall soon examine, was largely a Washington fabrication, that there would have been no crisis if Kennedy had done sooner what he did later. In this there is a direct parallel with the Cuban missile crisis.

Whatever his reason, Kennedy immediately began to alarm the American people. This is what Sorensen wrote:

> He wanted no one to think that the surface cordiality in Vienna justified any notion of a new "Spirit of Geneva, 1955" or "Spirit of Camp David, 1959." But he may have "over-managed" the news. His private briefings of the press were so grim, while Khrushchev in public appeared so cheerful, that a legend soon arose that Vienna had been a traumatic, shattering experience, that Khrushchev had bullied and browbeaten the President and that Kennedy was depressed and disheartened.[8]

That was certainly the impression he gave. So vivid was this impression that it stayed with James Reston of *The New York Times* until even a year after Kennedy's death. He wrote in the *Times Magazine* of November 14, 1964, that Kennedy "came into a dim room in the American Embassy shaken and angry. He had tried, as always, to be calm and rational with Khrushchev, to get him to define what the Soviet Union would and would not do, and Khrushchev had bullied him and threatened him with war over Berlin."

We do not know what Kennedy's private response was to his encounter with Khrushchev, for a politician often plays a role, and he may have wanted the world to think that Khrushchev was tough and had threatened war. But Charles Bohlen and Llewellyn Thompson, previous and current ambassadors to Russia, thought then that Khrushchev had been just "par for the course" and that Kennedy had overreacted.[9] Yet even if Kennedy, for whatever reason, wanted to portray the meeting as grim and Khrushchev as tough, he could hardly have wanted to appear intimidated. No President would want that, especially no President named Kennedy. This feeling may have contributed to a second overreaction, in which he tried to prove, in a typical American response, that he couldn't be pushed around. "Kennedy wished to make clear, in a favorite Washington phrase that spring, that Khrushchev must not crowd him too much." [10]

After stopping briefly at London to see Macmillan, Kennedy returned home. On June 6 he made a television report to the nation. Although he had regained his poise, his report was still somber:

> . . . I will tell you now that it was a very sober two days. There was no discourtesy, no loss of tempers, no threats or ultimatums by either side; no advantage or concession was either gained or given; no major decision was either planned or taken; no spectacular progress was either achieved or pretended. . . .
>
> Our most somber talks were on the subject of Germany and Berlin. I made it clear to Mr. Khrushchev that the security of Western Europe and therefore our own security are deeply involved in our presence and our access rights to West Berlin, that we are determined to maintain these rights at any risk, and thus meet our obligation to the people of West Berlin, and their right to choose their own future.
>
> Mr. Khrushchev, in turn, presented his views in detail, and his presentation will be the subject of further communications. But we are not seeking to change the present situation. A binding German peace treaty is a matter for all who were at war with Germany, and we and our allies cannot abandon our obligations to the people of West Berlin.[11]

Kennedy here attempted to give the impression that something was wrong in wanting to change the situation in West Berlin, even though the presence of Western troops in West Berlin was based on the terms of surrender and meant to last for only a limited time, not sixteen years. And he left the impression that Khrushchev was determined to exclude his former allies from participation in a peace treaty. But Khrushchev intended just the opposite; he wanted a general peace conference that would reach a formal agreement on Germany and Berlin, and threatened a unilateral peace treaty with East Germany *only* if the Western nations refused to participate. Further, Khrushchev specifically said means could be found to protect Western interests and invited Kennedy to make counterproposals.[12] It was, of course, desirable, important even, that Khrushchev not sign a unilateral peace treaty with East Germany. Yet in the past Russia had always backed away from carrying out such a threat after even a token concession of Western willingness to discuss the question. Kennedy not only declined to make such a minor gesture but would soon escalate the situation into a major international crisis with grim forebodings of nuclear war. In short, Kennedy in his June 6 speech and for weeks afterward made not the slightest gesture of conciliation on a matter that Khrushchev had made clear Russia regarded as one of primary importance to its national interest. Thus it is not surprising that on June 21 Khrushchev donned his army uniform and announced to the Soviet people that "we cannot delay a peace treaty with Germany any longer. A peaceful settlement in Europe must be achieved this year." And although Washington proclaimed alarm that Khrushchev announced an increase in military spending, this was clearly a Russian response to the dramatic military buildup already announced by Kennedy, and Khrushchev had called for "a peaceful settlement."

Although Kennedy said in his June 6 speech that Khrushchev's position would "be the subject of further communications," they were slow in coming. The State Department was supposed to make a quick reply to Khrushchev but it was sluggish, partly because of its customary bureaucratic inefficiency and partly because it was Achesonian on this matter and in no hurry to talk to the Russians. The reply took nearly six weeks and when it came out in mid-July it was, as Schlesinger described it, "a tired and turgid rehash of documents, left over from the Berlin crisis of 1958–59."[13] Schlesinger writes that Kennedy was exasperated, but he does not explain why the President did not do something to speed up the reply; he may not have done so because he himself was still trying to figure out what to do.

When he first returned from Vienna, Kennedy examined the Berlin contingency plans and found only two alternatives in case of a Russian move, both of which he regarded as unsatisfactory: a weak ground probe, or a nuclear attack. Accordingly, he was determined to increase American ground strength in central Europe, both to lessen Russia's superiority in conventional forces and "to convince Khrushchev that our vital interests were so deeply involved that we would use any means to prevent the defeat or capture of these forces." [14] This latter, of course, was just a strengthening of the old Eisenhower–Dulles concept of the tripwire. If the Soviets attacked United States troops, they would trigger a nuclear response. However wise this might have seemed in Pentagon war games, it is difficult to accept that anyone in Washington could have seriously believed that Khrushchev would attempt a military takeover of West Berlin. There is no reason to believe that he had any desire for so extreme a measure, and there is every reason to believe that he recognized that such an action presented incalculable dangers. To act as if it were a credible possibility was self-defeating, for the real problems, if they existed at all, were at an entirely different level.

Nonetheless, in the first weeks after Vienna the Acheson school was in the ascendancy. As the former Secretary of State saw it, Khrushchev's proposal had nothing to do with Berlin, Germany, or Europe. The Russian wasn't trying to rectify a local situation but was testing America's will to resist. The Acheson theory was that Khrushchev was hoping that, by making the United States back down on a sacred commitment he could weaken the country's world power and influence. A simple conflict of wills was involved and, until it was resolved, Acheson felt that any effort to negotiate the Berlin issue *per se* would be disastrous. He didn't see that there was anything to negotiate and felt that United States willingness to go to the conference table would be seen in the Kremlin as evidence of weakness and make the crisis even worse.

As Acheson saw it, let the Russians sign a peace treaty with East Germany. The United States would not quibble about access procedures, but if access itself were blocked, then the United States should start a series of military moves ranging from an airlift, through a ground probe in force, right up to nuclear warfare. Such resolve, Acheson thought, might cause Khrushchev to back down "but he added frankly that there was also a substantial possibility that nuclear war might result." This was the man that Joseph McCarthy accused of being soft on communists.

Kennedy seemed to share this apocalyptic view, which, despite its extremity, was quite the conventional Washington view of Soviet–American relations. It never seemed to occur to anyone that Russia might have limited goals in Berlin; each crisis was always a test of American resolve or American commitments, or some such rhetoric. In a long conversation with James Wechsler of the *New York Post,* Kennedy said he hoped that the Soviet Union would eventually recognize that the only alternatives were genuine negotiations or nuclear annihilation. But it was Kennedy who failed to recognize that it was the United States, by refusing to negotiate over Berlin, that was raising the possibility of a nuclear confrontation. He said to Wechsler that he feared Khrushchev might take his reluctance to engage in nuclear warfare as indicative of a loss of nerve. In a clear foreshadowing of the Cuban missile crisis, Kennedy said that the time might come when he would have to take the supreme risk to convince Khrushchev that conciliation did not mean humiliation. "If Khrushchev wants to rub my nose in the dirt, it's all over." [15] That sounds very much like adolescent *machismo.*

While there was little American opposition to Kennedy's simplistic analysis, *The Economist,* an impeccably anti-communist British weekly, saw clearly what was happening. It wrote on June 24: "Unless Mr. Kennedy takes a decisive grip on the wheel, the West is in danger of by-passing one possible line of compromise after another until it reaches a dead end where neither it nor Russia has any choice between ignominious retreat and nuclear devastation." But Kennedy did not seem to be seeking a compromise or a negotiated solution. In a press conference on June 28 he said the Berlin crisis was "Soviet-manufactured" and he refused to see the situation as a limited, local problem.

> This is not just a question of technical legal rights. It involves the peace and security of the people of West Berlin. It involves the direct responsibilities and commitments of the United States, the United Kingdom and France. It involves the peace and security of the Western world.[16]

On July 4 President Kennedy released at Hyannis a cordial Independence Day message from Nikita Khrushchev and Leonid Brezhnev, which made a hopeful reference to the Vienna talks. Kennedy responded with a routine, bloodless message. On July 5 Schlesinger was visited by a friend from the Soviet Embassy. The Russian expressed puzzlement over the American stand on Berlin. When Schlesinger said that the Russian guarantees on Berlin guaranteed nothing, the Russian said, "Well, if you do not consider these guarantees adequate, why don't you propose your own guarantees? All we want to do is to have a chance to discuss these things." [17] This moved Schlesinger to prepare a memo for the President, suggesting that too much emphasis was being put on military responses to the Berlin situation and not enough on the political. He suggested that the current planning was too much like preparing for a game of chicken. A number of others in the administration had similar views, and they began to draw up alternatives.

Yet the Acheson view remained dominant. On July 19 Kennedy held another of his frequent press conferences and again made a tough statement on Berlin. On July 25, his apocalyptic rhetoric soared to new heights. He made a chilling speech, an alarming speech that spread fear through the land. One can never fully recapture the dread of a fear long since faded. As Schlesinger wrote: "It is hard now to recall the forebodings of the late summer of 1961, to evoke again the pessimism that shrouded the government. . . . I found myself writing friends abroad, 'I feel more gloomy about international developments than I have felt since the summer of 1939.'" [18] His gloom came, perhaps, from the administration's assessment of the situation, but the national fear resulted from Kennedy's speech on national radio and television. A few paragraphs may help to recreate the atmosphere of that July night.

> West Berlin . . . above all . . . had now become—as never before—the great testing place of Western courage and will, a focal point where our solemn commitments stretching back over the years since 1945, and Soviet ambitions now meet in basic confrontation. . . .
>
> I hear it said that West Berlin is militarily untenable. And so was Bastogne. And so, in fact, was Stalingrad. Any dangerous spot is tenable if men—brave men—will make it so.

We do not want to fight—but we have fought before. And others in earlier times have made the same dangerous mistake of assuming that the West was too selfish and too soft and too divided to resist invasions of freedom in other lands. Those who threaten to unleash the forces of war on a dispute over West Berlin should recall the words of the ancient philosopher: "A man who causes fear cannot be free from fear."

We cannot and will not permit the communists to drive us out of Berlin, either gradually or by force. For the fulfillment of our pledge to that city is essential to the morale and security of Western Germany, to the unity of Western Europe, and to the faith of the entire Free World. Soviet strategy has long been aimed, not merely at Berlin, but at dividing and neutralizing all of Europe, forcing us back on our own shores. We must meet our oft-stated pledge to the free peoples of West Berlin—and maintain our rights and their safety, even in the face of force—in order to maintain the confidence of other free peoples in our word and our resolve. The strength of the alliance on which our security depends is dependent in turn on our willingness to meet our commitments to them.[19]

Kennedy did not stop with rhetoric. He announced that he was asking Congress for $3.25 billion more, raising to $6 billion his additional military requests since taking office only six months before. He went on to say that he was asking another quarter-million men for the Army, nearly 100,000 additional for the Navy and Air Force, ordering that draft calls be doubled, then tripled, and asking for authority to call up about 150,000 reservists. Then, most alarming of all to Americans, and perhaps to the Kremlin, both of whom may have feared that war was imminent, Kennedy asked for $207 million for an augmented civil-defense program.

. . . Tomorrow, I am requesting of the Congress new funds for the following immediate objectives: to identify and mark space in existing structures—public and private—that could be used for fallout shelters in case of attack; to stock these shelters with food, water, first-aid kits and other minimum essentials for survival; to increase their capacity; to improve our air-raid warning and fallout detection systems, including a new household warning system which is now under development; and to take other measures that will be effective at an early date to save millions of lives if needed.

In the event of an attack, the lives of those families which are not hit in a nuclear blast and fire can still be saved—*if* they can be warned to take shelter and *if* that shelter is available. We owe that kind of insurance to our families—and to our country. In contrast to our friends in Europe, the need for this kind of protection is new to our shores. But the time to start is now. In the coming months, I hope to let every citizen know what steps he can take without delay to protect his family in case of attack. I know that you will want me to do no less.

The implication was clear. Nuclear war was a real possibility. Almost overnight a new industry sprang up as ingenious businessmen advertised fallout shelters. And a new topic was added to the national dialogue, debated seriously on radio and television, in newspapers and from church pulpits: did a man have the moral right to shoot a neighbor who was trying to invade his family's fallout shelter? It was a shameful period, and the responsibility was entirely John Kennedy's. For whatever reason, he had chosen to alarm the nation in a speech that was moralistic, specious, and jingoistic. *It had absolutely no basis in fact.* No assessment of Kennedy as President and man can ignore that speech and what resulted from it.

As a New School student, Richard Abraham, wrote in a term paper in the spring of 1970, "The cruel paradox behind the shelter program and civil defense is that they perpetuate the myth of survival, and so long as nations believe it is possible to survive a nuclear war, the threat of all-out nuclear war will continue to be an important factor governing the relationships between nations."

To be sure, Khrushchev had threatened to sign a unilateral peace treaty with East Germany, *but only* if the West did not participate in talks. He said that Western interests in West Berlin could be preserved. He invited the West to propose its own guarantees if those offered by Russia were not adequate. And even if Khrushchev were to sign a unilateral peace treaty with East Germany, there was no evidence or reason to believe that the Russians would have used force to prevent Western access to West Berlin. Even if they had wanted to, they surely knew that to use force would have been supremely dangerous. Further, Kennedy knew that the United States was vastly stronger than the Soviet Union and that American intelligence estimates of Russian strength were being scaled down, not up. Yet he called for a massive military buildup on top of a massive military buildup, increasing not only international tensions but the possibility, and the probability, of resorting to military solutions for future political problems.

One can only assume that the speech was intended to cow the Soviet Union. Perhaps it had a different effect. Khrushchev was away from Moscow, at Sochi, discussing disarmament with John J. McCloy. The day before Kennedy's speech Khrushchev had seemed quite merry, but after it he told McCloy emotionally that Kennedy had presented an ultimatum and clearly intended hostilities. Nonetheless, he said, he still had confidence in Kennedy's judgment, that Kennedy would cool down and think things over. Yet one can only wonder whether the Berlin Wall and the resumed nuclear testing, both soon to come, were in some degree a response to the policy enunciated in Kennedy's hostile speech. Perhaps both developments were intended all along, but it is not fanciful to speculate that perhaps the speech was just what the Kremlin hard-liners were looking for.

The administration was distressed that the press played up the hard-line aspects of the speech and virtually ignored the passages that the anti-Acheson group evidently got inserted only with great effort. It is true that there were a few paragraphs of this nature: ". . . we shall also be ready to search for peace—in quiet exploratory talks—in formal or informal meetings. We do not want military considerations to dominate the thinking of either East or West." [20] Yet, in both tone and number, the tough words greatly dominate the soft. By the middle of August the administration still could not settle on a negotiating position. Dean Rusk went to Paris in early August to meet with his counterparts from Britain, France, and West Germany, hoping to work out a common position on the basis of which they could invite Russia to a four-power conference. Britain was eager for talks, West Germany was less reluctant than expected, but France thought that negotiations would be taken as an indication of surrender. De Gaulle and Acheson were of one mind. Since the United States did not really have a position of its own, nothing came of the Paris talks, but even Schlesinger wonders if the Berlin Wall would have gone up on August 13 if the Western allies had invited Russia to the Berlin talks.

Washington was well aware that the flow of refugees from East Berlin to West—some thirty thousand in July alone—was posing

a terrible problem for East Germany and Russia. Such a hemor-
rhage of talented people, most of them young, could not long be
tolerated by a government that was trying desperately to compete
with prosperous West Germany. It was obvious that almost any
government with the capacity to stop such a debilitating flow
would eventually do so. One cannot know the exact relationship
between the flood of refugees, so gleefully exploited by the United
States Information Agency and its Voice of America, and Khrushchev's determination to get a peace treaty with or without the
West, but it clearly had a significant bearing on the Berlin question. Thus Washington was not surprised that East Germany did
something. What did surprise the West, the Germans as well as
the Big Three, was the form of the communist response, the sudden construction of a physical barrier. The Western world was
shocked by the Wall (like the Pill, invariably capitalized), and, as
Schlesinger rousingly put it, Kennedy "instantly mobilized the resources of government." [21] Remarking that there was one chance
out of five of a nuclear exchange, Kennedy sent the Berlin Task
Force into continuous session. But everything it thought of was either too much or too little; it even took four days for a protest
note to reach Moscow. The West Berliners were understandably
alarmed and protested the feebleness of the American response,
but, as Kennedy wisely concluded, there was not much the United
States could do. Although some hard-liners suggested knocking
down the Wall, no responsible official, whether West German or
American, suggested such a dangerous course. Kennedy finally decided on some symbolic gestures. He sent Vice President Johnson
to Berlin to reiterate the American pledge of total support, and he
directed a 1500-man battle group to proceed from West Germany
over the *Autobahn* to West Berlin. There were some anxious
hours as it moved across East Germany, but there was no interference. Johnson greeted the troops and returned to Washington. In
his place Kennedy sent the retired General Lucius Clay, the symbol of American support during the Berlin blockade of 1948. Clay,
who had volunteered to help in any way he could, remained in
Berlin until well after the crisis was over.

These were grim days in Washington. "Get tougher, be hard.
That was the Kennedy dogma at midsummer, 1961." So wrote
journalist Hugh Sidey, who was close to John Kennedy. "As if

taking his own advice to heart, Kennedy named big-bomber man Curt LeMay to head the Air Force. It was a surprise to many that this old warrior would get the job at a time when the younger, smoother, more flexible generation of missile men was in vogue. But LeMay had the toughness Kennedy felt the country needed most." [22] (It was LeMay who, seven years later, ran as vice-presidential nominee with George Wallace.)

Difficult as it is now to recapture the mood of only a decade ago, Washington in those days, even more than the alarmed public, feared that there might be nuclear war.

> It had been Bob who sat one night late in the White House with his brother and talked about Berlin. The two Kennedys had discussed all the details, all the possibilities. John Kennedy had been more somber than ever. All his days had been spent planning the steps up to and into nuclear war, should it be required of this country. On that night as they talked, there was the eerie realization that war could be the product of a whim, a misunderstanding, a human mistake.[23]

Yet this is the way that the Kennedy realists were thinking. They all agreed that a Soviet blockade of West Berlin would necessitate first a Western move along the *Autobahn*. Yet there was disagreement. Some, like General Norstad, wanted a probe in order to cause a situation where the West could use nuclear weapons. But others, among them Kennedy and McNamara, wanted a probe in order to postpone the use of nuclear weapons. They all agreed that the West might eventually have to go on to nuclear war, yet again there was disagreement. Some wanted a single, conclusive salvo against Russia, and others favored a careful and discriminating attack.[24]

There is a strange, nightmarish quality to a discussion that is more concerned with the nuances of dropping nuclear bombs than in seeking ways to avoid their use. No administration before Kennedy's had faced—and, one hopes, none thereafter will face—with such equanimity the possibility of using nuclear weapons and (the context of the discussion makes it almost inevitable) using them first. This is hardly to suggest that Kennedy wanted to use them, but, as James Wechsler wrote with the President's personal approval in a piece publicly directed at the Kremlin, Kennedy had achieved "a certain composure about the brutal nature of the choice he may have to face in the solitude of some ghastly night." [25]

Yet even while the mood in Washington was tough and fearful, Khrushchev was saying on Soviet television on August 7, "We do not intend to infringe upon any lawful interests of the Western powers. Barring of access to Berlin, blockade of West Berlin, is entirely out of the question." One gets the feeling that within the Kennedy administration ideology had overcome reality. Yet gradually the Acheson school began to lose ground. Exactly why, the insiders do not say. Perhaps the reason was British pressure; Britain had wanted to talk all along. Perhaps it was influential Senators who wondered in public why a nuclear war was necessary to settle a diplomatic problem. Perhaps Kennedy himself began to be aware that history could hardly justify nuclear catastrophe on the basis that an agreement to talk things over constituted a fatal weakness of American resolve. Whatever the reason—maybe it was simply that common sense finally prevailed—Kennedy on August 21 informed Rusk that he should tell the allies that the United States planned before September 1 to issue an invitation to negotiations; the allies could either come along or not as they chose.

A few days later Rusk announced that negotiations with the Soviet Union would begin in mid-September with the convening of the United Nations General Assembly, when Foreign Minister Andrei Gromyko would be in New York. Inconclusive talks between Russia and the West began then and dragged on sporadically until 1971, when a compromise agreement on Berlin was reached. On October 17, 1961, in a long speech to the Twenty-second Congress of the Communist Party, Khrushchev reported that "the Western powers are showing some understanding of the situation, and are inclined to seek a solution to the German problem and the issue of West Berlin." Should this be so, "we shall not insist on signing a peace treaty before December 31, 1961." The crisis was over, although it took some months to fade completely away. As Schlesinger put it, ". . . in the end the substance of negotiations turned out to matter a good deal less than the willingness to negotiate." [26] What Schlesinger did not say: the "crisis" could have been entirely avoided if Kennedy had said in Vienna in early June what he said in Washington in late August.

In the meantime, military spending had leaped more than another $3.25 billion, 150,000 reservists were being called up, the Army increased by a quarter of a million men, the Navy and the Air Force together by 100,000, the nation had been frightened by Kennedy's July broadcast and many had gone on a binge of panic buying, hoarding food and water supplies, often in "fallout shelters" constructed by opportunistic, profiteering businessmen capitalizing on the fear Kennedy had spread. Of long-term consequence, the Pentagon was better equipped to participate in such adventures as Vietnam and the Dominican Republic, and the military-industrial complex was now stronger than ever. With regard to the Soviet Union, tensions had been increased, Russian military spending had been substantially raised, Russia's partial demobilization had been halted, and, although the exact degree of relationship cannot be demonstrated, the Berlin Wall was constructed and Russian nuclear testing resumed, with monster bombs that alarmed the entire world.

The admirers recorded the Berlin crisis as another Kennedy triumph and another step in the ongoing education that prepared him for his supreme triumph: the Cuban missile crisis. There is a mad logic here. The Bay of Pigs, although it could be called a disaster, prepared him for triumph. The Berlin "crisis," in which Kennedy approached the brink, could, by skillful presentation, be made into a triumph. And the Cuban missile crisis, in which Kennedy stood on the very edge of the brink, could be constructed as the greatest triumph of all. There is, to be sure, a consistency here, but it is possible that future historians will see that consistency in a different way from Kennedy's admirers.

. . . In the early stages of his public career his foreign policy speeches had a militant ring. Defense, in his view, was the bulk of diplomacy and disarmament was only a dream. But with increased perspective and responsibility came a renewed commitment to peace. Nothing gave him greater satisfaction in the White House than signing the Nuclear Test Ban Treaty.[1]

—THEODORE SORENSEN

CHAPTER SIX

Nuclear Testing

There is no doubt that Kennedy regarded the nuclear-test-ban treaty as one of his greatest accomplishments. For there is no doubt that he genuinely shared the widespread abhorrence of nuclear testing, an abhorrence that had given birth to the ban-the-bomb movement the world over, that had caused Adlai Stevenson in the 1956 campaign to call for an end to nuclear testing. (Vice President Nixon, four years later to be Kennedy's opponent, led the chorus against Stevenson, declaring that any restriction on nuclear testing would be "a fearful risk.") A year before his election, at a student convocation at UCLA on November 2, 1959, Kennedy spoke eloquently against the resumption of nuclear testing. He was responding to a call by Governor Nelson A. Rockefeller of New York, who wanted the United States to end the moratorium on testing begun by the Soviet Union in 1958 and joined by the United States and Britain. Kennedy said:

> While many competent scientists agree that there has been no great harm done to mankind as a whole from the amount of radiation created by bomb tests so far, it is also true that there is no amount of radiation so small that it has no ill effects at all on anybody. There is actually no such thing as a minimum permissible dose. Perhaps we are talking about only a very small number of individual tragedies—the number of atomic age children with cancer, the new victims of leukemia, the danger to skin tissues here and re-

94

productive systems there—perhaps these are too small to measure with statistics. But they nevertheless loom very large indeed in human and moral terms. Moreover, there is still much that we do not know—and too often in the past we have minimized these perils and shrugged aside these dangers, only to find that our estimates were faulty and the real dangers were worse than we knew.[2]

As a candidate in 1960 Kennedy pledged not to be the first to resume atmospheric testing and not to test underground until he had exhausted all reasonable possibilities for reaching agreement with the Soviet Union on a test ban. The first announcement in his first press conference as President was of a special group to prepare a new United States bargaining position and the actual draft of a test-ban treaty. But when he sent the crusty but indefatigable Arthur Dean to Geneva to discuss a treaty with the Russians, he discovered that they had moved even further away from the idea of a treaty enforced by a team of neutral onsite inspectors. The Russians had earlier appeared to accept a neutral commission, but now, angered by the United Nations role in the Congo, argued that no international body could be trusted unless the Soviet Union had a veto.

The question was raised by Kennedy at Vienna. Khrushchev reiterated that no international body could be trusted not to engage in espionage or allow the Americans to, and he repeated the Russian position that, in any case, no more than three onsite inspections could be allowed. The Americans had always argued that inspection was essential because it was not possible to determine without it whether seismic events were nuclear explosions or not. The Soviets, on the other hand, contended that national means of verification by scientific instruments were adequate. However, Khrushchev did tell Kennedy that Russia would not be the first nation to break the voluntary moratorium on testing.

As they conceded at Vienna, both leaders were under strong pressure to resume testing. In the United States the military, some Congressmen, and some scientists of the school of Dr. Edward Teller provided most of the pressure, and a Gallup Poll showed that the public favored testing two to one. In August 1961, during the height of the Berlin "crisis," even though General Maxwell Taylor, Kennedy's personal adviser on military matters, and the Joint Chiefs of Staff counseled Kennedy to begin testing immedi-

ately, he decided to hold off a while longer. He wanted the onus
to be on the Russians; he wanted it "absolutely clear—not only to
him but to the world—that he had done everything possible to ob-
tain a treaty, that the Soviets had not bargained in good faith or
really wanted such a treaty, and that the security of the free world
required this country to test." [3]

It is clear from this statement by Sorensen that Kennedy, despite what he said at UCLA about the perils of nuclear testing,
was prepared to resume testing first if he could build a good case
that Soviet intransigence was to blame. This despite the fact that
he was aware, as it is important to point out time and again, of
America's overwhelming military superiority. But Kennedy did
not have to make this difficult decision. On August 30 Khrushchev announced that Russia would begin a series of atmospheric
tests. Kennedy's intimates have written that he was furious at
being deceived by Khrushchev. The White House immediately issued, as no doubt the Kremlin would have done had the circumstances been reversed, a moralistic statement, asserting that the Soviet tests were a hazard to health (as they certainly were) and to
world peace, and a proof of hypocrisy and duplicity. Another
statement came the following day, after a meeting of the National
Security Council. This statement, for which there had been more
time for preparation, reached a higher rhetorical level, declaring
that the Soviet tests were "primarily a form of atomic blackmail,
designed to substitute terror for reason . . . testing not only nuclear devices but the will and the determination of the free
world." That may have been true, but there was no little hypocrisy
in the American statement, for Kennedy had been moving toward
the same decision. As for the charge that Khrushchev had deliberately deceived Kennedy at Vienna, that too may have been true.
On the other hand, it may not have been: Khrushchev may have
felt compelled to test after Kennedy's speech of July 25. John
McCloy reported later that Khrushchev had told him that he was
under strong pressure to resume testing, especially from his scientists, and that the Berlin crisis increased that pressure.[4] The Russian move seems to be another example of the dangers of Washington ethnocentrism, the apparent inability of United States
policy-makers to understand that their decisions might have un-
welcome consequences in other capitals.

For several days the United States exploited the opportunity presented by the Soviet Union. On September 3 Kennedy and Prime Minister Macmillan proposed an immediate three-power ban on atmospheric tests. With no favorable response immediately forthcoming, Kennedy on September 5 announced that the United States would resume underground testing. "In our efforts to achieve an end to nuclear testing, we have taken every step that reasonable men could justify. In view of the acts of the Soviet Government, we must now take these steps which prudent men find essential." The Soviets went ahead with their tests, carrying out more than forty in the atmosphere, including one monster bomb of more than fifty megatons. When Khrushchev announced that such a test was forthcoming, there was worldwide consternation, and the United Nations General Assembly, by a vote of 87 to 11, asked the Russians to refrain. They refused, and the explosion took place on October 30 at Novaya Zemlya. It was even larger than fifty megatons and the next day Khrushchev boasted, "Instead of fifty megatons it proved to be more, but we will not punish them [the scientists] for that." Thus within a few short months Kennedy had precipitated a Berlin crisis with its threat of nuclear war and Khrushchev had reopened the Pandora's box of nuclear tests.

The Soviet tests further increased the pressure on Kennedy to resume atmospheric tests, but a good number of his advisers argued that there was no need to resume testing. While the debate went on, Kennedy decided, immediately after the Soviets had detonated their monster bomb, to announce publicly that the United States was preparing for atmospheric "tests so as to be ready in case it becomes necessary to conduct them." [5] He pointed out that "we have many times more nuclear power than any other nation on earth and that these capabilities are deployed so as to survive any sneak attack on the United States or its Allies." And he declared that "no nuclear test in the atmosphere will be undertaken, as the Soviet Union has done, for so-called psychological or political reasons." However, it seems inarguable that the eventual decision to resume testing was for precisely those reasons.

Jerome Wiesner, the President's science adviser, said in December that the decision was primarily political, not military. "While these tests would certainly contribute to our military strength, they are not critical or even very important to our over-all military posture." And Hans Bethe, the pre-eminent theoretical physicist, reported to the President that the Soviet tests had been defensive in nature. He concluded that they had been used to develop "solid-fuel missiles similar to our Minuteman which could be put in hardened sites" as a defense against a counterforce (first) strike. "The major part of their test series, therefore, may well have reduced rather than increased the danger of war." [6]

The issue facing Kennedy was not that Khrushchev had endangered the health of millions by his massive tests. He had, but American tests would hardly help that situation. Nor was the question that Khrushchev had blustered during and after the tests. He had, but Kennedy knew, and Khrushchev knew he knew, how hollow these boasts were. Yet even though Kennedy accepted that Wiesner and Bethe were right, there was, as Schlesinger put it, "an unconscious hardening through the government, as if a final decision had been made." [7] The justification for resumption is fuzzy. Schlesinger suggests that Kennedy believed that the United States would not be endangered by one Russian series but might be by two. Even if that were so, why then could Kennedy not have waited until a second Russian series before resuming atmospheric tests?

With the decision all but made, Kennedy met with Prime Minister Macmillan in Bermuda just before Christmas. Not only did the United States want to use Britain's Christmas Island in the Pacific for the tests but it would be difficult for the United States to resume testing without the concurrence of its nuclear partner. Macmillan did all he could do to dissuade Kennedy then, and he persisted in his campaign through January and February 1962. Again, we see ambivalence in Kennedy. His advisers say time and time again that Kennedy did not want to test. Kennedy himself in a press conference on January 31 said that the biggest disappointment of his first year was the failure to get a test-ban treaty. Yet his administration moved relentlessly toward a decision to test. Macmillan's last try was fruitless, and his leading scientific adviser told Schlesinger that the Prime Minister was "a sad and embittered man" who believed that Kennedy's decision would "shatter the hopes of millions of people across the earth." [8]

At 7 p.m. on March 2, 1962, the President went on nationwide

radio and television to announce that the United States would resume atmospheric tests. Although Kennedy apparently recognized
that there was no military necessity for testing, he gave that as the
reason. And he employed some familiar rhetoric: "Should we fail
to follow the dictates of our own security, they [the Soviet lead-
ers] will chalk it up, not to goodwill, but to a failure of will.
. . ." However, Kennedy left the door ajar. He said the United
States would go to the Geneva talks, to begin twelve days later,
with a new disarmament proposal and would resubmit, along with
Great Britain, the proposed treaty for a comprehensive nuclear-
test-ban treaty. "If the Soviet Union should now be willing to accept such a treaty, to sign it before the latter part of April, and
apply it immediately—if all the testing can thus be actually halted
—then the United States and its ability to meet its commitment
would be safeguarded—and there would be no need for our tests
to begin." But "in the absence of a firm agreement that would halt
nuclear tests by the latter part of April, we shall go ahead with
our talks—striving for some new avenue of agreement—but we
shall also go ahead with our tests." If, however, the Soviet Union
did agree swiftly to a test-ban treaty, "that single step would be a
monumental step toward peace—and both Prime Minister Macmillan and I would think it fitting to meet Chairman Khrushchev
at Geneva to sign the final pact."

The Soviet Union was not prepared to depart from its long-held
position that a substantial number of onsite inspections were unnecessary and would amount to espionage, nor from its new position that in view of (what it considered) the United Nations' pro-
Western behavior in the Congo no neutral body could be trusted
to carry out onsite inspections, whatever the number. A test-ban
treaty, the Russians argued, had to be considered as part of a program for general and complete disarmament—thus switching 180
degrees from the position held for the previous three years. Earlier, when the United States had taken that position, Khrushchev
had asked correctly, "Is there any surer way of sabotaging the suspension of nuclear tests than by such conditions?" [9] It might seem
odd that the Soviet Union changed position so drastically and so
quickly, but neither side in the Cold War was a slave to consistency, and the postwar record is studded with instances where one
side took a firm, unwavering stand only to depart radically from it

when the other side approached it. It often seemed that both sides were more interested in propaganda positions than in genuine agreement.

When Russia rejected Kennedy's demand for a quick settlement, he ordered the tests to go on as scheduled. As a new day began over Christmas Island on April 25, the United States started a series of atmospheric tests that was to continue for six months. Then, just as Macmillan had feared, the Russians began yet another series of tests. It was the same dreary old story all over again. The Russians resumed testing because of the Berlin crisis and the big American military buildup. The Americans resumed because the Russians had resumed. The Russians then resumed again because the Americans had resumed. The atmosphere got more polluted, and people the world over again raised their voices against the testing by both sides.

As the summer of 1962 wore on, the Kennedy administration learned—and this only increased the President's skepticism—that neither side was profiting as much from the tests as either had hoped. This was an important factor in the movement, in late summer, toward eventual agreement on a test-ban treaty. Another was the recognition by the administration that the resumption of underground tests nearly a year before had not raised nearly the outcry that the atmospheric tests had. Obviously people were much more concerned about tests that polluted the atmosphere. (This difference was to have an unfortunate long-term effect.) Also, the United States was coming to the conclusion that it did not need as many onsite inspections as it had heretofore insisted were necessary. Khrushchev at Vienna the year before had restated the Russian position that three onsite inspections a year of unidentified underground seismic events were the maximum possible, and the United States had contended that twenty were required. But in July, speaking to reporters at the Geneva airport, Arthur Dean disclosed, without authorization from Washington, that a lesser number of onsite inspections was now being required. At Kennedy's instruction, American scientists were improving methods for the detection and identification of seismic events. Further, it was discovered that there were fewer earthquakes in Russia than had been supposed, and most of them took place in areas where underground testing would be difficult.

Kennedy confirmed these improvements at a press conference on August 1. However, he declared:

> . . . I must emphasize that these new assessments do not affect the requirement that any system must include provision for onsite inspection of unidentified underground events. It may be that we shall not need as many as we've needed in the past, but we find no justification for the Soviet claim that a test-ban treaty can be effective without onsite inspection. We have been conducting a most careful and intensive review of our whole position with the object of bringing it squarely in line with the technical realities. I must express the hope that the Soviet Government, too, will re-examine its position on this matter of inspection.
>
> In the past it has accepted the principle, and if it would return to this earlier position we, for our part, will be able to engage in an attempt to reach agreement on the number of onsite inspections which is essential.[10]

Notice the tone of this statement. It is businesslike, matter-of-fact, in contrast to the President's earlier statements about Russian duplicity, hypocrisy, atomic blackmail, etc.—another instance of Kennedy's ambivalence.

The developments of the summer of 1962 added up to two significant conclusions: that a comprehensive treaty might be more attainable than before; that if a comprehensive treaty were not possible, there would be considerable worldwide support for a treaty that banned tests in those environments where there could be widespread radioactive fallout—the atmosphere, outer space, and under water. In such a partial treaty the difficult sticking point of onsite inspections could be avoided. Prime Minister Macmillan agreed with this analysis, and on August 27 Kennedy released a joint statement saying that the American and British delegations at Geneva would present two proposed treaties: one, as before, a comprehensive treaty; and the second, a partial test ban.[11] Although the first was preferred, the second would be acceptable.

The Russians swiftly rejected both, the comprehensive because of the disagreement over onsite inspection, the partial because it would legalize underground testing and thus "raise the nuclear temperature." In turn, they proposed an immediate ban on other-than-underground tests and a moratorium on underground tests until a treaty covering them could be worked out. These the West rejected, understandably reluctant to enter into another moratorium when the Russians had broken the first. Yet, as history has demonstrated, the Russian position was sounder. The partial test-ban treaty eventually signed did not, as Kennedy said it would, "result in a definite downward turn in the arms race as it is represented by testing to develop weapons technology." As we shall see from a detailed discussion later, the partial test ban resulted in an accelerated arms race, with underground testing removed from the ban-the-bomb type of public criticism that had inhibited atmospheric testing. Had a moratorium on underground testing been accepted and had it been observed, the nuclear arms race would not be the worrisome thing it is today.

On August 29, at a press conference, Kennedy rejected one Soviet offer and accepted another. Rejecting the idea of a moratorium, Kennedy said, "They do not give assurance against an abrupt renewal of testing by unilateral action. This is the lesson of the Soviet Government's tragic decision to renew testing just a year ago. Nor can such informal arrangements give any assurance against secret underground testing." [12] But he did accept a Soviet proposal, made that morning in Geneva, that January 1, 1963, be established as a cut-off date for all nuclear tests, with the parties involved making a strenuous effort to agree on a treaty by then. However, the Cuban missile crisis soon intervened, paralyzing the test-ban talks for a time but in the long run paradoxically providing the primary motive force for their eventual success. But before détente came the brink. That is the subject of the next chapter.

John F. Kennedy entered and we all stood up. He had, as Harold Macmillan would later say, earned his place in history by this one act alone.[1]

—THEODORE SORENSEN

But the ultimate impact of the missile crisis was wider than Cuba, wider even than the Western hemisphere. To the whole world it displayed the ripening of an American leadership unsurpassed in the responsible management of power. . . . By his own composure, clarity and control, he held the country behind him. It was almost as if he had begun to shape the nation in his own image. . . .

It was this combination of toughness and restraint, of will, nerve and wisdom, so brilliantly controlled, so matchlessly calibrated, that dazzled the world. Before the missile crisis people might have feared that we would use our power extravagantly or not use it at all. But the thirteen days gave the world— even the Soviet Union—a sense of American determination and responsibility in the use of power which, if sustained, might indeed become a turning point in the history of the relations between east and west.[2]

—ARTHUR SCHLESINGER

CHAPTER SEVEN

The Cuban Missile Crisis

It has been widely accepted that the Cuban missile crisis was the occasion of John Kennedy's greatest triumph. I disagree. I believe that his decision to go to the brink of nuclear war was irresponsible and reckless to a supreme degree, that it risked the kind of terrible miscalculation that Kennedy was always warning Khrushchev about, that it was unnecessary, and that, if one assumes minimum competence, the Kennedy administration knew it was not necessary. I argue, in short, that Kennedy, without sufficient reason, consciously risked nuclear catastrophe, with all that implied for the people not only of the United States and Russia but of the entire world. This is a harsh conclusion, but I believe the following account will sustain such an indictment.

Kennedy's apologists have written that, although the Bay of Pigs was a disaster, it prepared him for triumph in the Cuban missile crisis. They have so often written about how this or that crisis educated Kennedy—Laos, the Bay of Pigs, the Berlin crisis—that one is tempted to conclude that perhaps the function of the Presidency is education, not governance. One cannot blame such writers for trying to protect their friend, but the hard fact is that the Bay of Pigs was the major cause of the Cuban missile crisis. It convinced Castro and Khrushchev that Cuba was in serious danger from the United States. Their fear can hardly be dismissed as exaggerated, particularly when it was reinforced by a series of increasingly hostile acts. The Bay of Pigs, as noted earlier, caused Khrushchev on April 17, 1961, to send an angry diplomatic note to Washington, pledging "all necessary assistance to Castro." (Nor was this the first such foreshadowing. As early as July 9, 1960, while Eisenhower was still President, Khrushchev had declared that "speaking figuratively, in case of necessity, Soviet artillerymen can support the Cuban people with rocket fire." [3])

If Khrushchev was committed to the defense of Cuba, and there is certainly no reason to doubt it, it is not surprising that he shared Castro's growing concern in the days and months following the Bay of Pigs. As early as April 20, 1961, rather than being chastened by the disastrous invasion, Kennedy had declared that "our restraint is not inexhaustible" in that speech in which he clearly hinted that the United States would not hesitate to use military action "should it ever appear that the inter-American doctrine of non-interference merely conceals or excuses a policy of nonaction—if the nations of this Hemisphere should fail to meet their commitments against outside communist penetration." [4] A week later he made another tough speech and on May 5, in a press conference, he said that the United States had no plans to train Cuban exiles as a Cuban force in this country or in any other country "at this time." To an alarmed Castro, this may not have sounded very reassuring.

Here, in chronological order, are some of the steps taken in

Washington that must have, in varying degrees, added to Castro's disquiet. In a press conference on August 30, 1961, the President, when asked about a recent statement of Castro's in which he said that the United States seemed afraid to negotiate with Cuba about problems of mutual concern, replied, "I've expressed my view that as long as Cuba makes itself a willing—the Cuban government makes itself a willing accomplice to the communist objectives in this hemisphere, that we could not have successful negotiations. And that, in my opinion, is what their status is today." Despite his proclamation in his inaugural address that the United States would never fear to negotiate, Kennedy refused to find out if talks were possible and if such talks might lead to improved Cuban–American relations.

On September 7, with Kennedy's support, Congress prohibited assistance to any country that aided Cuba unless the President determined that such assistance was in the national interest. Meanwhile, on September 20, a Soviet–Cuban communiqué proclaimed the "identity of positions of the Soviet Union and Cuba on all the international questions that were discussed." [5] Presumably the Soviet–Chinese split was not discussed, for on October 2 a Chinese–Cuban communiqué declared complete agreement on "the current international situation and the question of further developing friendship and cooperation." Castro was neatly straddling the chasm. And on December 2, Castro took what to many Americans was the last step. He declared that "I believe absolutely in Marxism. . . . I am a Marxist-Leninist and will be a Marxist-Leninist until the last day of my life." Some might take this statement as adequate justification for the previous and forthcoming hostile acts by the United States. Others might argue that Kennedy, as Khrushchev had told him at Vienna, was driving Castro deeper into the arms of the communists. In any case, Castro's moves were primarily rhetorical—his resources were limited—whereas Kennedy's moves had substance.

On December 6 the United States submitted a document to the Inter-American Peace Committee, discussing Cuba's ties to the communist world and its alleged threat to hemispheric security. This was the prelude to the severe political and economic measures soon to be taken, for only under unrelenting pressure from the United States would the Organization of American States

(OAS) move sharply against Cuba. On January 14, 1962, the Inter-American Peace Committee asserted that Cuba's ties with the communist countries were incompatible with inter-American treaties, principles, and standards—in short, that a sovereign state was not entitled to seek whatever ties it chose. In a press conference the next day President Kennedy said that he expected the Latin American foreign ministers to take action against Cuba at a meeting soon to open in Uruguay. His prediction was correct. Meeting at Punta del Este from January 22 through 31, the foreign ministers in effect ejected Cuba from the OAS. Although only Cuba voted against the resolution, six of the twenty-one nations abstained, among them the four most important in Latin America; Argentina, Brazil, Chile, and Mexico. Assuming, as one must, that the State Department played a major role in drafting that and other anti-Cuban resolutions, it is interesting that there is frequent reference to the "Sino–Soviet bloc" and the "Sino–Soviet powers," favorite bogy-man terms of Washington Cold Warriors that even the open hostility between Moscow and Peking could not retire.

Although the United States termed the conference a great success, it had not achieved the maximum United States goal, sanctions against Cuba. It was not possible to get approval for these, and even to get the necessary fourteen votes to exclude Cuba (there is considerable doubt that exclusion is possible under the OAS charter) the United States had to gather together a clutch of right-wing dictatorships, going so far as to submit to blackmail from Haiti to get its essential vote.[6] But even if success was not quite as great as claimed, the United States had succeeded in employing a technique that became fundamental to its anti-Castro crusade. It would, by sheer political and economic weight, force a measure through the OAS and then use this as public justification for what it was going to do anyway. Such authorization was not essential, but it provided a nice patina of legality that Washington much preferred to have.

Now, with the OAS in line, Washington felt free to act. On February 3, Kennedy declared an embargo on all trade with Cuba except for medical necessities. On February 20, Walt W. Rostow appeared before the NATO Council, urging its members in establishing their policies toward Cuba to take into account the OAS decisions at Punta del Este. On March 24 the United States excluded the import of goods made in whole or part of Cuban products. Kennedy had drawn an economic and political noose tight around Cuba. This, compounding the Bay of Pigs, was undoubtedly a basic factor in the Khrushchev–Castro decision. It is not known when the decision to put Russian missiles on Cuban soil was made or when the program began. A good guess would be mid-1962, for in late July there was a step-up in Soviet shipments to Cuba, following a visit to Moscow in early July by Fidel's brother Raúl, Minister of the Armed Forces. On August 24, Washington disclosed that the flow of Soviet military supplies and technicians was increasing, and on August 28, Moscow announced that the volume of maritime shipments to Cuba in 1962 would be double that of the previous year.

It was at about this time, with the Congressional elections impending, that the possibility of Russian missiles in Cuba was first raised publicly. On September 1, Senator Kenneth Keating of New York (later to be unseated by Robert Kennedy) began his criticism of the President's Cuban policy. The next day Keating stepped up his attacks on Kennedy's "do nothing" policy and suggested that an OAS mission be sent to Cuba to determine if Soviet missile bases were being established. That same day the Soviet Union announced that it had agreed to supply arms and technical specialists to train Cubans to meet threats from "aggressive imperialist quarters." The Kennedy administration, already handicapped by an uncooperative Congress, was concerned that the normal mid-term losses of the party in the White House might be increased if the Republicans could successfully make Cuba an issue despite Kennedy's hard-line approach. It therefore attempted to defuse the issue by declaring, as it continued to do for the next few weeks, that there was nothing new in Soviet–Cuban relations.

Since refugees, presumably the source of Keating's information, are notoriously unreliable, the Kennedy administration did not believe that surface-to-surface missiles with substantial range were in Cuba. The intelligence community knew that something was up, but the consensus had been that the Russians were putting in surface-to-air missiles (SAMs) to defend Cuba against air attack. Refugees would hardly be likely to have the sophisticated knowledge to distinguish between SAMs and longer-range missiles. Basic to this conclusion was the knowledge that the Russians, unlike the Americans, had never put their missiles outside the Soviet Union, even in those East European countries where their control was almost absolute. This, plus the assessment that even the impulsive Khrushchev would not take such a provocative action, caused American intelligence to dismiss the possibility that long-range missiles were going to Cuba. Despite this consensus, John McCone, who after the Bay of Pigs had succeeded Allen Dulles as director of the CIA, on August 22 had conveyed to Kennedy his hunch that long-range missiles were being put into Cuba. His theory was that SAMs were being installed to protect the missile bases, for missile bases that were not safe from conventional attack were of little value. He believed that the Russians had not installed missiles of substantial range in East Europe because they feared they might be turned against them. However, such missiles could be installed in Cuba with sufficient range to reach much of the United States but unable to reach the Soviet Union if turned around.[7] Although much of this theory seems fanciful, the most important part was correct. Soviet missiles of substantial range were going into Cuba.

Kennedy was concerned enough to order special daily intelligence reports, and these began on August 27, even before Keating stated his charges. Needless to say, such charges received big play in the news, and Kennedy was invariably asked about Cuba in his press conferences. He played down the offensive significance of the Russian assistance. Other Republicans gleefully seized on the issue, despite the fact that Kennedy was carrying on an anti-Castro campaign of such severity that it was criticized in Europe, where people had no difficulty in seeing who was David and who was Goliath. Kennedy was obviously in political trouble, however absurd it was to accuse him of not being tough enough on Castro. Writers sympathetic to Kennedy are quick to dismiss any possibility that politics might have been a factor in the President's decision to go to the brink; one gets the impression that they hope that if they do not discuss the political implications, other writers will not either. But Kennedy was supremely political, and this factor cannot be dismissed quite so swiftly, for it was inescapable.

In a press conference on August 29, the President was asked to comment on a suggestion by Senator Homer Capehart, the militant anti-communist Republican from Indiana, that the United States invade Cuba to stop the flow of troops and supplies. Kennedy attempted to brush off the question of troops and then went on to a discussion of "the mismanagement of the Cuban economy which has brought widespread dissatisfaction, economic slowdown, agricultural failures, which have been so typical of the communist regimes in so many parts of the world. So I think the situation was critical enough that they needed to be bolstered up." [8]

With a show of persistence rare at a presidential news conference, the reporter again asked Kennedy to comment on Capehart's suggestion. Again his answer was fuzzy: "I'm not for invading Cuba at this time. No, I don't—the words do not have some secondary meaning. I think it would be a mistake to invade Cuba, because I think it would lead to—that it should be very— an action like that, which could be very casually suggested, could lead to very serious consequences for many people." Again, Castro could hardly have been reassured by the use of the phrase "at this time." And, as we shall see, Robert Kennedy later disclosed that the United States government gave full consideration to the possibility of invading Cuba at the height of the crisis.

On August 31, Kennedy got the first hard evidence of SAMs from U-2 photographs taken two days earlier. The pace of events was beginning to quicken. On September 1, Keating made his first public charges. On September 2, in a communiqué marking a second visit by Che Guevara, Moscow declared that Cuba had requested help in the form of "armaments" and "specialists for training Cuban servicemen," to which the Soviet Union had responded because of threats from "aggressive imperialist quarters with regard to Cuba. As long as the above-mentioned quarters continue to threaten Cuba, the Cuban republic has every justification for taking necessary measures to insure its sovereignty and independence, while all Cuba's true friends have every right to respond to this legitimate request." [9] On September 4, Khrushchev sent Ambassador Anatoly Dobrynin to see Robert Kennedy with a personal message for the President: he would not stir up any trouble in Berlin or Cuba during the American elections. And, Dobrynin assured the Attorney General, the Soviet Union would hardly give to any nation the power to involve it in a thermonuclear war. One cannot know whether he was instructed to deceive the President's brother or whether he himself did not know of the missiles and shared the American intelligence community's firm conviction that Khrushchev would not send such missiles outside Russia.[10]

The President was not reassured, and he issued a statement that same day disclosing that the United States had learned that the Soviet Union had provided Cuba with a number of antiaircraft missiles with a slant range of twenty-five miles, the associated radar and electronic equipment, and several motor torpedo boats with ship-to-ship missiles with a range of fifteen miles. But more important was this section of the statement read to reporters by Press Secretary Salinger:

> There is no evidence of any organized combat force in Cuba from any Soviet bloc country; of military bases provided to Russia; of a violation of the 1934 treaty relating to Guantanamo; of the presence of offensive ground-to-ground missiles; or of other significant offensive capability either in Cuban hands or under Soviet direction. Were it to be otherwise, the gravest issues would arise.[11]

Notice here what was to become very significant—not ground-to-ground missiles that could be used offensively (or defensively) but "offensive ground-to-ground missiles." This is not merely a semantic exercise, for the purported fact that these were "offensive" missiles was absolutely crucial to the public justification of the extreme measures taken by President Kennedy. Whereas the Soviet missiles in Cuba were "offensive," the American Jupiter missiles in Turkey and elsewhere, aimed at Russia were "defensive." The Russians, of course, played the game too. Their missiles were "defensive" and ours were "offensive." The parallel is exact, although the Kennedy administration and its defenders never admitted it.

The important thing for the moment was that Kennedy was warning the Russians. The stage was not Kennedy's alone. On September 7 the Republican leaders of the Senate and House chimed in with separate statements. Senator Everett McKinley Dirksen and Representative Charles A. Halleck, whose joint television appearances had been labeled, with approximately equal proportions of affection and derision, the "Ev and Charlie Show," called for a joint resolution by Congress to authorize the President to use American armed forces as he deemed necessary. Inviting their Democratic counterparts to join them, they said, "This course of action by Congress will reflect the determination and clear purpose of the American people and will demonstrate to the world the firmness of this nation in meeting this problem." [12] Although they struck a statesmanlike pose, they were clearly trying to make political capital to help Republican candidates in the forthcoming Congressional elections. But Kennedy was not so easily outflanked, and that same day he sent a request to Congress asking for authorization to call up to 150,000 reservists for not more than twelve month's service. "In my judgment this renewed authorization is necessary to permit prompt and effective responses, as necessary, to challenges which may be presented in any part of the free world. . . ." [13]

It was now Moscow's turn. On September 11, Moscow issued a very long statement attacking the United States policy on Cuba. Although a bit overwrought in some passages, it did seem to communicate a genuine response to Kennedy's Cuban policy.

> The whole world knows that the United States of America has ringed the Soviet Union and other Socialist countries with bases. What have they stationed there—tractors? Are they perhaps growing rice, wheat, potatoes, or some other farm crops there? No, they have brought armaments there in their ships, and these armaments, stationed along the frontiers of the Soviet Union—in Turkey, Iran, Greece, Italy, Britain, Holland, Pakistan and other countries belonging to the military blocs of NATO, CENTO and SEATO—are said to be there lawfully, by right. They consider this their right! But to others the United States does not permit this even for defense, and when measures are nevertheless taken to strengthen the defenses of this or that country the United States raises an outcry and declares that an attack, if you please, is being prepared against them. What conceit! . . . [14]

The statement also said that there was "no need for the Soviet Union to shift its weapons for the repulsion of aggression, for a retaliatory blow, to another country, for instance, Cuba. Our nuclear weapons are so powerful in their explosive force and the Soviet Union has such powerful rockets to carry these nuclear warheads, that there is no need to search for sites for them beyond the boundaries of the Soviet Union." Moscow also made clear that an American attack on Cuba could mean nuclear war:

> We have said and we do repeat that if war is unleashed, if the aggressor makes an attack on one state or another, and this state asks for assistance, the Soviet Union has the possibility from its own territory to render assistance. . . . If this attack is made, this will be the beginning of the unleashing of war.

Although this passage does not explicitly say that no Russian missiles would be put into Cuba, it certainly reads as if it were meant to give that impression.

But the long statement was not only aggrieved complaint and storm warning. There was also an appeal "to the government of the United States, urging it to display common sense, not to lose self-control and to soberly assess what its actions might lead to if it unleashes war."

> Instead of aggravating the atmosphere by such actions as the mobilization of reserves, which is tantamount to the threat of starting war, it would be more sensible if the Government of the United States, displaying wisdom, would offer a kind gesture—would establish diplomatic and trade relations with Cuba, the desirability of which has been recently declared by the Cuban Government. If the American Government displayed this wisdom, the peoples would assess this properly as a realistic contribution of the United States to the relaxation of international tension, the strengthening of world peace.
>
> If normal diplomatic and trade relations were established between the United States of America and Cuba, there would be no need for Cuba to strengthen her defenses, her armed forces. For then nobody would menace Cuba with war or other aggressive actions, and then the situation would become normal.

Although the foreign policy of the Soviet Union in Eastern Europe, particularly in Hungary and Czechoslovakia, has hardly been one to allow it to lecture others, in this case it was right. Whatever Russia's share in aggravating the Cuban crisis by installing missiles, the indisputable fact is that the United States by its unrelenting hostility to a weak and isolated Cuba caused the confrontation in the first place. And notice the final paragraph of the quotation from the Russian note. It says, in effect, that if Cuba were not threatened by the United States, it would not need "to strengthen its defenses."

On September 13, President Kennedy opened his press conference with a statement on Cuba. He said that while the movement of Soviet military personnel had increased, the United States had it "under our most careful surveillance," and he repeated his earlier conclusion that "these shipments do not constitute a serious threat to any other part of this hemisphere." However, Kennedy said, if the United States ever found it "necessary to take military action against communism in Cuba, all of Castro's communist-supplied weapons and technicians would not change the result or significantly extend the time required to achieve that result." But he declared that "unilateral military intervention on the part of the United States cannot *currently* [emphasis added] be either required or justified, and it is regrettable that loose talk about such action in this country might serve to give a thin color of legitimacy to the communist pretense that such a threat exists." The point, however, was not whether the United States was actively planning military action against Cuba but whether Castro had a legitimate basis for the fear of such action. Given the Bay of Pigs and American actions of the previous months, Castro's fears were reasonable, certainly more so than Washington's fear a year earlier that the Soviet Union might take physical action to prevent Western access to West Berlin. Again, Washington seemed almost totally unable to see the world as others saw it. And again in this statement Kennedy repeated his warning that if American security were endangered, "this country will do whatever must be done to protect its own security and that of its allies."

In succeeding days Republicans increased the political pressure; Senators Barry Goldwater, John Tower, Hugh Scott, Kenneth Keating, and even Jacob Javits called for various tough measures, including a blockade. Former Vice President Nixon joined the chorus on September 18, calling for a "quarantine" of Cuba. On September 20 the Senate and on September 26 the House passed a resolution authorizing the use of arms if necessary. For their part, the Russians increased the tempo of their warnings. Foreign Minister Gromyko repeated them at the United Nations on September 21, and on September 28 Soviet President Leonid Brezhnev, on a visit to Yugoslavia, reiterated that an American attack on Cuba would mean war. These may have been bluffs designed to deter the United States, but Washington could hardly be sure that they were.

With the Russians rushing to complete the missile sites and the Americans increasing the U-2 flights that would soon disclose them, events were moving swiftly and relentlessly toward the Soviet–American nuclear showdown that mankind had feared for a generation. *Yet there was no need for this dread confrontation. It could have been avoided by normal diplomacy.* This was made clear in a speech by Cuban President Osvaldo Dorticos on October 8, even before the U-2 cameras on October 14 confirmed the presence of missile sites. For some reason Kennedy's biographers brush past this speech, although the Kennedy administration knew of its importance. Adlai Stevenson quoted it in a statement to the press on October 23.

> . . . finally, it is now apparent that President Dorticos of Cuba was admitting the existence of long-range nuclear weapons in Cuba when he told the General Assembly on October 8, "We have sufficient means with which to defend ourselves; we have indeed our inevitable weapons, the weapons which we would have preferred not to acquire and which we do not wish to employ." [15]

It is certainly true that this constitutes an admission by Dorticos, and one might assume that the Kennedy administration would have gone back to the speech and read it with particular care once, a week later, it became clear to what Dorticos was referring. Assuming normal competence by the high-powered team called together by Kennedy to consider policy, and assuming that if its members had somehow overlooked the speech, lower-level people would have called attention to it, the Kennedy administration could hardly have missed its significance. In his speech Dorticos quoted a statement made some days earlier by the Cuban Council of Ministers, one obviously approved by Castro.

> Were the United States able to give Cuba effective guarantees and satisfactory proof concerning the integrity of Cuban territory, and were it to cease its subversive and counterrevolutionary activities against our people, then Cuba would not have to strengthen its defenses. Cuba would not even need an army, and all the resources that were used for this could be gratefully and happily invested in the economic and cultural development of the country.
> Were the United States able to give up proof, by word and deed, that it would not carry out aggression against our country, then, we

declare solemnly before you here and now, our weapons would be unnecessary and our army redundant. We believe ourselves able to create peace.[16]

In short, if the United States guarantees Cuba's territorial integrity, Cuba will get rid of its nuclear weapons. Since that was precisely the agreement between Kennedy and Khrushchev that ended the fearful confrontation, it is inescapable that Kennedy did not have to go to the brink to have the missiles removed. A diplomatic avenue was expressly offered by the Cubans. Thus, it is difficult to avoid one of two conclusions: either the Kennedy administration somehow missed the significance of the Dorticos speech —which is incredible—or Kennedy decided to take the risk of nuclear war, real, but, as he believed, limited, for reasons beyond just the removal of the missiles. Here it is instructive to look back at the Berlin crisis. There, as we saw, Kennedy shared Acheson's view that the crisis had little or nothing to do with Berlin; it was a test of American resolve. Now, with Cuba (again with Acheson in a key advisory role), Kennedy again took the view that the issue was not primarily Cuba but another test of American determination, demonstrating anew the American instinct to rush from the particular to the general. Even before the Kennedy administration had hard knowledge of the missile sites, it had yet again dismissed the possibility of Cuban–American talks to ease tensions between the two countries. It saw the issue not primarily as one of Cuban–American relations but as a crucial episode in the Cold War. This is clear from Adlai Stevenson's prompt response to Dorticos:

The President of Cuba professes that Cuba has always been willing to hold discussions with the United States to improve relations and to reduce tensions. But what he really wishes us to do is to place the seal of approval on the existence of a communist regime in the Western Hemisphere. The maintenance of communism in the Americas is not negotiable. . . .

If the Cuban regime is sincere in its request for negotiations and wishes to lay its grievances before the appropriate forum—the Organization of American States—I would suggest the Cuban government might start by some action calculated to awake the confidence of the inter-American system.[17]

In short, the United States flatly refused to talk with Cuba. Cuba was not supposed to exercise its sovereign right to associate with whatever nations it chose, and if it wanted to air its grievances it should do so not in the United Nations, where there were friendly and neutral states as well as enemies, but in the OAS that was an instrument of the very power against whom it had legitimate grievances.

We have seen that even before his election Kennedy uttered the rhetoric of the anti-communist crusader. We have seen how he moved swiftly to build up American military might even though it was, as he knew, "sufficient beyond doubt" by many times. We have seen how he authorized the Bay of Pigs, and we have seen how he exaggerated the Berlin crisis, moving toward nuclear confrontation and then backing away. But even though he did back away then, he still believed that a confrontation might be necessary. As he told James Wechsler of the *New York Post,*

> . . . What worried him was that Khrushchev might interpret his reluctance to wage nuclear war as a symptom of an American loss of nerve. Some day, he said, the time might come when he would have to run the supreme risk to convince Khrushchev that conciliation did not mean humiliation. "If Khrushchev wants to rub my nose in the dirt," he told Wechsler, "it's all over." But how to convince Khrushchev short of a showdown? "That son of a bitch won't pay any attention to words," the President said bitterly on another occasion. "He has to see you move." [18]

Given the *machismo* quality in Kennedy's character, his fervent anti-communism, and his acceptance of the basic assumptions of American postwar foreign policy, it is not fanciful to conclude that he was not adverse to a showdown. When Khrushchev foolishly and recklessly put missiles into Cuba, he gave Kennedy the opportunity for a showdown, not in Berlin, where the Russians had all the strategic advantages, but only ninety miles from the United States, where the Russians had to operate at the end of a long and vulnerable supply line.

Two days after the Dorticos–Stevenson exchange at the United Nations, Senator Keating returned to the attack, asserting on October 10 that he had "100 per cent reliable" information that the Russians were building six intermediate-range missile sites. Although it is not crucial to this discussion, there is some reason to believe that the government was indeed slow in concluding that there was a strong possibility that missile sites were being constructed. As is so often the case, the administration had a vested interest in proving the Republican attackers wrong, so it tended to overlook evidence that did not suit it. However, hard evidence was soon to come. On October 14 a U-2 flight over western Cuba came back with photographs. They were analyzed that night and the next day, and by late in the afternoon of Monday, October 15, the beginnings of a missile site had been detected near San Cristobal. The analysts were fairly certain of their findings by evening, and McGeorge Bundy was notified. He decided that there was nothing the President could do immediately but order more photographs, so Bundy, himself giving that order, did not notify the President, feeling, no doubt correctly, that a good night's sleep was more important in view of the decisions that would soon have to be made.[19]

On Tuesday morning, October 16, Bundy gave Kennedy the startling news. The President was furious; if, after all his denials and protestations, Khrushchev could pull this, how could he ever be trusted again on anything? Throughout the various accounts of these fearful days there is frequent reference to the Russians' "deceit," "duplicity," etc. There was deception involved, to be sure. But it is not clear whether Khrushchev or Gromyko or others with specific knowledge ever said, before the sites were spotted, explicitly that ground-to-ground missiles were not being installed in Cuba. Certainly, according to various accounts, the Russians usually said that offensive weapons were not being sent to Cuba. If that was all they said, then the debate is semantic. But even if there were specific denials of ground-to-ground missiles, the reader will have to decide for himself whether or not they fall into the category of justifiable military secrecy, as beloved by American warriors as by any others. Neither the Americans nor the Russians normally disclosed the character of military moves when they believed it in the national interest that they remain secret. Nor had Kennedy, as we have seen, always been entirely candid in his public statements about, for instance, Laos and Cuba.

It was the fact of the missile sites that was paramount, not the stealth of their installation. In any case, after the Keating disclosures, the Russians must have expected from their own bitter experience with U-2s that the sites would soon be spotted, however much they might have hoped to present the United States with a *fait accompli*. However, just as it would be unrealistic to expect the Russians to tell the Americans exactly what they were doing in Cuba, it would be unrealistic to expect the United States not to make effective use of charges of "deceit" and "duplicity" in the propaganda battle that soon erupted.

Before again picking up the chain of events, it is necessary to point out something that Kennedy's admirers do not, for obvious reasons, stress. Castro had every right to ask for, and Khrushchev had every right to offer—whichever came first—the installation of Russian missiles on Cuban soil. Not only was this permissible by international law, but it was the United States that had established the precedent by installing Jupiter missiles in Turkey, right next to Russia, in Italy, and elsewhere. The American missiles had been "practically forced on" Turkey and Italy by the Eisenhower administration.[20] On the other hand, if it makes any difference, there is evidence that Cuba asked for the Russian missiles. Castro said so in an interview with Lee Lockwood in 1965.

> Naturally the missiles would not have been sent in the first place if the Soviet Union had not been prepared to send them. But . . . we made the decision at a moment when we thought that concrete measures were necessary to paralyze the aggressiveness of the United States, and we posed this necessity to the Soviet Union.[21]

Nonetheless, there is all the difference in the world between having the right to do something and deciding to do it. Just as Washington often does not take into adequate consideration Moscow's response to an American action, so too in this case Khrushchev failed to see what should have been obvious. (Since one cannot know what goes into decisions in the Kremlin, it is possible that Khrushchev too was seeking a confrontation. But if he was, it is scarcely credible that he would have wanted that kind of confrontation in a place so terribly disadvantageous to the Soviet Union.) Khrushchev, or certainly his advisers, should have recognized from even the most superficial knowledge of American postwar foreign policy and American politics that no President (least of all one with Kennedy's character and record) could tolerate the

installation of Russian missiles in Cuba, particularly right before
an election. However unfair it might be for the Americans to expect the Russians to live under the shadow of United States missiles in Turkey yet refuse to permit a reciprocal situation, that was
simply the way it was. This must have seemed outrageous to the
Russians. Certainly it seemed unfair to millions in other nations,
even to some Americans, but it was the reality of the situation.
Khrushchev had miscalculated badly. The question then for Kennedy was not whether to remove the missiles but how.

Kennedy's first instinct was to take some kind of military action, perhaps to bomb the missile sites, but before reaching a decision he called into being an *ad hoc* group that came to be known
as the ExCom. It was composed of a constantly shifting combination of top officials from the White House, the State Department,
the Pentagon, plus Attorney General Kennedy, Treasury Secretary
Dillon, and Dean Acheson. Although it took them several days of
intense, and tense, discussions to settle on the course eventually
taken, two decisions were made quickly. The first (the most important and dangerous) was that a political and diplomatic solution should not be sought. This is what has since been written by
Adam Yarmolinsky:

> From the discovery of the missiles on October 14 until October
> 28, when Khrushchev promised to remove them, the executive com-
> mittee of the National Security Council (ExCom) spent at least
> 90% of its time studying alternate uses of troops, bombers and war-
> ships. Although the possibility of seeking withdrawal of the missiles
> by straightforward diplomatic negotiation received some attention
> within the State Department, it seems scarcely to have been aired
> in the ExCom.[22]

One of the few participants persistently to urge a diplomatic approach was Adlai Stevenson, who suggested, among other things,
that the missiles on Cuba could be swapped for those, already obsolescent, in Turkey and Italy. For this Stevenson again became
the object of Acheson's scorn. In a piece in the *Saturday Evening
Post* some weeks later, he was accused of having advocated "a
Munich." (The authors, Charles Bartlett and Stewart Alsop, both
close to Kennedy, denied that the President was the source of the
story, as did Kennedy himself, whereas Otto Friedrich, an editor
of the *Post,* has written that he was.) More important than the at-

tack on Stevenson, evidently by a number of the hard-liners in the ExCom, was the fact that he was right and they were wrong. Although anti-communist, Stevenson was not virulently so, and it is difficult to believe that if he had been elected President in 1960, or earlier, there would have been the dangerous Berlin crisis or that the United States would have become involved in either of the Cuban crises or so deeply in Vietnam.[23]

Stemming from this decision not to seek a political/diplomatic solution was the decision to announce simultaneously, if at all possible, that the United States had uncovered the Russian move and what it intended to do about it. This "was not so inconsequential as it sounded—it expressed the President's determination not to be dragged along in the wake of events, but to control them."[24] This has a nice ring to it, but with the elections only a couple of weeks away, it is hard to believe that Kennedy was not concerned that the Republicans might finally smoke out convincing proof of the presence of Soviet missiles. This would have been a political disaster, probably costing the Democrats a number of Congressional seats, even if Khrushchev remained silent, thus keeping his pledge not to embarrass the administration before Election Day. It would be even worse if a public furor made Khrushchev feel that he had to come forward and proclaim himself as the defender of tiny, beleaguered Cuba. No, it would be much better if Kennedy could strike first, accusing Khrushchev of a deceitful and dangerous plot against hemispheric security *and* disclosing a dynamic plan to frustrate the communist plot. This move would have a double advantage: it would put Khrushchev in his place for once and for all, and it would blunt the Republican charge, perhaps even help Democratic candidates. Although Kennedy's admirers play down the political aspect, it is almost inconceivable that it was not a factor—almost certainly not the major one, but a factor nonetheless.

The ExCom spent long, contentious hours in discussion while Kennedy carried on his campaign travel and the ExCom members tried to stick close to their normal routine so as to preserve secrecy. Obviously, a first consideration was Khrushchev's intentions. According to Sorensen, there were five basic theories:[25]

1. The missile installation was a Cold War move to test American resolve and to discredit American strength and reliability as

an ally. If it succeeded, Khrushchev could then move boldly on West Berlin or in Latin America.

2. If the United States responded by attacking Cuba, its energies would be diverted. This diversion plus worldwide censure and division at home would free Khrushchev to move elsewhere, again in Berlin or Latin America.

3. The installation was intended to defend Cuba, in which Khrushchev now had the same kind of credibility stake as did the United States in supporting its weaker allies.

4. The missiles were intended as a bargaining counter. Khrushchev in a summit or United Nations confrontation could bargain away the missile bases for a favorable settlement in Berlin or a reduction of American overseas bases.

5. The Soviet Union wished to improve its military posture by positioning missiles that were both much cheaper than intercontinental missiles and able to avoid most of the American early-warning system.

Kennedy believed that while the third and fifth theories might have some validity, they were insufficient motives for so drastic a move. He leaned, for reasons I have discussed earlier, toward the first theory, of which the second and fourth were merely variations. Again, Washington could not resist the conviction that any Soviet–American dispute was not limited to the question at hand but represented a fundamental test of American courage. This conviction has been a basic cause of the Cold War and a fundamental block to improved relations between the United States and the Soviet Union and China. Much of the death, destruction, and misery, much of the international tension and domestic turmoil of the past quarter-century has been born of Washington's conditioned reflex to spring immediately from the particular to the general. And now Kennedy was doing it again.

Documentary proof of Khrushchev's intentions may be long in coming, and Russia's consistency before, during, and after the crisis in maintaining that its sole motivation was to defend Cuba is hardly sufficient. Often the simplest explanation is the best, and it is not unlikely that Cuba's defense was a predominant motive, although Khrushchev may well have hoped for valuable fringe benefits in Latin America and throughout the world. But the crucial question was: What dangers could result from the missiles? This was the question raised by theory number five. Although such missiles would offer certain advantages, "these Cuban missiles alone, in view of all the other megatonnage the Soviets were capable of unleashing upon us, did not substantially alter the strategic balance *in fact*. . . ." [26] On a television program two weeks after the crisis, Deputy Defense Secretary Roswell Gilpatric put it this way: "I don't believe that we were under any greater threat from the Soviet Union's power, taken in totality, after this than before." [27]

A blunt public ultimatum, issued to the impulsive leader of a powerful nation at a dangerous moment, can be justified, if ever, only at a time of supreme physical danger. Yet the United States was not in any immediate physical danger, and the Kennedy administration knew it. Furthermore, it was entirely confident that Khrushchev had neither the intention nor even the desire to *use* the missiles he was putting into Cuba. Kennedy put it this way in a television interview on December 17, 1962:

> They were planning in November to open to the world the fact that they had these missiles so close to the United States; not that they were intending to fire them, because if they were going to get into a nuclear struggle, they have their own missiles in the Soviet Union. But it would have politically changed the balance of power. It would have appeared to, and appearances contribute to reality.[28]

There is no doubt that Khrushchev made a serious and dangerous miscalculation, nor is there any doubt that, given the political realities, Kennedy had to get the missiles removed. But Kennedy did not have to add to Khrushchev's miscalculation an even more dangerous one of his own. Even though there was every reason to hope that Khrushchev would back away from a military confrontation under such disadvantageous circumstances, there was no certain way to predict his response to a public ultimatum. It was, of course, possible that Kennedy might in the end have to resort to military pressure to remove the missiles, but why was it necessary to do so in the very first instance, even if Dorticos had not already indicated the basis for a diplomatic solution? Kennedy embarked on a dangerous path with unforeseeable consequences not because of immediate physical danger but because missiles on Cuba "would have politically changed the balance of power." He took an unpardonable mortal risk without just cause. He threatened the lives of millions for appearances' sake.

To get back to the narrative, on Thursday, October 18, the President held what was billed as a routine meeting with Soviet Foreign Minister Gromyko, who was in the United States for the United Nations General Assembly session. It was a long meeting, and the White House let it be assumed that Berlin was the major topic. But foremost in Kennedy's mind was Cuba. Although tempted to pull the U-2 photos out of his desk and confront Gromyko with them, Kennedy stuck to his plan. But he warned the Russians by reading aloud his earlier warnings of September 4 and 13. Assuming that Gromyko knew of the missiles, he must have concluded from this warning that Kennedy also knew of them, yet he too stuck to his plans and merely assured the President that the Russian military aid "was by no means offensive," that "if it were otherwise, the Soviet government would never become involved." [29] Kennedy deliberately neglected a perfect opportunity to seek a diplomatic solution.

Having decided not to seek a diplomatic solution by approaching Russia and/or Cuba, Kennedy and the ExCom had to settle on another approach. They had, it was estimated "about ten days before the missiles would be on pads ready for firing. The deadline defined the strategy. It meant that the response could not, for example, be confided to the UN, where the Soviet delegation would have ample opportunity to stall action until the nuclear weapons were in place and on target. It meant that we could not even risk the delay involved in consulting our allies. It meant that total response had to fall on the United States and its President." [30]

That is nonsense. Since the Kennedy administration knew that the Cuban missiles were not a significant military factor and since it was confident that they would not be fired, completion of their installation was an artificial deadline. It was of no immediate consequence, except for whatever political capital Khrushchev could make of it. The reasons for not relying on the United Nations were different. In the first place, Russia could make a good case that it was doing only what the United States was doing in Turkey, Italy, and elsewhere. Second, the United Nations as a whole would hardly take the alarmist view of the situation held by Washington. Many United Nations members, even allies, had long thought that the United States was entirely too preoccupied with Cuba.

Consulting with allies might well, as the administration argued, have meant a break in the secrecy that Kennedy had decreed, and the allies, by urging a more cautious approach, might have hampered Kennedy's freedom of action. But beyond these points, this question of consultation is a very serious one. Kennedy was preparing to go to the brink of a nuclear war that, if it erupted, would inevitably involve NATO allies at great human cost, yet he excluded them from such a fateful decision. To paraphrase the American colonists, it would be nuclear war without representation. Neither friend nor foe would be notified until Washington had decided, unilaterally, what to do.

Within the ExCom the idea of a "surgical strike" by bombers was at first appealing. However, there were too many dangers. Such a strike could be effective, if at all, only if it were a surprise. This would mean the death and wounding of Russians as well as Cuban military men and could affect civilians as well. Robert Kennedy was adamantly opposed. It would be "a Pearl Harbor in reverse." [31] It would be wrong and it would cause revulsion all over the world. Furthermore, it might well trigger a nuclear response from Russia. So too might an invasion. Yet even while the discussions were under way orders went out to all the military services. Ships were concentrated in the Caribbean, troops in Florida, and the Air Force was ready. Preparations were also made for nuclear war if the situation should come to that. Gradually, however, sentiment moved away from endorsement of a military strike to the idea of a blockade. Although there was a feeling that a blockade might be too slow, it seemed less risky and the other options were still available if it did not work. Someone with a touch of public-relations genius proposed that the term "quarantine," earlier suggested by Richard Nixon, be used. It seemed less belligerent and had a nice medical sound to it. Nonetheless, a blockade by any other name is still an act of war. Thus the stage was set for what was probably the most dramatic and most frightening presidential address in the history of the republic. The nation knew that something serious was up. It knew it had to do with Cuba, but the secrecy had held. Kennedy's speech on Monday night, October 22, came as a complete and numbing surprise.

The President got directly to the point:

> Within the past week, unmistakable evidence has established the fact that a series of offensive missile sites is now in preparation on that imprisoned island. The purpose of these bases can be none other than to provide a nuclear strike capability against the Western Hemisphere. . . .
> This secret, swift, and extraordinary buildup of communist missiles—in an area well known to have a special and historic relationship to the United States and the nations of the Western Hemisphere, in violation of Soviet assurances, and in defiance of American and hemispheric policy—this sudden, clandestine decision to station strategic weapons for the first time outside of Soviet soil—is a deliberately provocative and unjustified change in the status quo which cannot be accepted by this country, if our courage and our commitments are ever to be trusted again by either friend or foe.[32]

Kennedy announced that action was necessary to secure the "withdrawal or elimination" of the missiles from Cuba.

> . . . action is required—and it is under way; and these actions may only be the beginning. We will not prematurely or unnecessarily risk the costs of worldwide nuclear war in which even the fruits of victory would be ashes in our mouth—*but neither will we shrink from that risk at any time it must be faced.* [Emphasis added.]

The President outlined the steps he was ordering. Among them was the establishment of a "quarantine"—blockade—of all "offensive" weapons, a blockade that would "be extended, if needed, to other types of cargo and carriers." There would also be increased surveillance of Cuba. "Should these offensive military preparations continue, further action will be justified. I have directed the Armed Forces to prepare for any eventualities; and I trust that in the interest of both the Cuban people and the Soviet technicians at the sites, the hazards to all concerned of continuing this threat will be recognized."

Then the most alarming statement of all, reinforcing the impression that the world was on the brink of nuclear war:

> . . . It shall be the policy of this Nation to regard any nuclear missile launched from Cuba against any nation in the Western Hemi-

sphere as an attack by the Soviet Union on the United States, requiring a full retaliatory response upon the Soviet Union.

Again and again Kennedy's admirers have written that the President did not want to humiliate Khrushchev or back him into a corner. Robert Kennedy put it this way:

> Neither side wanted war over Cuba, we agreed, but it was possible that either side could take a step that—for reasons of "security" or "pride" or "face"—would require a response by the other side, which in turn, for the same reasons of security, pride or face, would bring about a counter-response and eventually an escalation into armed conflict. That was what he [the President] wanted to avoid. . . . We were not going to misjudge, or miscalculate, or challenge the other side needlessly, or precipitously push our adversaries into a course of action that was not intended or anticipated.[33]

Yet how does that square with the facts? President Kennedy went on radio and television, accused Russia of deception and deliberate provocation, ordered a blockade, and told Khrushchev that he must back down or be faced with further steps, including, if necessary, nuclear war. However one chooses to describe it, this was an ultimatum, and a public and humiliating one at that. It was given, for all practical purposes, with no warning. Ambassador Dobrynin got the text of the President's message at 6 p.m., only an hour before the President spoke, and it was conveyed to the Russian Foreign Office in the Kremlin a few minutes later—after midnight, Russian time.

Khrushchev did not share the view that his pride had been spared. Both in public statements and in a private message to Kennedy he accused the United States of piratical acts. In a private letter received by Kennedy on October 23, he accused the President of threatening him and the Soviet Union and he said Russia would not observe the blockade. "The actions of the USA with regard to Cuba are outright banditry or, if you like, the folly of degenerate imperialism." He said the United States was pushing mankind "to the abyss of a world missile-nuclear war." The USSR would not order its ship captains to obey the commands of the American Navy, and if any effort were made to interfere with Soviet ships, "we would then be forced for our part to take the measures which we deem necessary and adequate in order to protect our rights. For this we have all that is necessary." [34] Khrushchev may have meant Soviet submarines that were detected moving into the area. He certainly did not sound like a man whom it would be profitable to press further.

It was, as no one can doubt, the United States that was putting on the pressure, not the Soviet Union. It seems not to have occurred to the President that Khrushchev might believe that Russia was in the right in sending missiles to Cuba and that to attempt to use an act of war to force him to back down was to take a dangerous risk of triggering a military response. Kennedy was asking for unconditional and public surrender from a proud and powerful adversary that may well have believed itself in the right and the United States in the wrong.

However, Kennedy did succeed in taking the political offensive. At the United Nations, where the public contest was fought, Adlai Stevenson succeeded in capturing the role of prosecutor for himself, forcing Valerian Zorin into the role of defendant. Russia obviously had a creditable case: that it was helping defend Cuba against the demonstrated hostility of the United States, that it was doing no more in Cuba than the United States had done in Turkey. Nonetheless, Stevenson, materially aided by the American press, read and listened to by the United Nations delegates every day, kept the offensive, culminating in the now-famous until-hell-freezes-over speech: [35]

> . . . Well, let me say something to you, Mr. Ambassador, we do have the evidence. We have it, and it is clear and incontrovertible. And let me say something else. These weapons must be taken out of Cuba. . . . You, the Soviet Union, have sent these weapons to Cuba. You, the Soviet Union, have created this new danger—not the United States. . . .
>
> Finally, Mr. Zorin, I remind you that the other day you did not deny the existence of these weapons. But today, again, if I heard you correctly, you now say that they do not exist, or that we haven't proved they exist.
>
> All right, sir, let me ask you one simple question. Do you, Ambassador Zorin, deny that the USSR has placed and is placing medium- and intermediate-range missiles and sites in Cuba? Yes or no? Don't wait for the translation, yes or no?
>
> ZORIN: I am not in an American courtroom, sir, and therefore I do not wish to answer a question that is put to me in the fashion in

which a prosecutor puts questions. In due course, sir, you will have your answer.

STEVENSON: You are in the courtroom of world opinion right now, and you can answer yes or no. You have denied that they exist, and I want to know whether I have understood you correctly.

ZORIN: Continue with your statement. You will have your answer in due course.

STEVENSON: I am prepared to wait for my answer until hell freezes over, if that's your decision. And I am also prepared to present the evidence in this room.[36]

With that, Stevenson aides set up easels in the corner of the Security Council chamber and showed, with great effect, huge blowups of the missiles. This dramatic confrontation, watched by millions on television, made Stevenson a national hero, even with those who in the past had accepted the absurd Republican charges that he was somehow soft on communism. But Stevenson himself later concluded that he had gone a bit overboard and, in responding to the drama of the moment, had backed Zorin too far into a corner.

Although the attention of a fearful world was focused on the United Nations Security Council, where the visible drama was being played out before television cameras, the vital decisions were being made in Washington and Moscow. Nonetheless, the United Nations did have an important function. It was at the United Nations on Tuesday, October 23, that the Cuban Ambassador, Dr. Mario Garcia-Inchaustegui, repeated the Dorticos statement of October 8: "Were the United States able to give proof, by word and deed, that it would not carry out aggression against our country, then, we declare solemnly before you here and now, our weapons would be unnecessary and our army redundant." If there had been any earlier doubt as to the meaning of these words, it was now removed. And at the United Nations the word was passed in specific terms: if the United States would guarantee Cuba's territorial integrity, Cuba and the USSR would agree to remove the missiles.

Nonetheless, Kennedy continued to press for unconditional surrender with all its unforeseeable consequences. But then there was a timely, and crucial, intervention by U Thant, Acting Secretary General following the death the year before of Dag Hammarskjöld. With Soviet ships nearing the United States blockade line 500 miles off Cuba, Thant, on Wednesday, October 24, sent identical messages to Kennedy and Khrushchev. Stressing that it was essential to avoid an aggravation of the situation that might lead to war, and essential to provide time for negotiations, Thant asked for "the voluntary suspension of all arms shipments to Cuba, and also the voluntary suspension of the quarantine measures. . . ." He also asked that work be stopped on the missile sites and pointed to the Dorticos statement as a possible basis of agreement.

Khrushchev immediately accepted U Thant's proposal. Some have argued that he seized upon it as a way to save face, to claim that he had stopped his ships in response to Thant's appeal rather than to Kennedy's ultimatum. That may be so, but there is no more reason to believe that than to believe that he would have attempted to force the blockade had not Thant made his appeal. He may have responded to Thant's appeal because he was genuinely seeking a way to avoid a physical clash that could easily—and swiftly—escalate to nuclear war. This was his purpose, he said in reply to Bertrand Russell, who had sent him a message: "May I humbly appeal for your further help in lowering the temperature. . . . Your continued forbearance is our great hope." In reply to Russell, Khrushchev said:

> . . . I should like to assure you that the Soviet Government will not take any reckless decisions, will not permit itself to be provoked by the unwarranted actions of the United States of America and will do everything to eliminate the situation fraught with irreparable consequences which has arisen in connection with the aggressive actions of the United States Government. We shall do everything in our power to prevent war from breaking out. We are fully aware of the fact that if this war is unleashed, from the very first hour it will become a thermonuclear and world war. This is perfectly obvious to us, but clearly is not to the Government of the United States which has caused this crisis. . . .
>
> The Soviet Government considers that the Government of the United States of America must display reserve and stay the execution of its piratical threats which are fraught with the most serious consequences.
>
> The question of war and peace is so vital that we should consider useful a top-level meeting in order to discuss all the problems which have arisen, to do everything to remove the danger of unleashing a

thermonuclear war. As long as rocket nuclear weapons are not put into play it is still possible to avert war. When aggression is unleashed by the Americans such a meeting will already become impossible and useless.[37]

Kennedy's replies to Thant and Russell were somewhat different in substance and tone. To Thant he wrote on October 25:

> . . . As we made clear in the Security Council, the existing threat was created by the secret introduction of offensive weapons into Cuba, and the answer lies in the removal of such weapons.
> In your message and in your statement to the Security Council, you have made certain suggestions and have invited preliminary talks to determine whether satisfactory arrangements can be assured.
> Ambassador Stevenson is ready to discuss these arrangements with you.
> I can assure you of our desire to reach a satisfactory and peaceful solution of the matter.[38]

Still no suggestion that the United States was prepared to accept anything short of unconditional surrender.

Russell's message to Kennedy, although extreme, represented an important school of thought in British public opinion: "Your action desperate. . . . No conceivable justification. We will not have mass murder. . . . End this madness." [39] Although one cannot question the aged philosopher's sincerity, or perhaps even his essential correctness, his telegram was provocative. It was not surprising that Kennedy replied in these terms:

> . . . While your messages are critical of the United States, they make no mention of your concern for the introduction of secret Soviet missiles into Cuba. I think your attention might well be directed to the burglars rather than to those who have caught the burglars.[40]

On Thursday, October 25, some of the Soviet ships stopped or turned around, presumably because of Khrushchev's acceptance of U Thant's proposal and the elaboration of it made on that day. In this "continuation of my message of yesterday," Thant said:

> . . . I would like to bring to Your Excellency's attention my grave concern that Soviet ships already on their way to Cuba might chal-

lenge the quarantine imposed by the United States and produce a confrontation at sea between Soviet ships and United States vessels which could lead to an aggravation of the situation. What concerns me most is that such a confrontation and consequent aggravation of the situation would destroy any possibility of the discussions I have suggested as a prelude to negotiations on a peaceful settlement. In the circumstances I earnestly hope that Your Excellency may find it possible to instruct the Soviet ships already on their way to Cuba to stay away from the interception zone for a limited time only, in order to permit discussions of the modalities of a possible agreement which could settle the problem peacefully in line with the Charter of the United Nations.

I am confident that, if such instruction could be issued by Your Excellency, the United States authorities will take action to ensure that a direct confrontation between their ships and Soviet ships is avoided during the same period in order to minimize the risk of any untoward incident taking place.

If I could be informed of the action taken by your Government on the basis of this appeal, I could inform President Kennedy that I have assurances from your side of your cooperation in avoiding all risk of an untoward incident.[41]

Thant also sent a similar message to Kennedy, in which he asked the President to instruct United States naval vessels to avoid a confrontation.[42]

Kennedy replied the same day that he would accept the proposal if Khrushchev did, but again he stressed the urgent need that the Soviet missiles be removed.[43] Khrushchev replied affirmatively the next day (Soviet replies often took longer because of the time difference between New York and Moscow) but he asserted that "we have given this order in the hope that the other side will understand that such a situation, in which we keep vessels immobilized on the high seas, must be a purely temporary one; the period cannot under any circumstances be of long duration." [44]

The decision was much easier for Kennedy than for Khrushchev, for if Khrushchev stopped his ships, for whatever reason, it meant that the blockade was effective. Whether Thant's appeal was the reason or only the occasion for Khrushchev's not forcing the blockade, the Acting Secretary General is responsible for the breathing space that avoided confrontation at sea—and possible escalation into nuclear war. American writers have generally underestimated Thant's crucial contribution to the settlement of the missile crisis.

The crisis was almost over, although, as we shall see, it was briefly to enter a stage even more dangerous than before. On Friday, October 26, the United States received, via two unorthodox channels, proposals that seemed to mean a peaceful end to the crisis. The more unusual came through John Scali, the experienced and talented diplomatic correspondent for the American Broadcasting Corporation, who received a telephone call from Aleksandr S. Fomin of the Soviet Embassy. The Soviet diplomat said it was imperative that they meet immediately. At a restaurant Fomin asked Scali if the State Department would be interested in settling the crisis on this basis: 1) the missiles would be shipped back to Russia under United Nations supervision; 2) Castro would pledge not to accept offensive weapons; 3) the United States would pledge not to invade Cuba. Scali thought this was a possible basis for a settlement and rushed off to the State Department with the Russian proposal.

Somewhat less unorthodox and more important was a proposal direct from Khrushchev himself. In a personal letter to Kennedy —Khrushchev a year earlier had begun writing such letters to the President—the Premier appealed for an end to the crisis in the most urgent and emotional terms. Some have suggested that when Khrushchev wrote the letter he was so unstable or emotional that the message was incoherent. Robert Kennedy addressed this directly:

> There was no question that the letter had been written by him personally. It was very long and emotional. But it was not incoherent, and the emotion was directed at the death, destruction, and anarchy that nuclear war would bring to his people and all mankind. That, he said again and again, and in many different ways, must be avoided.[45]

Although Khrushchev's letter has yet to be made public, it can be reconstructed to a considerable degree, particularly from the accounts given by Robert Kennedy and by Elie Abel in *The Missile Crisis*. He said the time had come to rise above "petty passions" and stop the drift toward war before it was too late. He said that the forthcoming elections were "transient things," but that "if indeed war should break out, then it would not be in our power to stop it, for such is the logic of war." Khrushchev wrote that it was obvious that he and Kennedy could not agree on the significance of the Soviet missiles, but he insisted that they were not offensive weapons, that they would never be used to attack the United States:

> You can be calm in this regard, that we are of sound mind and understand perfectly well that if we attack you, you will respond the same way. But you too will receive the same that you hurl against us. And I think that you also understand this. . . . This indicates that we are normal people, that we correctly understand and correctly evaluate the situation. Consequently, how can we permit the incorrect actions which you ascribe to us? Only lunatics or suicides, who themselves want to perish and to destroy the whole world before they died, could do this.

Khrushchev assured Kennedy: "We want something quite different . . . not to destroy your country . . . but despite our ideological differences, to compete peacefully, not by military means." He said there was no need to stop the Soviet ships en route to Cuba, for they carried only nonmilitary cargo; the missiles were already there. This was Khrushchev's first acknowledgment that there were indeed Soviet missiles in Cuba. He said that he could not be sure that Kennedy would believe this, but he hoped the President would not stop Soviet ships, for that would be piracy. If the ships were stopped, Russia would be forced to defend them, as it had the right to do under international law, and no man could know where this might lead.

Then Khrushchev made directly the proposal suggested by President Dorticos on October 8, by Cuban Ambassador Garcia-Inchaustegui on October 23, and informally by Mr. Fomin to John Scali that same day:

> . . . If assurances were given that the President of the United States would not participate in an attack on Cuba and the blockade lifted, then the question of the removal or the destruction of the missile sites in Cuba would then be an entirely different question. Armaments bring only disasters. When one accumulates them, this damages the economy, and if one puts them to use, then they destroy people on both sides. Consequently, only a madman can be-

lieve that armaments are the principal means in the life of a society. No, they are an enforced loss of human energy, and what is more are for the destruction of man himself. If people do not show wisdom, then in the final analysis they will come to a clash, like blind moles, and then reciprocal extermination will begin.[46]

Then Khrushchev made his proposal specific. No more such weapons would be sent to Cuba and those already there would be withdrawn or destroyed. In return, the United States would end the blockade and agree not to invade Cuba. And Khrushchev again asked Kennedy not to interfere with the Soviet ships. Then came these emotional, eloquent, and sensible words:

. . . If you have not lost your self-control and sensibly conceive what this might lead to, then, Mr. President, we and you ought not to pull on the ends of the rope in which you have tied the knot of war, because the more the two of us pull, the tighter that knot will be tied. And a moment may come when that knot will be tied so tight that even he who tied it will not have the strength to untie it, and then it will be necessary to cut that knot, and what that would mean is not for me to explain to you, because you yourself understand perfectly of what terrible forces our countries dispose. Consequently, if there is no intention to tighten that knot, and thereby doom the world to the catastrophe of thermonuclear war, then let us not only relax the forces pulling on the ends of the rope, let us take measures to untie that knot. We are ready for this.

When the crisis was over a few days later, most of the world agreed that Kennedy had won a great victory by outbluffing Khrushchev, but a reading of the paragraph above and a less chauvinistic view of the facts can lead to another conclusion. True, it was Khrushchev who backed away from nuclear confrontation, but unless *machismo* is to be the ultimate standard of statesmanship, it was Khrushchev who sacrificed pride to avoid nuclear war and it was Kennedy who was pushing the world to the brink of the catastrophe that has been man's dread since the mushroom cloud spread over Hiroshima a generation before. Nor was Khrushchev's action the surrender that it has been pictured. Even *in extremis* Russia refused to accept the blockade, shot down a U-2 over Cuba, and insisted that Kennedy pledge not to invade Cuba. One of Khrushchev's major reasons was certainly to defend that threatened island. In that he succeeded entirely and, as we shall see, he received even more. Khrushchev, despite the popular view, did not cave in; he held out for—and got—a reasonable settlement.

On that Friday night Kennedy and his advisers went to bed with an enormous sense of relief. For the first time in eleven nights the threat of nuclear war did not hang over them. But the next morning they concluded that the crisis was still on—and more dangerous than ever. On Saturday morning, when the ExCom convened, there was a new letter from Khrushchev, one obviously the product of the Russian Foreign Office. It was quite different from the Premier's personal letter: "We will remove our missiles from Cuba, you will remove yours from Turkey. . . . The Soviet Union will pledge not to invade or interfere with the internal affairs of Turkey; the United States to make the same pledge regarding Cuba." [47]

All those close to the situation have written that the crisis thereby went into, as Robert Kennedy put it, its "most difficult twenty-four hours." "To add to the feeling of foreboding and gloom, Secretary McNamara reported increased evidence that the Russians in Cuba were now working day and night, intensifying their efforts on all the missile sites." Perhaps the tension and exhaustion of the previous days caused the ExCom to take so pessimistic a view, for in retrospect it is difficult to see what else could have caused it. Even if Khrushchev had stiffened his offer somewhat, "the fact was," Robert Kennedy observed, "the proposal the Russians made was not unreasonable and did not amount to a loss to the United States or to our NATO allies." [48] Indeed, the President had directly ordered several months earlier that the Jupiter missiles be removed from Turkey and Italy because they were obsolescent. But his orders had not been carried out because Turkey was reluctant, possibly for economic reasons (a big American payroll was involved) to have them removed. Once again Kennedy found himself hung up on the concept of American honor. He did not want to risk nuclear war for missiles that were no longer of any real military value, but he shared the general view of the ExCom that to remove them now under Russian pressure would undermine the faith of the NATO alliance in America's word. Then there were those Congressional elections just a few days off. What political capital the Republicans would make of Kennedy's "surrender"! The ExCom sought unsuccessfully to find some formula by which the Turkish missiles could be removed without appearing that the United States was giving way to Soviet pressure. Alarm was heightened when it received the bad news that antiaircraft fire, presumably a Russian SAM, had shot down an American U-2 pilot, Major Rudolf Anderson, Jr., one of the two pilots whose mission on October 14 had first disclosed the presence of the Soviet missiles.

There was certainly just cause to mourn the death of a brave man who had performed such a great service, but the fact was that there was no reason for the Russians and the Cubans to stop their military preparations until Khrushchev learned whether or not Kennedy would accept his proposals. Indeed, there was good reason to continue them, for if Kennedy did not accept, the likelihood was that the crisis would intensify, with the possibility, even the probability, that the Americans would take military action. In any case, it was clear by now that the Russians would not initiate military action but would only respond to American moves. But Washington did not see things that way.

Then Robert Kennedy had a brilliant idea, one that contributed signally to the sudden end of the crisis. Ignoring the speculation about the second Khrushchev note—that he had changed his mind, or that the hard-liners in the Kremlin had taken over or had forced Khrushchev to take a tougher position—the President's brother suggested replying to the first, more acceptable letter, and ignoring the second. It is possible that the second letter was actually first but had been delayed in the bureaucratic machinery so that it was overtaken by Khrushchev's personal message.

The President agreed and sent this message:

> I have read your letter of October 26th with great care and welcomed the statement of your desire to seek a prompt solution to the problem. The first thing that needs to be done, however, is for work to cease on offensive missile bases in Cuba and for all weapons systems in Cuba capable of offensive use to be rendered inoperable, under effective United Nations arrangements.
>
> Assuming this is done promptly, I have given my representatives in New York instructions that will permit them to work out this weekend—in cooperation with the Acting Secretary General and your representative—an arrangement for a permanent solution to the Cuba problem along the lines suggested in your letter of Octo-

ber 26th. As I read your letter, the key elements of your proposals
—which seem generally acceptable—are as follows:

1. You would agree to remove these weapons systems from Cuba
under appropriate United Nations observation and supervision; and
undertake, with suitable safeguards, to halt the further introduction
of such weapons systems into Cuba.

2. We, on our part, would agree—upon the establishment of adequate arrangements through the United Nations to ensure the carrying out and continuation of these commitments—(a) to remove
promptly the quarantine measures now in effect and (b) to give assurances against an invasion of Cuba. I am confident that other nations of the Western Hemisphere would be prepared to do likewise.

If you will give your representative similar instructions, there is
no reason why we should not be able to complete these arrangements and announce them to the world within a couple of days.
The effect of such a settlement on easing world tension would ena-
ble us to work toward a more general arrangement regarding "other
armaments" as proposed in your second letter which you made public. I would like to say again that the United States is very much interested in reducing tensions and halting the arms race; and if your
letter signifies that you are prepared to discuss a détente affecting
NATO and the Warsaw Pact, we are quite prepared to consider
with our allies any useful proposals.

But the first ingredient, let me emphasize, is the cessation of
work on missile sites in Cuba and measures to render such weapons
inoperable, under effective international guarantees. The continuation of this threat, or a prolonging of this discussion concerning
Cuba by linking these questions to the broader questions of European and world security, would surely lead to an intensification of
the Cuban crisis and a grave risk to the peace of the world. For this
reason I hope we can quickly agree along the lines outlined in this
letter and in your letter of October 26th.[49]

Notice that without mentioning Turkey, Kennedy, in the last
paragraph, excludes it from the deal. This—publicly—satisfied
the American concept of honor, that it must never seem to respond to pressure, and it is this public firmness that contributed to
the general assessment that Khrushchev backed down. Yet when
Robert Kennedy delivered the letter to Ambassador Dobrynin at a
Saturday-night meeting in the Justice Department, the question of
Turkey was raised by the Russian. This was Robert Kennedy's
reply:

. . . I said that there could be no *quid pro quo* or any arrangement made under this kind of threat or pressure, and that in the last analysis this was a decision that would have to be made by NATO. However, I said, President Kennedy had been anxious to remove those missiles from Turkey and Italy for a long period of time. He had ordered their removal some time ago, and it was our judgment that, within a short time after this crisis was over, those missiles would be gone.[50]

There is no way to disguise the fact that this, however informal, was a *quid pro quo,* and no doubt the anxious Dobrynin evaluated it as such in his cable to Moscow. And the fact is that a few months later the Jupiter missiles were quietly removed from Turkey and Italy. Stevenson, despite having been castigated as a "dove"—it was in this controversy that the terms "dove" and "hawk" were born—was right, and Khrushchev did get all he asked for in the second, stiffer letter: an end to the blockade, a pledge guaranteeing Cuba's safety, and the removal of the Jupiter missiles. Since the recognition of this would diminish Kennedy's "triumph," his admirers have understandably skirted this point.

Yet despite President Kennedy's acceptance of Khrushchev's proposal, the crisis was not over. When the news came that Major Anderson had been shot down,

At first, there was almost unanimous agreement that we had to attack early the next morning with bombers and fighters and destroy the SAM sites. But again the President pulled everyone back. "It isn't the first step that concerns me," he said, "but both sides escalating to the fourth and fifth step—and we don't go to the sixth because there is no one around to do so. We must remind ourselves that we are embarking on a very hazardous course." [51]

Despite this sensible concern, there is complete agreement by those close to the situation that Kennedy was on the very edge of a decision to increase the military pressure on the Russians, with measures ranging from broadening the blockade to include nonmilitary goods to an air strike and an invasion. Although no one can say how the Russians would have responded, obviously any of these steps risked a military response with the gravest danger of escalation to nuclear war. With the elements of a peaceful solution right at hand, Kennedy was both increasing the pressure and demanding an immediate reply. This was neither sensible nor prudent; it jeopardized at terrible risk the very agreement that mutual concessions had made possible. No one was closer to the situation than Robert Kennedy. This was what he told Ambassador Dobrynin that Saturday night. They are chilling words.

> . . . Because of the deception of the Soviet Union, our photographic reconnaissance planes would have to continue to fly over Cuba, and if the Cubans or Soviets shot at these planes, then we would have to shoot back. This would inevitably lead to further incidents and to escalation of the conflict, the implications of which were very grave indeed. . . . We had to have a commitment by tomorrow that those bases would be removed. I was not giving them an ultimatum but a statement of fact. He should understand that if they did not remove those bases, we would remove them. . . .
>
> I said President Kennedy wished to have peaceful relations between our two countries. He wished to resolve the problems that confronted us in Europe and Southeast Asia. He wished to move forward on the control of nuclear weapons. However, we could make progress on these matters only when this crisis was behind us. Time was running out. We had only a few more hours—we needed an answer immediately from the Soviet Union. I said we must have it the next day.[52]

This did not make sense. Kennedy had just agreed to Khrushchev's proposals, and it was just a matter of time, a day or so perhaps, before the crisis was to be resolved peacefully, yet the United States was issuing what, despite Robert Kennedy's words, was another ultimatum. Why could not the President's brother have conveyed the President's message, added the concession on Turkey that made agreement even more certain, and confined himself to an urgent but friendly hope that the issue could be swiftly resolved?

When the Attorney General returned to the White House, he and the President were pessimistic. The President ordered to active duty twenty-four Air Force troop-carrier squadrons to be ready for an invasion. He "had not abandoned hope, but what hope there was now rested with Khrushchev's revising his course within the next few hours. It was a hope, not an expectation. The expectation was a military confrontation by Tuesday and possibly tomorrow. . . ."[53] Or, as Roger Hilsman put it, ". . . an actual invasion of Cuba might be no later than forty-eight hours away."[54]

This did not make sense either. With agreement, by any reasonable expectation, only a day or so away, Kennedy was preparing, by military action, to pull that knot "so tight that even he who tied it will not have the strength to untie it, and then it will be necessary to cut that knot, and what that would mean is not for me to explain to you, because you yourself understand perfectly of what terrible forces our countries dispose." Kennedy was in such a hurry that he seemed prepared to jeopardize everything. One can only assume that continued tension and exhaustion caused such behavior, for there was no need for Khrushchev to revise his course: he had already offered and Kennedy had accepted a reasonable proposal. One can only believe that Kennedy would have seen the folly of pulling the knot tighter if Khrushchev had delayed for a day or so.

Fortunately, Khrushchev was not provoked by the Attorney General's language; perhaps he was under similar pressure himself and understood how extreme tension affected even brave and calm men. On Sunday, October 28, the welcome words came from the Kremlin, broadcast by Radio Moscow to save time: Khrushchev had accepted Kennedy's understanding of his proposals. The missiles would be removed and no more sent, with the United States, for its part, to end the blockade and guarantee Cuba's territorial integrity.[55] The crisis was over.

It took a few months, however, to tie up the loose ends. Castro, perhaps angered because he had been so largely ignored, refused to allow United Nations observers into Cuba, despite a flying trip to Havana by U Thant. But that difficulty was overcome by Russia's, and Cuba's, tacit agreement to let American U-2s serve to verify that the sites were dismantled and the missiles shipped back to the Soviet Union. However, the Soviet Union and Cuba argued that the IL-28 bombers should not be included in the deal; the United States, largely for political reasons, insisted, and Khrushchev eventually gave in. It is interesting that an entire decade later that kind of semantic debate continued. In early 1971, during the Strategic Arms Limitation Talks, the Soviet Union insisted that American fighter-bombers in Western Europe capable of carrying nuclear bombs be included within the scope of the talks.

The United States, however, argued that such bombers should not be included since their sole purpose was to "defend" NATO countries. The question had not been resolved at this writing and, in general terms, it probably never will be, for it is always the other side's weapons that are offensive.

What finally can be said about the Cuban missile crisis? First, it is obvious that both Khrushchev and Kennedy made serious miscalculations. Although Khrushchev was entirely justified by international law in sending the missiles to Cuba, he was not justified by a more important law, common sense. He should have known that no American President could permit such a thing even if, as was the case, the missiles did not materially change the military balance of power. Although Khrushchev and Castro did have legitimate fears of American hostility, Khrushchev could have protected Cuba by less extreme means. He could have made a public pledge that an attack on Cuba would be regarded as an attack on the Soviet Union, or he could have sent a limited force of Russian soldiers to serve as a trip-wire, as American troops did in Western Europe. There might well have been other measures short of sending missiles.

But if Khrushchev's move was reckless, Kennedy's response was even more so. Granted that political realities made it necessary for Kennedy to rid Cuba of the missiles, he could have done it diplomatically. It is difficult to escape the conclusion that, as with Berlin, he deliberately built up the crisis, possibly to influence the elections, possibly to force the showdown with Khrushchev that he had long thought might be necessary. He gambled when there were too many unpredictable things that could have gone fatally wrong. His public and surprise ultimatum to Khrushchev risked nuclear war and, because it was wholly unnecessary, risked it to a degree beyond forgiveness. Clearly, however great his reluctance, Kennedy did seem, on the evidence of his friends, more willing than Khrushchev to take that last fatal step. One can only wonder, if their roles had been reversed, if Kennedy would have been able to accept public humiliation as the cost of avoiding nuclear war. For there is no doubt that in the eyes of much of the world, however unwarranted such a conclusion, Khrushchev was humiliated and Kennedy was triumphant. This despite the fact, as historians will surely note, that Khrushchev got all he had asked for in his "second," tougher message: an end to the blockade, the removal of American missiles from Turkey and Italy, and a guarantee of Cuban security. When the crisis was over, the status quo with Cuba no longer existed. It is true that there were no Soviet missiles in Cuba, but there were none there before. In this regard, no change; but before the crisis, Cuba's safety was not assured; after the crisis, it was. History will decide who, in tangible terms, gained the most. And even Kennedy's public triumph at the cost of Khrushchev's humiliation may have been as hollow as it was illusory. This humiliation, or the appearance of it, may well have contributed to Khrushchev's overthrow two years later. It is difficult for an American to know what Khrushchev's ouster meant to the people of the Soviet Union, but it did mean the loss of a man who, despite his failings, despite his foolish behavior in sending missiles to Cuba, genuinely sought the American–Soviet détente essential to world peace, and sought it with more imagination and purpose than did his successors. But what might have been, had Kennedy lived, had Khrushchev remained in power, can never be known. What was observable, however, was the move toward détente that followed the sobering missile crisis; but again the situation is not as simple as it once appeared.

As for the missile crisis itself, the reader must judge for himself whether Kennedy was prudent or reckless. Perhaps the standard for prudent behavior was best expressed by Kennedy himself.

> . . . Above all, while defending our own vital interests, nuclear powers must avert those confrontations which bring an adversary to a choice of either a humiliating retreat or a nuclear war. To adopt that kind of course in the nuclear age would be evidence only of the bankruptcy of our policy—or of a collective death-wish for the world.[56]

John Kennedy believed that his course during the Cuban missile crisis conformed to this essential standard. I disagree.

> . . . Kennedy's stand in the Cuban missile crisis, said a Euro-
> pean political leader in my office, may well be like the Greek
> stand against the Persians at Salamis in 400 B.C.—not only a
> great turning point in history, but the start of a true Golden
> Age.[1]
>
> —THEODORE SORENSEN

CHAPTER EIGHT

Détente

It is not necessary to go as far as the unnamed European leader to
recognize that the Cuban missile crisis was indeed a milestone in
the dreary history of the Cold War, but whether it was genuinely a
turning point we can never know. Nonetheless, a great deal happened in the year that was all that was left to Kennedy. There was
a tangible move toward détente, culminating in the partial-nuclear-
test-ban treaty. In language and deed the President moved toward friendlier relations with Russia, but in neither language nor
deed was he consistent. Nor was even the test-ban treaty the
achievement it at first seemed. And overshadowing all in that last
year was Vietnam, which, after Kennedy's death, was to postpone
any real Soviet–American détente for at least another decade.
What Kennedy might have done had he lived, we cannot know.
What he did in those final months, we can examine.

Before going on to Soviet–American relations after the missile
crisis, it is necessary to note that the Congressional elections
turned out much better than Kennedy had feared. While he had
expected to lose ten or fifteen seats in the House and perhaps gain
one or two in the Senate, the Democrats lost only four in the
House and gained that many in the Senate. Whereas the Republicans had been exploiting the Cuban issue before October 22, they
were obviously hurt by it thereafter. What had been a major liabil-
ity had turned after Kennedy's "victory" into a major advantage.

The conventional view has been that both Kennedy and Khru-

143

shchev were sobered by the crisis and determined that their nations should never again come that close to nuclear war. This may
be an oversimplification. No doubt Kennedy did recognize to a
greater degree than before how easy it was to set off a chain of
events that could lead almost inevitably to a catastrophe that no
one wanted. It is no doubt true that he was more eager to ease international tensions and, in particular, to seek a nuclear-test-ban
treaty to, as he often said, put "the genie back in the bottle." And
of Khrushchev, it has often been asserted that he had been taught
a lesson, that an aggressive, bellicose policy was not productive in
face of Kennedy's determination and strength. But that is just the
rewarming of the old Washington myth that the Russians always
back down when faced by American resolve. There is considerable doubt that Khrushchev "backed down" in Cuba and ample
evidence that he had been actively seeking détente ever since Kennedy took office. His warm messages when Kennedy was elected
and inaugurated, the release of the RB-47 fliers, the series of private letters, frank but friendly, that he initiated in September
1961—these outweigh in the balance his occasionally angry
speeches, even his reckless sending of missiles to Cuba, and these,
after all, it could be argued, were responses to initiatives by Kennedy that the Kremlin regarded as hostile. Khrushchev's emotional
and eloquent appeal for reason in his letter of October 26 that signaled the end of the missile crisis certainly seems consistent with
what has been learned of his earlier letters. However naïve it may
seem to some, it is possible to be convinced that Khrushchev in
his own impulsive, inconsistent way was genuinely seeking peace
and believed—this is a measure of his faith in Kennedy—that the
President would eventually respond. No doubt the missile crisis
was a sobering experience to Khrushchev, as it was to Kennedy,
but I am convinced that the crisis did not so much teach him a
lesson as reinforce one he had already learned. For Khrushchev,
whatever his degree of participation in the horrors of Stalinism,
and however inconsistent his support of a liberalizing trend
within the Soviet Union, did seem to be convinced of the need for
better Soviet–American relations and to pursue that conviction
with more vigor and imagination than any ruler of Soviet Russia
before him or since. While it is true, and good, that Kennedy
learned from the missile crisis, he had more to learn, for his pol-

icy until then had been more adventurous than Khrushchev's.

The first goal was obvious: to limit the nuclear-arms race. At first the prospects looked promising. Neither side had learned as much as it had expected from the series of tests just ending. Kennedy had agreed to the American tests only to find after their completion that those who had opposed them were right, but it will come as no surprise that the defenders of the tests argued that the lack of results just proved the necessity for more tests. Nonetheless, "in response to Khrushchev's talk of new accords after the Cuban crisis," Kennedy established a test-ban treaty as the first priority.[2] It is important to note that, again, it was Khrushchev who took the initiative. Informal talks soon began, from which the Soviet Union got the impression that the United States was willing to lower its insistence on onsite inspections from seven or eight to three. In this belief, Khrushchev sent Kennedy another of his private letters.

"It seems to me, Mr. President," Khrushchev wrote to Kennedy on December 19, 1962, "that the time has come now to put an end once and for all to nuclear tests, to draw a line through such tests." We believe, Khrushchev continued, that national means of detection are sufficient to police underground as well as atmospheric tests; but we understand your need for "at least a minimum number" of inspections for the ratification of the treaty. "Well, if this is the only difficulty on the way to agreement, then for the noble and humane goal of ceasing nuclear weapons tests we are ready to meet you halfway." Citing the Kuznetsov–Dean conversations, Khrushchev proposed agreement on two to three annual inspections limited to earthquake areas. If this were to be accepted, "the world can be relieved of the roar of nuclear explosions."[3]

Khrushchev had his hawks, just as did Kennedy, and he explained to the visiting Norman Cousins, editor of the *Saturday Review,* how he got agreement from his colleagues. He told the Council of Ministers that

> we can have an agreement with the United States to stop nuclear tests if we agree to three inspections. I know that three inspections are not necessary, and that the policing can be done adequately from outside our borders. But the American Congress has convinced itself that onsite inspection is necessary and the President

cannot get a treaty through the Senate without it. Very well, then, let us accommodate the President.[4]

There is no reason to doubt the Soviet conviction that onsite inspections were not necessary. As we have seen, seismic technology was improving and Kennedy's top science adviser, Jerome Wiesner, and his associates had arrived at the "firm opinion . . . that the possibility of five inspections per year would have provided adequate security against clandestine nuclear testing." [5] Robert McNamara was ready to accept six. But Kennedy was having more trouble than Khrushchev in getting support, not only outside the executive branch but within it. The Joint Chiefs of Staff were against a comprehensive ban (one in all environments) under almost any conditions and were particularly opposed to only six onsite inspections. So was the right wing of the Congress and the public: Senator Everett Dirksen, the Illinois Republican, the nuclear scientist Edward Teller, and Admiral Lewis Strauss, former head of the Atomic Energy Commission. They were joined by Governor Nelson A. Rockefeller of New York.

The accounts of all this are a bit uncertain in the books about Kennedy, but it does seem that somehow there had been an honest misunderstanding, that the Americans engaged in the informal talks, Arthur Dean and Jerome Wiesner, had not meant to give the impression that the United States would accept just three inspections. Nonetheless, Kennedy was encouraged by Khrushchev's letter and told him so, while explaining that there unaccountably had been some misunderstanding. There were ways to overcome the Russian fear that onsite inspections were an opportunity for espionage, the President said. He suggested that representatives of both sides meet for technical discussions.

Khrushchev accepted this proposal, but the Russians complained bitterly that the Premier had risked his political prestige within the Kremlin only to be embarrassed when Kennedy reneged because of rising political opposition at home. Khrushchev told Norman Cousins at his Black Sea retreat that he had convinced the Council of Ministers to agree to three onsite inspections with the guarantee that this would lead to a test-ban treaty, only to have the United States counter with an offer of eight.

So once again I was made to look foolish. But I can tell you this: it won't happen again. . . . We cannot make another offer. I cannot go back to the Council. It is now up to the United States. Frankly, we feel we were misled. . . . When I go up to Moscow next week I expect to serve notice that we will not consider ourselves bound by three inspections. If you can go from three to eight, we can go from three to zero.[6]

This was the kind of misunderstanding that has been endemic throughout the Cold War. The two sides were so suspicious of each other that misunderstandings occurred even when both sides genuinely wanted agreement. Kennedy believed Khrushchev had deceived him about the Cuban missiles, while Khrushchev believed they were necessary because of his suspicions of Kennedy based on the Bay of Pigs invasion. Here Khrushchev thought Kennedy had welshed on a deal, yet Kennedy was genuinely and urgently eager to get a test-ban treaty. Indeed, at many of his press conferences in the early months of 1963, Kennedy made a point of stressing the need for a treaty and of being as hopeful as possible. Still, even here, his ambivalence reasserted itself. On one hand, he announced on January 26 that "during the present discussions in Washington and New York on the nuclear-test-ban treaty among the Soviet Union, the United Kingdom and the United States, I have asked the Atomic Energy Commission to postpone underground shots in Nevada." He went on to say that "we are maintaining the capability and readiness to resume our test program at any time" and then balanced his earlier generous statement by saying that "we have no intention of again accepting an indefinite moratorium on testing, and if it is clear that we cannot achieve a workable agreement we will act accordingly."[7] In a news conference on March 6, Kennedy again stressed the need for an adequate number of onsite inspections.

I want to say that we have made substantial progress, as a result of a good deal of work by the United States Government in recent years, in improving our detection capabilities. We have been able to determine that there are a substantially less number of earthquakes in the Soviet Union than we had formerly imagined. We have also been able to make far more discriminating our judgments from a long distance of what would be perhaps an atomic test and what would be an earthquake. But we have not been able to make those discriminations so effective that we can do without onsite inspections and without a sufficient number to prevent a series of tests being carried out which would be undetected. I can assure you that no agreement will be accepted which would permit any such conditions.[8]

During these early months of 1963, Kennedy, in his public statements, showed a great deal more interest in pushing for a treaty than did Khrushchev. Although Khrushchev had provided the initial impetus, he seemed to be sulking in his tent because of the misunderstanding over the number of onsite inspections. The third man involved, Prime Minister Harold Macmillan, who with such eloquence and passion had tried to convince Kennedy not to resume testing, had not diminished in his persistence. In March and April the President and the Prime Minister exchanged a series of draft proposals to Khrushchev, and a few days after the Russian had told Norman Cousins that the next step was up to the United States, he received a new British–American proposal. It pointed out that the West had reduced from twenty to seven the number of onsite inspections it felt was necessary. And the Kennedy–Macmillan message said that while each nation had a duty to its own security, they felt that their duty to humanity required one more genuine attempt to stop testing and to prevent the spread of nuclear weapons. To this end, they suggested the sending of very senior representatives to Moscow to speak directly with Khrushchev.

Khrushchev's response was not enthusiastic. He acted as if he had heard all this before. The Western proposals had been learned by heart just as Russians used to learn the "Pater Noster." He still regarded the demand for onsite inspections as a ruse for NATO intelligence agencies. Khrushchev had consented in December to two or three inspections, not because he thought they were necessary but solely to help the President out with the Senate. Yet this great Soviet concession had been met only with Western haggling over the number of inspections and how they should be conducted. Khrushchev said that, judging by their proposals, the Western leaders could not be serious; maybe they were only going through the motions for domestic political reasons. But on the crucial point Khrushchev did respond favorably: the West could send representatives to Moscow; the Russians were prepared to try any-thing. Instead of continuing this wearisome debate point by point, Kennedy and Macmillan wisely skipped all that and in a joint reply on May 30 suggested that the British and American repre-sentatives go to Moscow at the end of June or early in July.

This was the background to the finest speech in John Kennedy's career, delivered on June 10, 1963, at American University. Theodore Sorensen may not have been overstating when he said it was "the first Presidential speech in eighteen years to succeed in reaching beyond the Cold War."

> . . . Unlike most foreign policy speeches—none of which was as sweeping in concept and impact as this turned out to be—official departmental positions and suggestions were not solicited. The Pres-ident was determined to put forward a fundamentally new empha-sis on the peaceful and the positive in our relations with the Soviets. He did not want that new policy diluted by the usual threats of destruction, boasts of nuclear stockpiles and lectures on Soviet treachery.[9]

This speech, in which the President said he did not want "a Pax Americana enforced on the world by American weapons of war," is so important that it demands substantial quotation.

> Some say that it is useless to speak of world peace or world disarmament—and that it will be useless until the leaders of the So-viet Union adopt a more enlightened attitude. I hope they do. I be-lieve we can help them do it. But I also believe we must re-examine our own attitude—as individuals and as a Nation—for our attitude is as essential as theirs. And every graduate of this school, every thoughtful citizen who despairs of war and wishes to bring peace, should begin by looking inward—by examining his own attitude to-ward the possibilities of peace, toward the Soviet Union, toward the course of the Cold War and toward freedom and peace here at home. . . .
>
> Let us re-examine our attitude toward the Soviet Union. It is dis-couraging to think that their leaders may actually believe what their propagandists write. . . . Yet it is sad to read these Soviet statements—to realize the extent of the gulf between us. But it is also a warning—a warning to the American people not to fall into the same trap as the Soviets, not to see only a distorted and desper-ate view of the other side, not to see conflict as inevitable, accom-

modation as impossible, and communication as nothing more than an exchange of threats.

No government or social system is so evil that its people must be considered as lacking in virtue. As Americans, we find communism profoundly repugnant as a negation of personal freedom and dignity. But we can still hail the Russian people for their many achievements—in science and space, in economic and industrial growth, in culture and in acts of courage.

Among the many traits the peoples of our countries have in common, none is stronger than our mutual abhorrence of war. Almost unique, among the major world powers, we have never been at war with each other. And no nation in the history of battle ever suffered more than the Soviet Union suffered in the course of the Second World War. At least twenty million lost their lives. Countless millions of homes and farms were burned or sacked. A third of the nation's territory, including nearly two-thirds of its industrial base, was turned into a wasteland—a loss equivalent to the devastation of this country east of Chicago.

Today, should total war ever break out again—no matter how—our two countries would become the primary targets. It is an ironic but accurate fact that the two strongest powers are the two in the most danger of devastation. All we have built, all we have worked for, would be destroyed in the first twenty-four hours. And even in the Cold War, which brings burdens and dangers to so many countries, including this Nation's closest allies—our two countries bear the heaviest burdens. For we are both devoting massive sums of money to weapons that could be better devoted to combating ignorance, poverty and disease. We are both caught up in a vicious and dangerous cycle in which suspicion on one side breeds suspicion on the other, and new weapons beget counterweapons.

In short, both the United States and its allies, and the Soviet Union and its allies, have a mutually deep interest in a just and genuine peace and in halting the arms race. Agreements to this end are in the interests of the Soviet Union as well as ours—and even the most hostile nations can be relied upon to accept and keep those treaty obligations, which are in their own interest.

So, let us not be blind to our differences—but let us also direct attention to our common interests and to the means by which those differences can be resolved. And if we cannot end now our differences, at least we can help make the world safe for diversity. For, in the final analysis, our most basic common link is that we all inhabit this small planet. We all breathe the same air. We all cherish our children's future. And we are all mortal.

. . . Let us examine our attitude toward the Cold War, remembering that we are not engaged in a debate, seeking to pile up debating points. We are not here distributing blame or pointing the finger of judgment. We must deal with the world as it is, and not as it might have been had the history of the last eighteen years been different.

We must, therefore, persevere in the search for peace in the hope that constructive change within the communist bloc might bring within reach solutions which now seem beyond us. We must conduct our affairs in such a way that it becomes in the communists' interest to agree on a genuine peace.[10]

President Kennedy capped his speech with two important announcements: first, that he, Prime Minister Macmillan, and Premier Khrushchev had agreed that high-level talks would soon begin in Moscow to seek early agreement on a treaty banning nuclear tests in all environments; second, to "make clear our good faith and solemn convictions on the matter," the United States would not conduct atmospheric tests as long as other states did not do so. "We will not be the first to resume. Such a declaration is not a substitute for a formal binding treaty, but I hope it will help us achieve one. Nor would such a treaty be a substitute for disarmament, but I hope it will help us to achieve it."

Khrushchev later told Averell Harriman that it was "the greatest speech by an American President since Roosevelt." [11] Perhaps that was because the Russians recognized more fully than most Americans—more fully, certainly, than Kennedy's aides—that the speech constituted an admission that the United States postwar policy, Kennedy's own policy, had been wrong. What the President had done was to ask the people of the United States to accept a new policy without conceding—and what politician could have made such a staggering admission—that the unrelenting, hard-line policy of Truman, Eisenhower, and Kennedy had been a major factor in the birth and growth of the Cold War. But it is not necessary for a President to beat his breast and murmur "Mea culpa." It is necessary only that he do the right thing. Although present-day critics of American foreign policy could certainly find things wrong with Kennedy's speech, it was, given the context of the times, given his and the nation's history, magnificent. It seemed for a glorious moment that Kennedy's ambivalence was finally ended, that the peacemaker had triumphed over the Cold Warrior. But was that so? Despite the evidence of that splendid statement of June 10, 1963, we cannot be sure. Death deprived him, and us, of the time necessary to find out, and even the evidence available questions the conviction that Kennedy had finally become the man that many have believed him always to have been.

On June 6, just four days before the American University speech, Kennedy appeared at the Marine Corps recruit depot in San Diego. His words were far different.

> . . . Since 1945 and the end of the Second World War, the whole cause of freedom has depended upon the United States. We have been the keystone of the arch—the 180 million Americans carrying on a worldwide struggle against the Sino–Soviet bloc, composed of more than a billion people, have been able to maintain the independence of this country and dozens who are allied with it.[12]

Even more dramatic were Kennedy's words in Berlin just a couple of weeks after American University. Speaking to a huge crowd in the Rudolf Wilde Platz, the President declared:

> Two thousand years ago the proudest boast was *"civis Romanus sum."* Today, in the world of freedom, the proudest boast is *"Ich bin ein Berliner."*
> . . . There are many people in the world who really don't understand, or say they don't, what is the great issue between the free world and the communist world. Let them come to Berlin. There are some who say that communism is the wave of the future. Let them come to Berlin. And there are some who say in Europe and elsewhere we can work with the communists. Let them come to Berlin. . . .[13]

It is possible that in speaking words in direct contradiction to those of the American University speech, Kennedy was merely responsive to his audiences, Marines and West Berliners, that his true thoughts were spoken at American University. But since the June 10 speech was the deviation from a pattern long since established, might not the reverse be true? And there was the steadily increasing involvement in Vietnam. Yet the American University speech made such sense and in its simple eloquence seemed so much deeper than just another finely tooled product of Ted Sorensen's skill that one feels that the speech was genuine, that it represented a great and welcome change in Kennedy's thinking about Soviet–American relations. That seemed to be Khrushchev's judgment, for he responded eagerly. On July 2 he offered a partial-test-ban treaty—banning tests in the atmosphere, in outer space, and under water—saying that, if the West accepted, "the question of inspection no longer arises." [14] And he said he did not insist at this time on a moratorium on unpoliced underground tests. Khrushchev was prepared to go even further; he wanted a nonaggression pact between NATO and the Warsaw Pact. He said that a nuclear test ban "combined with the simultaneous signing of a non-aggression pact" would mean a "fresh international climate." It has always been debatable which comes first, the chicken of international tension or the egg of an arms buildup. As Khrushchev recognized, the only way out of that tangle is to tackle both at once or, at least, in close sequence.

Although there is no reason to doubt the sincerity of Khrushchev's eagerness to establish better relations with the United States, he was obviously, then and always, also concerned about China. While good relations with the United States were invaluable in themselves, they would also mean that his rear was secure during the conflict with China that was certain to endure. In fact, even as Britain and the United States on one hand and Russia on the other were preparing for the talks that would soon lead to the test-ban treaty, the Soviet Union and China were engaged in talks. They were held in Moscow in deep secrecy and ended without a communiqué. On July 14, the day before Averell Harriman and Lord Hailsham arrived in Moscow, the Central Committee of the Soviet Communist Party issued a long, emotional statement. Asserting that Mao Tse-tung was prepared to sacrifice millions of lives in a nuclear war, the Russians declared that they could not "share the views of the Chinese leadership about creating 'a thousand times higher civilization' on the corpses of hundreds of millions of people." The Russians seemed to take all the Chinese statements seriously, forgetting, as they should know better than anyone, that hyperbole has always been a supreme communist art form.

Harriman took the lead for the West in the test-ban negotiations and kept in constant touch with Washington. Kennedy was intensely interested in the talks and discussed them every day with his top advisers. He instructed Harriman to separate the two questions proposed by Khrushchev earlier in the month: the test ban and the NATO–Warsaw Pact nonaggression treaty. Kennedy was not very interested in the nonaggression pact; he did not see that it offered much advantage to the United States, and Dean Rusk and the Joint Chiefs of Staff feared that any such pact would mean the death of NATO, their most cherished toy. Their reasoning was beautifully circular. NATO was necessary for the defense of the West. If there were a nonaggression pact genuinely observed by both sides, there would be no need for NATO, but if there were no NATO, the West would be endangered. The instrument had become more precious than the purpose it was designed to serve. There were, however, legitimate reasons for trying to separate the two questions. A nonaggression pact could not be reached without the complicating, time-consuming participation of all the NATO members. This could delay a nuclear treaty for months or longer. Also such a pact might complicate the Senate ratification of the test-ban treaty, and, as we shall see, this too was a difficult matter. But, given the attitude of Kennedy and his administration, they may have wanted the separation for other reasons as well, and there is no reason to be confident that, had Kennedy lived, he would have welcomed substantial talks on a nonaggression pact.

In any case, Khrushchev agreed to this separation, and the talks went swiftly; a treaty was initialed by Harriman, Hailsham, and Andrei Gromyko on July 25, 1963. It ducked the question of on-site inspections by excluding from the treaty underground tests. All others could be detected and identified without such inspections. The treaty has been hailed as Kennedy's greatest achievement, one that fittingly capped his "triumph" in the Cuban missile crisis. Yet the treaty depended fully as much on Nikita Khrushchev, who sacrificed much for it. It meant he had accepted, for the foreseeable future, permanent Soviet inferiority in nuclear weaponry, for without atmospheric tests it would be difficult for the Russians to catch up. This was no inconsiderable sacrifice, and one wonders if any American President, had the circumstances been reversed, would have made such a sacrifice.

More important, time has eroded the conviction, genuinely held in 1963, that the partial-nuclear-test-ban treaty was a major step toward ending the arms race. In his radio-television address on the initialing of the treaty, President Kennedy declared that "now, for the first time in many years, the path of peace may be open. No one can be certain what the future will bring. No one can say whether the time has come for an easing of the struggle. But history and our own conscience will judge us harsher if we do not now make every effort to test our hopes by action, and this is the place to begin." [15] Khrushchev seemed to agree, for he promptly showered Washington with proposals: not only the nonaggression pact but a freezing or, "still better," cutting of defense budgets, measures to prevent surprise attacks, the reduction of foreign forces in both Germanys. One is tempted to conclude that during the Khrushchev years the road to Soviet–American détente had been waiting for an American President to set foot upon it.

Again, what might have happened if Kennedy had lived, if Khrushchev had remained in power, is a matter of speculation, but the internal American debate on the test-ban treaty is a matter of hard fact. It was not, as we look back on it now, an encouraging debate. The concessions made by Kennedy to the hard-liners, concessions that he thought necessary to ensure the treaty's ratification, seriously, perhaps fatally, undermine the conclusion that the treaty was Kennedy's greatest achievement.[16]

Although Kennedy in his speech to the nation presented the test-ban treaty as the first step on the path toward peace, he presented it to the Pentagon and to the Congress not as a step toward ending the arms race but as a lasting triumph in it, as an acknowledgment of American nuclear superiority and as a way to maintain it. Not only did the exclusion of underground testing avoid the problem of onsite inspection but it permitted a form of testing in which the United States was more skilled and could better afford. Since Kennedy genuinely seemed to fear that it would be difficult to get the two-thirds majority necessary for Senate ratification, he stressed just those aspects of the test ban that weakened its effect. And since he feared public opposition by the top military might torpedo the treaty, he made a series of concessions to the Joint Chiefs of Staff perhaps more significant than the treaty itself.[17] Even so, a number of admirals and generals opposed it either in Senate hearings or in public.

As Secretary McNamara told the Senate, "By limiting Soviet testing to the underground environment, where testing is more dif-

ficult and more expensive and where the United States has substantially more experience, we can at least retard Soviet progress
and thereby prolong the duration of our technological superiority." [18] When it came his turn to testify, General Maxwell
Taylor, since August 1962 Chairman of the Joint Chiefs, told the
Senate that "the most serious reservations" of the Chiefs were
based on "the fear of a euphoria in the West which will eventually
reduce our vigilance." They feared, in short, that peace would
cause us to lose our enthusiasm for preparing for war. Thus, they
attached "safeguards" to their support, and Kennedy gave "unqualified and unequivocal assurances" that their conditions would
be met.[19] This is the Kennedy—and the McNamara—who established firm civilian control over the military. These conditions, as
read by General Taylor, are so significant that they must be
quoted verbatim.

> (a) The conduct of comprehensive, aggressive, and continuous
> underground nuclear test programs designed to add to our knowl-
> edge and improve our weapons in all areas of significance to our
> military posture for the future.
> (b) The maintenance of modern nuclear laboratory facilities and
> programs in theoretical and exploratory nuclear technology, which
> will attract, retain, and insure the continued application of our
> human scientific resources to these programs on which continued
> progress in nuclear technology depends.
> (c) The maintenance of the facilities and resources necessary to
> institute promptly nuclear tests in the atmosphere should they be
> deemed essential to our national security or should the treaty or any
> of its terms be abrogated by the Soviet Union.
> (d) The improvement of our capability, within feasible and prac-
> tical limits, to monitor the terms of the treaty, to detect violations,
> and to maintain our knowledge of Sino–Soviet activity, capability
> and achievements.[20]

This is an extraordinary document. It is no wonder that Senator
George McGovern declared:

> Indeed, Mr. President, the administration has been called upon to
> give so many assurances of our continued nuclear efforts after
> treaty ratification that a casual observer might assume that we are

approving this treaty so that we can accelerate the arms race and beef up the war-making facilities of our country.[21]

More than a casual observer could reach that conclusion. Not only did these "safeguards" call for an aggressive program of underground testing, but they provided—in section (c)—that the United States could conduct atmospheric tests, "should they be deemed essential," even if the Soviet Union had not abrogated the treaty. Further, these safeguards not only undercut the purposes of the treaty but, in the words of General Earle Wheeler, Army Chief of Staff, would "in my opinion . . . cost sums of money over and above the sizable military budget that the chairman pointed out this morning." And Curtis LeMay, Air Force Chief of Staff, chimed in, "I would agree that the military budget will probably go up as a result of the treaty, not down." [22] Such was the logic of the Cold War: more is less, less is more.

As I. F. Stone discovered, there were more than twice as many American tests in the seven years after the treaty as there were in the eighteen years before it, and there is good reason to believe that the United States has conducted more tests than it has announced. On the other hand, according to figures of the Atomic Energy Commission, the Soviet Union conducted many fewer tests than the United States in the period between August 5, 1963, when the test-ban treaty took effect, and April 1970.[23] The conclusion is inescapable: as far as the United States is concerned, the treaty caused an increase in testing, not the decrease that the world expected and Kennedy led it to expect. And Kennedy, in succumbing to military pressures, was largely responsible. This alone would be sufficient to question whether the Moscow Treaty was the great achievement Kennedy's admirers have termed it. But there is even more to question.

Since it was the fear of atmospheric tests that provided most of the impetus to the vigorous ban-the-bomb movements all over the world, the end to atmospheric tests all but eliminated public pressure to stop nuclear tests. Thus the United States and the Soviet Union have felt free to conduct as many underground tests as they chose. (Both France and China refused to sign the Moscow Treaty, and each has conducted a few atmospheric tests.) These underground tests have enabled the nuclear-arms race to continue as dangerously as ever, with the consequent disputes over the ABM, MIRV, etc. Whatever Kennedy felt he had accomplished with the partial-test-ban treaty, he most assuredly did not put "the genie back in the bottle."

Only a comprehensive treaty could have done that, and Kennedy would not take the risk. Khrushchev had offered three onsite inspections. Jerome Wiesner and a group of scientists were convinced that five, not the minimum of seven offered by Kennedy, were sufficient. Further, the science of detecting and identifying underground explosions was steadily improving. Yet Kennedy, as we saw at the Bay of Pigs, Berlin, and the Cuban missile crisis, was prepared to take far greater risks toward war than he was toward peace. It is possible, of course, that if he had accepted Khrushchev's proposal of three inspections, the Russians would have found a way to back out of it. Khrushchev too had his military hard-liners. But there is no reason to believe that Khrushchev's offer was not genuine because, if for no other reason, underground testing benefited the United States more than the Soviet Union. If Kennedy had taken that risk—certainly a slight one and certainly less dangerous than what has resulted from his not taking the risk —and if a comprehensive treaty had resulted, then he would have merited the gratitude of all mankind for all time to come, as would have Khrushchev.

Even if Kennedy had feared the opposition of the hard-liners in the military, in the Congress, and in public life generally, his gifts as a public persuader were so extraordinary that he almost certainly could have been able to rally overwhelming public support for a comprehensive treaty. The partial treaty, on September 24, passed the Senate by 80 to 19. There is no reason to believe that a comprehensive treaty would not have passed, even if the margin had been somewhat less handsome. In any case, it was worth the risk, for the partial treaty, whatever hopes Kennedy had for it, was like a medicine that does not cure the disease but merely suppresses the symptoms for a while. With all the harm that has come from underground testing, it might have been better to have had no treaty at all for a while longer in the hope that continued public pressure would have resulted in a comprehensive treaty.

But it is difficult to make a final judgment on the Moscow

Treaty. After all, it did end the poisonous atmospheric testing and it did contribute to the short-lived spirit of détente. If Kennedy had lived, if Khrushchev had remained in power to push his wide-ranging proposals, things might have been different. There are too many ifs. One thing is certain, however. The Moscow Treaty did not achieve what the world expected of it, and Kennedy's refusal to confront his own hard-liners, his reluctance to spend his political capital a year before running for re-election are major reasons. And Khrushchev, although he demonstrated considerable sensitivity to Kennedy's political problems, could perhaps have stretched a bit further and offered another one or two onsite inspections, with the expectation that improving technology would soon convince the Americans that no onsite inspections were necessary. But Kennedy and Khrushchev cannot be blamed for the fact that absolutely no serious effort has been made in recent years to extend the test ban to underground blasts. That responsibility rests with Johnson and Nixon, Brezhnev and Kosygin, both sides demonstrating the poverty of their dedication to ending the arms race.

After the Moscow Treaty, in the final months of Kennedy's life, even while things were getting worse in Vietnam, they were getting better with the Soviet Union. During the summer the "hot line," an emergency communications link, was installed, connecting the White House and the Kremlin. In a swing through the West in September, the President, to an enthusiastic reception, made peace the theme of his speeches. And at the United Nations on September 20 he declared, "If this pause in the Cold War merely leads to its renewal and not its end—then the indictment of posterity will rightly point its finger at us all. But if we can stretch this pause into a period of cooperation—if both sides can now gain new confidence and experience in concrete collaboration for peace—if we can now be as bold and as farsighted in the control of deadly weapons as we have been in their creation—then surely this first small step can be the start of a long and fruitful journey." [24]

On the very day that the Senate ratified the test-ban treaty, the White House began considering the sale of surplus grain to the Soviet Union, and in October it decided to go ahead, with only limited public outcry. Also the United Nations General Assembly, with United States and Soviet support, passed a resolution calling on all states to refrain from "placing in orbit around the earth any objects carrying nuclear weapons or any other kinds of weapons of mass destruction" and from "installing such weapons on celestial bodies." [25] And that fall a Gallup Poll reported that the American people for the first time regarded the Democrats as the peace party, an ironic conclusion at a moment when the United States was slipping deeper and deeper into the Vietnam war, one that would last as long as all United States foreign wars combined.

There was a feeling of détente in the air, and the American people were beginning to respond to it. Yet Kennedy was slow to lose his ambivalence. In one of his last analyses of Soviet–American relations, speaking at the University of Maine on October 19, he said, "Let us distinguish between our hopes and our illusions, always hoping for steady progress toward less critically dangerous relations with the Soviets, but never laboring under any illusions about communist methods or communist goals." [26]

If that was the ambivalent Kennedy, on November 18, just four days before his death, spoke the Cold Warrior.

. . . I think Americans can take satisfaction in realizing that without the United States, without the effort of the 190 million people of this country, our effort not only today but ever since 1945, not only in this administration but in the two previous administrations, it is the United States, and on many occasions the United States alone, which has prevented this globe from being dominated by our enemies. If it was not for the assistance which we have rendered to millions of people, if it were not for the alliances which we have made in SEATO, our association with CENTO, our alliances in NATO, our alliances in the inter-American system, long ago this globe of ours would have seen the communist advance sweep over much of what is now free. And it is free because the people of this country who lived so long in isolation have chosen to bear their share of the burden, and I believe we must continue to do so. . . .[27]

Which Kennedy would have prevailed? That one, who sounded just like the Kennedy of the first, hawkish days of the administration, or the one who on June 10 called on the American people to "re-examine our attitude toward the Cold War"? The Cold Warrior Kennedy had been more characteristic throughout his public life, but maybe he was now at a point of transition where he swung back and forth between his new attitude and his old. We can never know which would have prevailed. One hopes it would have been the new, but the weight of evidence, of inertia, of character, was on the side of the old. John Kennedy the conciliator might have prevailed over John Kennedy the Cold Warrior, but it is glib to assert without doubt that this would have been so. And even if it had been so, there was still John Kennedy the counter-revolutionary.

. . . In the final analysis, it is their war. They are the ones who have to win it or lose it. We can help them, we can give them equipment, we can send our men out there as advisers, but they have to win it, the people of Vietnam, against the communists. . . . All we can do is help, and we are making it very clear, but I don't agree with those who say we should withdraw. That would be a mistake. . . .[1]

—JOHN F. KENNEDY

CHAPTER NINE

Vietnam

Although the Cuban missile crisis was the most dangerous moment of the Kennedy administration, it is now but a dramatic episode in the history of the nation and in the personal histories of those who lived through those anxious thirteen days. Vietnam is Kennedy's most lasting legacy, and the sad irony is that Kennedy was one of the first American political figures to perceive in the early 1950s the difficulty of United States intervention. As early as 1951 young Congressman John Kennedy journeyed to Asia and, on his return, warned that "in Indochina we have allied ourselves with a colonial regime that had no real support from the people." [2] And in April 1954, when President Eisenhower was moving toward his decision not to try a last-ditch rescue of the French at Dienbienphu, Senator Kennedy took the floor to warn of the dangers of intervention. He spoke words that must have come back to haunt him:

To pour money, matériel, and men into the jungles of Indochina without at least a remote prospect of victory would be dangerously futile and self-destructive. Of course, all discussion of "united action" assumes the inevitability of such victory; but such assumptions are not unlike similar predictions of confidence which have lulled the American people for many years and which, if continued, would present an improper basis for determining the extent of American participation.

Yet even while Kennedy recognized the difficulties, the anti-communist triumphed over the realist, or perhaps it would be more accurate to say that the anti-communist confused the realist!

> To check the southern drive of communism makes sense but not only through reliance on the force of arms. The task is rather to build strong native non-communist sentiment within these areas and rely on that as a spearhead of defense rather than upon the legions of General de Tassigny. To do this apart from and in defiance of innately nationalistic aims spells foredoomed failure.[3]

This was Kennedy's crucial misconception. He recognized the irresistible force of nationalism, yet he believed it could be exploited from outside to defeat communism. He believed that the United States could manipulate the strong emotions of a downtrodden people so as to enlist them in America's crusade, not theirs. Much misery has resulted from the inability of John Kennedy, and other American leaders before him and since, to recognize that communism is not a monolithic, indivisible force. Communism and nationalism can be synonymous, as they have been with Ho Chi Minh or Tito or, later, Castro or, most important, Mao Tse-tung, but whatever their rhetoric, whatever their devotion to the principles of Marxism–Leninism, these communist leaders always put their countries first. In one place, and one place only, are communism and nationalism synonymous with the Soviet Union, and that is in the Soviet Union. And only in those countries within the grasp of the Red Army has there been any need to pretend otherwise.

Between 1951, when he was a young congressman, and 1961, when he was President, still young but presumably sophisticated and pragmatic, Kennedy did not learn that essential lesson. This is not so surprising when one considers that it was learned by very few people indeed. Americans seemed unable to recognize that a people, in the exercise of their national fervor, might want a communist to lead them. With that profound, matter-of-fact arrogance that America knows best, Eisenhower and Dulles chose Ngo Dinh Diem to lead South Vietnam, and Kennedy later decided, until he changed his mind toward the end, to keep him in power. It was

Americans, not Vietnamese, who chose Diem. And it was Americans, not Vietnamese, who were surprised when Diem acted like an autocratic despot. There was no other way he could act, for that is what he was, a mandarin, whereas Ho Chi Minh was a national hero, not because he had used guile and force to win his position—as no doubt he did—but because he had come to represent national Vietnamese aspirations. A successful revolution, his followers know, is its own justification. Outside intervention could mean only chaos or the artificial and temporary stability of repression. The terrible irony—as so many have pointed out—is that the nationalism of Vietnam was the best barrier to any possible Chinese expansion because it was natural, whereas intervention weakened that barrier.

Although the people of Vietnam had their own urgent necessities, Kennedy, like Eisenhower and Truman before him, believed that Vietnam was an arena for the Cold War. People in Indochina would continue to suffer, be made homeless, and die not in pursuit of their own goals but because an elite safe in Washington was to will it so. Kennedy's defenders have argued that he inherited the situation in Vietnam and, as with the Bay of Pigs, had no real choice but to continue where Eisenhower left off. But Eisenhower's "commitment" to Diem had been sketchy, and what is the point of having elections if one President must necessarily follow the course of the previous one? The reasons for Kennedy's policy in Vietnam are simple: he was an anti-communist American leader who had little comprehension of the revolutionary world caused by the breakup of the great European empires.

The Vienna meeting between Kennedy and Khrushchev is thought of as the birthplace of the Berlin crisis, but the Berlin crisis, like the missile crisis, was a transient affair, however dangerous. Vienna is more important for the light it throws on the Vietnam war. Assuming that published accounts of the Vienna meeting are substantially correct, as there is every reason to believe they are, Kennedy demonstrated a deep and dangerous misunderstanding of the postwar world. He confused revolution, in countries where revolution was inevitable and desirable, with communist conspiracy. Kennedy's basic thesis was that while change was inevitable in the world, East and West must be careful to avoid confrontations that could lead to nuclear war. Khrushchev agreed that confrontations should be avoided but wondered how that was possible if the United States saw revolution everywhere as the result of a Soviet conspiracy. He said that it was the United States that was responsible for revolutions by supporting reactionary governments; it was the United States that was turning Castro into a communist by its economic sanctions against Cuba. Again and again Kennedy argued that the world balance of power must not be changed, that the addition of new countries to communist ranks would upset the equilibrium that preserved peace. Khrushchev disagreed. He said that the addition of such states would be only a drop in the bucket, but that such revolutions were the expression of popular will and that any attempt to stop them from outside could trigger a chain reaction that might lead to war.

Khrushchev warned that the worst thing that the United States could do was get involved in guerrilla wars. Such action was hopeless. It was better to let history take its course. Khrushchev said it was impossible for the Soviet Union to implant its ideas in the new nations, that changes would be brought about by the will of the people. The Soviet Union could not be held responsible for indigenous revolutions, nor could it be held responsible for the adoption in these circumstances of communist ideas. There was no way to immunize against ideas; they could travel anywhere. Khrushchev asked if Kennedy meant that communism could exist only in those countries already communist and that if communism developed elsewhere the United States and the Soviet Union would be in conflict. If that was so, there was no way to avoid conflict.

The conclusion is simple. Even if Khrushchev was sanctimonious in his devotion to the principle of revolution—the Soviet Union had hardly welcomed it, or even evolution in the mildest forms, within its East European empire—his analysis was essentially correct: in the postwar years revolutions have been largely indigenous in character. Kennedy, on the other hand, was preaching the merits of the status quo, however much he may have denied it. He said he recognized the need for change but in fact, like Truman and Eisenhower, he recognized the validity of only the kind of change acceptable to the United States. Real change, messy, chaotic change, change almost inevitably involving communism or communists, was not acceptable. Kennedy, the first President born in this century, the modern President, was a counterrevolutionary. For it is only as counterrevolutionary that his policies in Cuba and Vietnam, and even in insignificant British Guiana, make sense. The great buildup in conventional war-making capacity, his passion for the Green Berets, the "counterinsurgency" programs—all these make sense only as preparation for counterrevolution. Perhaps he did not even know it himself; perhaps he genuinely believed in change and simply did not understand that the gradual, slow evolution he wanted was no longer possible in modern circumstances. Nor did Kennedy understand that the Soviet–American rivalry was essentially a distinct phenomenon. He shared the belief with Truman and Eisenhower that *any* communist government was a threat to American security, when in fact it was often the attempt to prevent such a government that damaged the United States. Truman's "success" in Greece eventually led to the tortures of a right-wing militaristic junta. Kennedy's vain attempt to crush Castro led to the brink of nuclear war, and his effort to enlist South Vietnam in the anti-communist cause set off a train of tragic consequences that has yet to run its course. The cool, prudent Kennedy, who so often warned Khrushchev of the dangers of miscalculation, was himself guilty of two enormous miscalculations, miscalculations that were entirely representative of the American ethos at the time: the conviction that the United States had the right to change the natural course of events within other sovereign countries; and the belief that it had the power to do so.

When Kennedy was a candidate for presidential office, Vietnam was not a preoccupation with him. In the index to the collection of his campaign speeches from August 1 to Election Day, Vietnam is listed only twice and all Indochina only nine times. It was Cuba, soon joined by Laos, that was his major concern during his first months in office. But soon he had to consider the deteriorating situation in Vietnam. There were two prescriptions offered by his advisers: one predominantly military, the other predominantly political. These led to internal conflict, "and the struggle within the administration became increasingly bitter," McGeorge Bundy calling Vietnam "the most divisive issue in the Kennedy administration." [4] But the dispute was one of tactics; one searches in vain throughout the wide literature available to find any substantial debate as to whether the United States had any business being in Vietnam in the first place. This is the way it was put by Roger Hilsman: "If Vietnam does represent a failure in the Kennedy administration, it was a failure in implementation." Kennedy and the Kennedy men may have thought they were pragmatists but they were just as dogmatic as John Foster Dulles and, because more adventurous, more dangerous.

It is not surprising that those advocating military methods won the debate. Dean Rusk, who as Secretary of State should have been the leading proponent of a political solution, himself tended to think of Vietnam as a military problem. And the State Department as an institution was widely outmatched by the Defense Department. The stronger Defense grew under Kennedy and McNamara, the greater was its influence. The inevitable tendency for a stronger military to play a stronger role was reinforced by the unequaled personal influence within the administration of McNamara. The Pentagon could provide the pseudo-precision—with charts and maps and lists of such tangibles as aircraft carriers, howitzers, helicopters, etc.—that appealed to the President, whereas State could only talk subjectively of personalities and parties and possibilities, notably imprecise stuff. One can formulate an iron rule for American—perhaps for any nation's—foreign policy: the more available military methods are, the more likely they are to be used. Peace through Strength becomes Intervention through Capability.

In those first months the Kennedy administration groped for a strategic concept. One, which at least had the virtue of consistency, was Walt W. Rostow's suggestion that "the ultimate source of aggression" should be attacked. Members of the Kennedy and Johnson administrations consistently spoke of "aggression from the North" (Dean Rusk in particular) and resolutely refused to face the elementary fact that the war in Vietnam was a civil war. Dean Rusk, insisted upon comparing the Vietnam situation to Munich, a wholly false analogy. A better one might have been the Spanish Civil War. In that war, although the United States avoided even entirely proper assistance to the Loyalist government, at least it did not actively intervene on the totalitarian side. An administration full of historians and political scientists ignored the lessons of both fields. But it was no doubt useful, in attempting to play one more time on the nation's anti-communist impulse, to talk of "aggression."

Another "strategic concept" for Vietnam also featured police and military measures. "But the approach was essentially political. What was needed to meet the guerrilla threat successfully, we felt, were reformers to organize mass parties and social and political programs that could become the basis for modernization." [5] This plan overlooked the fact that this ground had already been staked out by Ho Chi Minh and the communists. An arrogant, dictatorial mandarin such as Ngo Dinh Diem, a militant Catholic in a Buddhist land, was hardly likely to be a passionate reformer. And it should be noted that Kennedy's "liberal" administration wanted reforms not primarily for their benefits to the Vietnamese people but because they would strengthen the Diem regime's capacity to fight the war. Even a cursory reading of the Kennedy literature makes that conclusion inescapable.

Shortly after he took office, Kennedy was shocked by a report on Vietnam prepared not long before by General Edward Lansdale, a shadowy but legendary officer with the CIA who had been Magsaysay's adviser in the successful campaign to tame the Hukbalahap rebels in the Philippines. Lansdale reported that despite seven years of United States economic, logistic, and political assistance, the Viet Cong was rapidly gaining strength and controlling increasing areas of the countryside. Kennedy decided that something had to be done. He quickly relieved Ambassador Elbridge Dubrow, who had carried so many complaints to Diem from the Eisenhower administration that he was no longer welcome at the Presidential Palace, and replaced him with Frederick Nolting, a nice comfortable foreign-service officer whose assignment was to win Diem's confidence and persuade him to undertake the reforms that would justify continued American support. He was to succeed fully in the first assignment and to fail completely in the second.

Meanwhile, Kennedy agreed to increase the number of American military advisers in Vietnam—about 600 when he took office —and to step up economic and military aid programs. His own task force recommended combat troops, but he settled on the increase of advisers. These, however, now served on the battalion as well as the regimental level and could advise on combat, on both the conventional and unconventional levels, as well as on training. On April 29, 1961, just days after the Bay of Pigs fiasco and while the crisis in Laos was at a crucial stage, he approved the recommendation for a 100-man increase in American advisers and some additional logistical support. The Pentagon Papers said, "The only substantial significance that can be read into these April 29 decisions is that they signaled a willingness to go beyond the 685-man limit of the United States military mission in Saigon." [6] That is something of an understatement, because this was the first step in an escalation that was to continue throughout the Kennedy years. And as the papers pointed out, publicity would have entailed "the first formal breach of the Geneva agreements," so the move was kept quiet. This, too, established a pattern followed by Kennedy and his successors. The public was either not informed or actually deceived.

In May Kennedy sent Vice President Lyndon Johnson to Saigon, partly to get an independent report, partly to assure Diem of his support, and partly to put pressure on Diem to carry out the reforms that always died somewhere between the agreement and the execution. Even while Johnson was still on his trip, in fact only a couple of days after he left, Kennedy decided to accept a further recommendation that 400 Special Forces troops (later known better as Green Berets) be sent to Vietnam to carry on covert warfare. As recorded in National Security Action Memorandum 52, Kennedy also instructed that the following steps be carried out:

1. "Dispatch . . . agents to North Vietnam" for intelligence-gathering.

2. "Infiltrate teams under light civilian cover to southeast Laos to locate and attack Vietnamese communist bases and lines of communications."

3. "In North Vietnam, using the foundation established by intelligence operations, form networks of resistance, covert bases and teams for sabotage and light harassment."

4. "Conduct overflights for dropping of leaflets to harass the communists and to maintain morale of North Vietnamese population, and increase gray [unidentified-source] broadcasts to North Vietnam for the same purposes."

5. Train "the South Vietnamese Army to conduct ranger raids

and similar military actions in North Vietnam as might prove necessary or appropriate." [6]

The Pentagon Papers also show that Kennedy approved "the use in North Vietnam operations of civilian air crews of American and other nationality, as appropriate, in addition to, Vietnamese." The memorandum also instructed Ambassador Nolting to negotiate a "new bilateral arrangement [treaty] with Vietnam." Such a treaty and the secret incursions into Laos and North Vietnam were both violations of the 1954 Geneva agreements. By July, Hanoi began to protest these incursions to Britain and Russia, co-chairman of the Geneva conference.

Most important, Kennedy instructed Johnson to "encourage" Diem to request American ground troops. Diem's initial response to the secret urging was to decline. He said that he did not want United States troops except in the case of direct aggression by North Vietnam, pointing out that such troops would violate the 1954 Geneva accords. Later, Diem wrote to Kennedy that he wanted increased material support, that the dispatch of United States troops would lend support to the communist charge that he was a front for American imperialists. However, with the military situation continuing to deteriorate, Diem in October did ask for United States troops. [7]

Exercising his Texan's talent for hyperbole, Johnson proclaimed Diem as "the Winston Churchill of Southeast Asia." On his return to Washington, Johnson told the President that time was running out and a basic decision had to be made. "We must decide whether to help these countries to the best of our ability or throw in the towel in the area and pull back our defenses to San Francisco and a 'Fortress America' concept. More important, we would say to the world in this case that we don't live up to our treaties and don't stand by our friends. This is not my concept. I recommend that we move forward promptly with a major effort to help these countries defend themselves." [8] This not only foreshadowed Johnson's own actions as President but increased the pressure on Kennedy to step up United States intervention.

But that May, Kennedy got advice based on much longer experience in Vietnam, advice that, had it been taken, would have prevented an indelible stain on Kennedy's record. Infinitely more important, it probably would have spared the people of Indochina incalculable death, destruction, and pain and spared America not only the lives of 50,000 men but the turmoil and divisiveness caused by the Vietnam war. On May 31, 1961, Kennedy, en route to his Vienna talks with Khrushchev, stopped in Paris for a couple of days to see Charles de Gaulle. The old French President urged his young American counterpart to learn from France's misfortune and not become entangled in Vietnam.

> For you, intervention in this region will be an entanglement without end. From the moment that nations have awakened, no foreign authority, whatever its means, has any chance of imposing itself on them. You are going to see this. For, although you find officials who, by interest, agree to obey you, the people will not consent and moreover are not calling for you.
>
> The ideology that you invoke will not change anything. Even more, the masses will confuse it with your will to exert power. That is why the more you commit yourself there against communism, the more communists will appear to be champions of national independence, the more they will receive help and, first of all, that which comes from desperation.
>
> We French have experienced this. You Americans wanted, yesterday, to take our place in Indochina. You want to assume a succession to rekindle a war that we ended. I predict to you that you will, step by step, be sucked into a bottomless military and political quagmire despite the losses and expenditures that you may squander.
>
> What you, we and others should do in this unfortunate Asia is not to substitute ourselves for states on their own soil but to give them what they need to get out of poverty and humiliation, which are, there as elsewhere, the causes of totalitarian regimes. I say this to you in the name of our West.[9]

In his memoirs, De Gaulle added these sad, prophetic words: "Kennedy is listening to me, but events will show that I did not convince him." Khrushchev, a couple of days later, said these same things, but Kennedy, to his terrible loss and ours, paid heed to neither adversary nor ally.

While it was the Johnson trip to Saigon that got the headlines, a more important visit was made by Professor Eugene Staley of the Stanford Research Institute. Working closely with Ngo Dinh Nhu, Diem's brother, closest adviser, and head of the secret-police apparatus, Staley developed the idea of "strategic hamlets." It was a welcome idea in Washington, where Kennedy's enthusiasm for "counterinsurgency" was spreading. The President was an avid reader of Mao Tse-tung and Ernesto "Che" Guevara, and the strategic hamlets seemed to be the way to deprive the Viet Cong guerrillas of the people. Mao, as everyone must now know, had written that "guerrillas must move among the people as fish swim in the sea." According to the Nhu–Staley plan, the peasants would work in the fields by day, and by night, when the Viet Cong normally exerted its control, the peasants would move into the safety of the strategic hamlets. This would deprive, so it was thought, the Viet Cong of essential food, supplies, and shelter. It was an ingenious plan.

> By touching the villages Nhu and his friends touched at the very foundations of Vietnamese peasant culture, where the local group, bound in its bamboo collar, had remained the basic unit, the raw material of public life, and even the basis of private life. The village, even more than the individual, was an entity. It was the village that had to pay taxes, and the village that negotiated with the central power. Everything derived from that entity, and all came down to it. It was the expression of that "harmony beneath the heavens" that any society imbued with Confucianism considered essential.
> By attacking this unity, Nhu was, strictly speaking, more revolutionary than the Viet Minh, who had never dared touch that cell as its base. But though his "revolution" overturned a society, it brought no solution to the problems facing that society. It was an end in itself, and claimed to play a strategic role only in connection with a purely circumstantial task: the struggle against the guerrillas, who the little people of the Vietnamese countryside saw as dangerous brothers rather than as enemies.[10]

Although the strategic-hamlet program had some success at first, it eventually suffered the fate of all the other ingenious schemes devised in Washington and Saigon that promised an early and successful end to the war. In every case—the concentrated use of helicopters, the bombing of the North, the invasions of Cambodia and Laos—the Viet Cong has learned how to cope. Either that or the plans turned out to have inherent faults, in theory or execution, so that in the long run none of these "miracles" worked.

The strategic hamlets were part of a wider Kennedy program

of counterinsurgency. Indeed, that term became a watchword in Washington during the Kennedy years. The President set up an interdepartmental counterinsurgency committee under one of his favorite advisers, General Maxwell Taylor, with his brother, the Attorney General, as his personal representative on the committee. Taylor was keen on the idea, not only on its own supposed merits but because it gave the Army an increased role. He, like many Army officers, had been upset because the Air Force and the Navy had pushed the Army aside in recent years. The Pentagon, reluctantly, the CIA, State, and the United States Information Agency were all involved. Special counterinsurgency schools were set up in Washington, and it was a mark of favor to be sent to one; bureaucrats scrambled frantically for such preferment.

At the Fort Bragg Special Forces School, at the war colleges, and elsewhere in the military, there was a serious study of guerrilla warfare in Greece, the Philippines, Malaya, etc. From it "came general agreement on the nature of guerrilla warfare and on the idea that meeting it successfully would require an emphasis on political, economic and social action into which very carefully calibrated military measures were interwoven." [11] The President took such an interest in the counterinsurgency forces that he flew down to Fort Bragg to inspect them and personally supervised the selection of new equipment—for instance, sneakers instead of heavy combat boots, with flexible steel inner soles after they proved vulnerable to bamboo spikes. Over the objections of the Pentagon, he ordered these Special Forces to wear the distinctive green berets by which they soon became known. He even kept one on his White House desk. "I like these berets. The Special Forces need something to make them distinctive. My father even wears one now." [12] The contemporary young President had chosen as his favorite new idea counterrevolution, the classic, and usually futile, reflex of defenders of the status quo.

Kennedy did not count on the Special Forces to win guerrilla wars abroad, "for he knew that guerrillas depend on the local countryside and must be combated primarily by local countrymen. . . . But the United States, believed Kennedy, could effectively supply training, arms and leadership for this new yet ancient kind of warfare." [13] Such an effort was doomed from the beginning. An effective guerrilla movement can be successfully countered only

174 / COLD WAR AND COUNTERREVOLUTION

by the adoption of programs that remove the grievances that caused the guerrillas to take the field in the first place. Kennedy and his top advisers were right in recognizing that widespread reform was necessary in South Vietnam but naïve in expecting that Diem, who had perpetuated the intolerable conditions, would carry out such reforms. Diem was only acting true to his nature in responding with repression to the people's—and the Americans' —demands for reform. This has been the melancholy history of American foreign policy in Asia and Latin America. Those leaders supported by the United States because they are the most anti-communist are almost always those whose programs, or lack of them, do the most to encourage leftist movements. The policy, whatever its short-term successes, is self-defeating in the long run. The United States almost invariably finds itself on the wrong side in the civil strife that comes sooner or later. What a joy it would be if some day the United States found itself on the right side— the people's side.

While the debate within the administration centered on how best to intervene, Kennedy got some more advice not to intervene at all. Again it came from a man of stature, General Douglas MacArthur, who was a luncheon guest at the White House. "You know what MacArthur said at lunch? He said that we shouldn't put one American soldier on the continent of Asia—we couldn't win a fight in Asia. I thought some of the Republicans were going to choke when he said that." [14] MacArthur, like General Matthew Ridgway, who had counseled against American intervention in 1954, would never forget the lesson of Korea. They were members of the Never Again club of military leaders, who swore that never again would the United States get sucked into land combat on the Asian mainland. But it took only eight years for others in the Pentagon to forget that bitter and expensive lesson.

Throughout 1961 the situation in Vietnam continued to deteriorate. Theodore H. White, the journalist close to many in the Kennedy administration, wrote to Washington in August: ". . . The guerrillas now control almost all the southern delta—so much so that I could find no American who would drive me outside Saigon in his car even by day without military convoy." He reported "political breakdown of formidable proportions" and then raised the essential point: ". . . what perplexes hell out of me is that the

Commies, on their side, seem to be able to find people willing to die for their cause." [15] If nothing else could persuade Kennedy to stay out of Vietnam, this should have. If there is any absolute test of the strength of a cause, it is whether or not men willingly sacrifice their lives for it. Men were willing to die for the cause personified by Ho Chi Minh; they were not willing to die for that personified by Ngo Dinh Diem. It was as simple as that. If Diem could not recruit effective support from among his own people, he did not deserve support from outside, nor would outside support, at any reasonable level, do any good.

In October Kennedy sent Maxwell Taylor and Walt Rostow to Saigon. They came back with a report that the situation was serious but not hopeless. They recommended increased economic assistance, a step-up in military advisers, the use of Americans for airlift and air reconnaissance operations, even the dispatch of as many as 10,000 combat troops. They noted Diem's shortcomings but specifically rejected the idea of his being replaced. John Kenneth Galbraith was also asked to stop in Saigon on his way back from Washington to his post as Ambassador to India. He wrote that there was not "the slightest practical chance" that the reforms being urged on Diem would be carried out and that any long-term success would depend on Diem's being replaced.

Nonetheless, Kennedy had faith in Taylor and Rostow—and in McNamara, who concurred with their views. So he followed their recommendations, except for sending the combat troops. His reason for not sending the combat troops was sadly prophetic.

> . . . They want a force of American troops. They say it's necessary to restore confidence and maintain morale. But it will be just like Berlin. The troops will march in; the bands will play; the crowds will cheer; and in four days everyone will have forgotten. Then we will be told we have to send in more troops. It's like taking a drink. The effect wears off, and you have to take another. [16]

So Ambassador Nolting and General Paul Harkins, the new military commander, embarked on a campaign of wooing Diem by professions of unwavering support, hoping to steer him gently into the necessary reforms. This, of course, was self-defeating, for the more they pledged American support, the less reason he saw for doing what they asked, since they were going to support him anyway. On those rare occasions when Kennedy or one of his traveling envoys exerted pressure, Diem responded—often with stories in the government-controlled press—that the United States had a nerve to interfere in South Vietnam's domestic affairs. Considering that only American interference kept Diem in power, such a response required no little nerve on his part.

It is worth noting that on that October mission General Taylor represented the Pentagon and Walt Rostow the White House. There was no one of remotely comparable stature from the State Department. Schlesinger, Sorensen, and Hilsman all bemoan in their books that then and thereafter the military outweighed the diplomatic, that unfortunately, as Sorensen put it, the President's "effort to keep our own military role in Vietnam from overshadowing our political objectives was handicapped by the State Department's inability to compete with the Pentagon." [17] But that was President Kennedy's fault; it was up to him to establish priorities and to ensure that one department did not prevail over another. If the Pentagon dominated State, it was only because Kennedy permitted it.

That autumn of 1961 is, for several reasons, crucial to any study of the Kennedy administration and the Vietnam war. On October 5 a special national intelligence estimate reported "that 80–90 per cent of the estimated 17,000 VC had been locally recruited, and that there was little evidence that the VC relied on external supplies." [18] Even if one were to accept the Kennedy administration's indefensible contention that the war was an international one between two different nations, the administration's own figures show that there was little help from the North, certainly nothing to compare in even the remotest degree with American aid to the South. Blaming Hanoi for the collapsing situation in South Vietnam was simply a smokescreen to hide the fact that Diem was being defeated by foes within his own half of the country, with little outside help. In order to justify further aid to Diem, it was necessary for the Kennedy administration to provoke the old American conditioned reflex to the menace of communism. If the American people came to realize that Diem's large, well-equipped army (paid for, supplied, and trained by the United States) was being defeated by a few thousand rebels, it might come to feel that Diem did not deserve help. But if Diem was the victim of "communist aggression"—well, that was different.

Yet even though Kennedy was willing to reawaken old fears, as he had done in his campaign and did with Laos and Cuba after taking office, he did not want the people to know precisely what he was doing. He certainly did not want them to realize that the United States was slipping deeper and deeper into the Indochinese quagmire. Thus, when the press began to ask whether Maxwell Taylor's trip to Saigon meant that Kennedy was considering sending combat troops to Vietnam, the administration deliberately— and successfully—set out to deceive the press and the public. Carefully managed news leaks caused the press to report that military leaders were reluctant to send troops to Vietnam and that this question was "near the bottom of the list" of things Taylor would consider during his trip. The fact was, according to the Pentagon Papers, that sending large numbers of combat troops was at the very top of the list of things he would consider. Indeed, the administration had been considering, and the military had recommended, sending substantial forces since the first weeks of the administration. As the Pentagon Papers said, the leaks were "simply untrue"; the administration was consciously deceiving the American people.[18]

On November 8 a memo from Defense Secretary McNamara said the Pentagon supported Taylor's recommendation that an 8000-man task force be sent to Vietnam. But the memo warned that the task force "probably will not tip the scales decisively," meaning that "we would be almost certain to get increasingly mired down in an inconclusive struggle." As the Pentagon Papers said, "In short, the President was being told that the issue was not whether to send an 8000-man task force, but whether or not to embark on a course that, without some extraordinary good luck, would lead to combat involvement in Southeast Asia on a very substantial scale."[18] Although, as we saw, Kennedy did not send the troops then, he did, however reluctantly, embark on a course that made inevitable their dispatch later.

Three days later, McNamara and Rusk joined in another memorandum that scaled down the immediate recommendations but scaled up the anti-communist rhetoric. In this memorandum, almost totally accepted by Kennedy, Rusk and McNamara wrote:

The loss of South Vietnam would make pointless any further discussion about the importance of Southeast Asia to the Free World;
we would have to face the near certainty that the remainder of
Southeast Asia and Indonesia would move to a complete accommodation with communism, if not formal incorporation within the
communist bloc.[18]

This is a good exposition of the "domino theory," to which
Kennedy subscribed. As must be said, perhaps to the point of tedium, Kennedy and his advisers saw communism almost exactly as
did John Foster Dulles: as a monolith with no respect for national
frontiers. It seemed not to occur to them that communism, in certain circumstances, might be desirable or perhaps inevitable, that
nationalism was a natural foe of monolithic communism, and that a
sophisticated American foreign policy could work with and
strengthen that nationalism.

But Kennedy did recognize that a war against communism in
South Vietnam could not succeed until the Diem regime carried
out extensive reforms. In a message to Ambassador Nolting the
administration demanded "concrete demonstration by Diem that
he is now prepared to work in an orderly way [with] his subordi-
nates and broaden the political base of his regime." Kennedy
wanted it to become an American war. "We would expect to share
in the decision-making process in the political, economic and military fields as they affect the security situation." [18]

Diem was disappointed that combat troops weren't forthcoming
but "took our proposals rather better than I expected." Perhaps
that was because he recognized that the sending of support troops
and increased numbers of advisers would almost inevitably lead to
combat troops. But he obviously did not like the idea of taking orders from the United States. Like any national leader, he wanted
to use foreigners, not be used by them. He soon went into one of
his famous sulks, which was promptly reported back to Washington. Kennedy then made a fatal mistake. If one accepts the view
that the United States was right to intervene in a civil war, such
intervention could be justified only if there were a reasonable
chance of success. Success depended, as Kennedy and all his top
advisers recognized, on substantial reforms. Yet Kennedy in December 1961 backed down on his demand for reforms; he was not
prepared to tell a stubborn Diem: Reform or else. And having

backed down then, Kennedy was not able later to convince Diem, at an even more critical moment, that he meant it when he insisted on essential reforms. Because of the supremacy of the Pentagon over the State Department, Kennedy already tended to see Vietnam as more of a military than a political problem. Since Diem was fairly cooperative on military matters and stubborn on political, the Kennedy administration concentrated on the symptom (the Vietcong rebellion) and not on the cause—Diem's repressive, corrupt rule. This was perhaps inevitable, given Kennedy's preoccupation with communism, but he was hardly alone. Truman and Eisenhower before him and Johnson and Nixon after him were the same. Their first concern was not the welfare of whatever people were involved, but in smashing communism or later, when that proved impossible, in saving face. The irony, of course, is that they would have been more effective had they been more concerned with the people and less with ideology. This virulent anti-communism has led not only to suffering in Greece and Guatemala and Cuba and the Dominican Republic and Vietnam but to many of the terrible problems that today confront Americans at home.

The infusion of American money and military advisers, and particularly of helicopters, did in 1962 seem to be making a critical difference. For some months, until the Viet Cong got used to them, the guerrillas were terrified by helicopters. It seemed for a while that the war was going well. Washington, then as now, preferred to believe the optimistic reports, not the pessimistic ones, and to believe that temporary successes were permanent. For the next two years there was a succession of optimistic reports from Washington that "we have turned the corner" or that "there is light at the end of the tunnel" or "the tide has turned" or—one of the many such statements that McNamara must recall when he awakens in the middle of the night—"every quantitative measurement we have shows we're winning the war."

In his 1963 State of the Union message, Kennedy said on January 14 that the "spearpoint of aggression has been blunted in Vietnam." But the President preferred not to talk about Vietnam any more than he had to. He hardly wanted to tell the American people that the Diem regime almost entirely rejected the reforms that could have justified it as a government, that the United States was supporting a corrupt, repressive, incompetent regime. As with the succeeding Johnson and Nixon administrations, Kennedy preferred to operate away from public scrutiny. Even Sorensen admits that this was a mistake, a tactical mistake.

> A full-scale articulation by the President of the country's long-range political and economic aims for Southeast Asia might have strengthened this neglected non-military side. The Taylor report recommended a major television address. But unwilling to give Vietnam a status comparable to Berlin, the President chose to keep quiet.[19]

The Berlin "crisis" has long since been forgotten by most people, yet for more than a decade people were to die in Indochina —more than 50,000 Americans and incalculable tens of thousands of Asians—because of the intervention Kennedy started. One can only conclude that Kennedy, like Johnson and Nixon after him, was not candid with the American people because candor would handicap his freedom to act, restrict his "options." Despite his frequent eloquent statements on the need for an informed public, Kennedy recognized that an uninformed, or misinformed, public was easier to manipulate. This was entirely in the tradition established by the elite who have managed American foreign policy since the end of World War II. The extent of this deception, although it had long been obvious, was documented by the Pentagon Papers, a secret study, portions of which were printed by *The New York Times* and other newspapers in June 1971, some months after this manuscript had been completed.

The tragedy, and even that word is inadequate, is that the National Liberation Front (Viet Cong), although dominated by communists, was seeking an end to the war that should have been acceptable to the Kennedy administration, for similar terms were acceptable in Laos. The NLF was almost entirely southern in character and regarded itself as distinct from North Vietnam. At its first congress, in early 1962, the NLF stated that reunification of Vietnam was something for the future, that the "reunification of the Fatherland will be solved step by step on the basis of the aspirations and interests of all sections of the people of South Vietnam as well as the people of North Vietnam, on the principles of freedom and democracy, negotiations and agreement between the two sides." [20]

The NLF said it would join no military alliances, would accept aid from any nation that offered it without political conditions, and advocated the formation of "a peace and neutrality zone comprising Cambodia, Laos and South Vietnam." And Hanoi, although it maintained that Vietnam was a single unit, asserted in an official publication that it would be willing to accept a neutralized South Vietnam. It may be, of course, that much of this was window-dressing, but there was only one way to find out: to enter negotiations with the NLF. This Kennedy refused to do. There was no point to negotiations unless Diem and Kennedy were prepared to concede a significant share of participation in the government to the NLF. This neither Kennedy nor his successors nor Diem nor his successors were prepared to do. This is what the fighting has been about for a decade: who is to govern in Saigon. As long as the United States by force of arms refused to let the NLF share significantly in the Saigon government, the fighting would continue, unless the NLF and North Vietnam lost the determination and stamina that sustained them for a quarter of a century.

There is a similarity here to the Cuban missile crisis. Even before the missile crisis developed, President Dorticos in his United Nations speech indicated the way to a peaceful solution. With Vietnam, just at the time that Kennedy was authorizing substantial American intervention, the NLF was signaling the way to a peaceful solution. That signal was ignored and so was the signal that foretold what would happen if it was. The NLF congress warned that if the "aspirations of the people in South Vietnam are not heeded" and "if the United States imperialists and their agents obdurately go further and further into a bloody military adventure of aggression in South Vietnam," then:

> In case of necessity, the people of South Vietnam and the South Vietnam National Front for Liberation will use their legitimate and effective right to appeal to the people and government of North Vietnam, to peace- and democracy-loving peoples and governments the world over, irrespective of political system, requesting that active support, including material and manpower support, be afforded to the just struggle of the people of South Vietnam.

Whereas Kennedy at the last moment agreed to Khrushchev's proposals to end the missile crisis, he refused even to discuss those offered by the NLF. Kennedy recognized finally that Soviet strength was too great to attempt to win unconditional surrender in Cuba. But he was unaware of the strength of the NLF, despite the warnings of Khrushchev, De Gaulle, and MacArthur. He made one of those fatal miscalculations he was always warning Khrushchev about. The Vietnam war, and all its terrible consequences, are Kennedy's responsibility, for he launched America on the course of war. Johnson is responsible for escalating the war and Nixon for widening it, but it was John Kennedy who started it.

Thus early in 1962 Kennedy refused a chance to negotiate an end to the war; he preferred to step up United States intervention. American aid began pouring into Vietnam, but Diem resisted the reforms that were supposed to be the quid pro quo, and his brother, Ngo Dinh Nhu, ordered Saigon newspapers to print anti-American stories. This is how the situation was described by David Halberstam, who won a Pulitzer Prize for his *New York Times* reportage.

> . . . After a few days of this—plus sulking on the part of Diem— the Americans decided not to push for reforms; they would back Diem strongly and hope that the sheer force of military equipment would help to turn the tide. So, the Americans began to give in to the Ngo family on virtually everything. Having failed to get reforms, our officials said that reforms were taking place; having failed to change the tactics of the military, they talked about bold new tactics which were allegedly driving the communists back. For the essence of our policy was: *There is no place else to go.*[21]

The Kennedy administration embarked, with the enthusiastic support of United States officials in Saigon, on a public-information policy of deception, distortion, and secrecy. The public was misinformed and Congress was supine, its customary state in foreign-policy matters, one in which it languished until well into the Johnson administration, when the dimensions of the disaster became so obvious that even Congress could no longer ignore it. Very few Americans knew what was going on: a few intellectuals who contributed to such publications as *The Nation,* the *New Republic,* and *The Progressive;* a few liberals and radicals found mainly on university faculties; and a few fine journalists such as

Halberstam of *The New York Times* and his predecessor, the almost legendary Homer Bigart, Neil Sheehan of United Press International, Malcolm Browne, Peter Arnett, and Horst Faas of Associated Press, James Robinson of NBC, and Charles Mohr and
Mert Perry of *Time,* although the copy of the latter two was often
distorted by editors in New York.

The Kennedy administration did all it could to undercut these
correspondents, who wrote that the war was being lost while the
administration was trying to convince the country that it was being
won and wasn't much of a war anyway. Hawkish journalists such
as the late Marguerite Higgins wrote pieces attacking the young
Saigon reporters. Pierre Salinger at the White House and press officers at the State and Defense Departments did all they could to
discredit with the Washington press corps the reports of their colleagues in Saigon. Kennedy even went so far, just a month before
his death, to suggest to the young new publisher of *The Times,*
Arthur Ochs Sulzberger, that he might want to reassign Halberstam because he had become too close to the story. Sulzberger declined. There is no way to fudge this issue. The President and his
administration tried to deceive the press, so as to deceive the nation, and when that failed tried to pressure it into line. Kennedy
may have been thinking of the 1964 election.[22]

By the end of 1962 the improvement in the military situation
had come to an end, as the resourceful Viet Cong had learned to
cope with the greatly increased American assistance. Nonetheless,
this was only slowly recognized by the United States establishment
in Saigon, which continued to issue optimistic reports. "In Washington, the President, who had other matters on his mind, accepted the cheerful reports from men in whom he had great
confidence."[23] But in this bland dismissal of a serious problem,
Schlesinger does not explain what was more important than the
only war in which the United States was then engaged.

In the early months of 1963 the tide was turning again, again in
favor of the Viet Cong, but still Saigon and special teams sent
from Washington were reporting that things were going well, although not as well as had been hoped. The State Department announced that 30,000 Viet Cong had been killed in 1962, twice as
many as the entire estimated force at the beginning of the year.
McNamara reported that "we have turned the corner in Vietnam,"

and General Harkins asserted that the war would be won "within a year." Perhaps the most creative optimism came from Dean Rusk, who on April 22, 1963, spoke of a "steady movement toward a constitutional system resting on popular consent." In view of what was soon to happen in South Vietnam, one can only marvel at that. Despite these reports, civilian affairs—in which the Kennedy administration had all but given up on reforms—began to slide downhill fast. Disaster came on May 8, when South Vietnamese troops fired into a Buddhist crowd in Hue. Eight were killed, and the swelling demonstrations that were immediately organized by Buddhist militants affected the prosecution of the war, demonstrated the bankruptcy of the administration's attempt to cajole Diem into reforms, and set in train the series of stunning and horrifying events that ended with the assassination of Diem and his brother.

The worst moment came on June 11. Diem and his brother had responded to the events of early May in true dictatorial fashion. First, they lied, trying to blame the deaths on a fictional Viet Cong agent who threw a grenade into the crowd. When that falsehood was immediately rejected, the next response was repression. This widened the chasm between the Catholic rulers and the Buddhist majority. Repression begat demonstration, which begat further repression. On June 11, 1963, another demonstration began. At first it seemed like any other, but it soon became grotesquely different. Sitting in the center of the chanting Buddhists was an aged priest, Thich Quang Duc. Doused with gasoline, he sat calmly in the cross-legged "lotus" position. He struck a match and set himself ablaze, setting off cries of horror. For what must have seemed like an endless time, Quang Duc sat immobile and silent, until he keeled over, dead. Malcolm Browne had been warned of the demonstration and took the Associated Press photograph that spread the horror of the moment the world over. Many people, no doubt, can still close their eyes and see that photograph. The repercussions of the event were immense, and they grew stronger yet as other Buddhist monks and nuns joined in a series of self-immolations. Kennedy knew he had to do something, but he and his advisers could not decide what to do. The tactic of sweet reason had entirely failed to convince the Ngo family that reforms were essential. Nor could Kennedy attack Diem publicly without discrediting the pro-Diem propaganda that his and Eisenhower's administrations had so tirelessly promoted. And any public criticism by the President would have had incalculable effects on the South Vietnamese political situation.

But the Diem regime was no longer publicly supportable, particularly when the beautiful Madame Nhu, Diem's sister-in-law, openly delighted in the self-immolations. "I would clap hands at seeing another monk barbecue show. . . ." [24]

> . . . the pyres the monks had immolated themselves on consumed and destroyed the power of the Ngos, because they managed to transform the growing antipathy against them on the part of international, and primarily American, public opinion into a veritable feeling of horror.[25]

In that terrible summer of 1963 the Kennedy administration was able to do something: adopt the time-honored tactic of the owners of professional athletic teams. When the team isn't doing well, fire the coach. Dean Rusk was for asking Henry Cabot Lodge to succeed the hapless Frederick Nolting as Ambassador in Saigon. Kennedy took to the idea immediately. It was a magnanimous gesture toward the Brahmin politician who had twice suffered political defeats at Kennedy's hands, losing his Senate seat in 1952 and his election as Richard Nixon's running mate in 1960. Perhaps more important, such an appointment would involve a national figure who was not only a leading Republican but, as Eisenhower's United Nations Ambassador, an unimpeachable hard-line anti-communist. His appointment would help protect the administration's flank from attacks by the right.

While Kennedy was coming to the decision to invite Lodge to take the impossible job in Saigon, it became clear that something had to be done about the deteriorating press situation. Although Kennedy did not like the press reports coming from Saigon, there was little that could be done other than to hinder the correspondents as much as possible in Vietnam and try to discredit their reports in Washington. The Diem regime, however, did not have to be so subtle. On July 7 South Vietnamese police attacked a number of American newsmen. This, of course, resulted in a protest by the American press corps, which was sent directly to the President. Press Secretary Pierre Salinger recommended that the President immediately respond with a telegram that Robert Manning, Assistant Secretary of State in charge of public information, was on his way to Saigon to look into the situation. Kennedy agreed, and Manning (who later became editor of *The Atlantic Monthly*) flew quickly off to Vietnam. He confirmed what he already knew: that the press situation was bad indeed and in his candid report to Dean Rusk conceded that criticism of the administration was valid.

> The press problem in Vietnam is singular because of the singular nature of the United States involvement in that country. Our involvement is so extensive as to require public, i.e., press, scrutiny, and yet so hemmed in by limitations as to make it difficult for the United States government to promote and assure that scrutiny. The problem is complicated by the long-standing desire of the United States government to see the American involvement minimized, even represented, as something less than in reality it is. The early history of the handling of the situation is marked by attitudes, directives, and actions in Washington and in the field that reflect this United States desire.[26]

Manning called for "relaxation of some—but not all—of the strictures still imposed on American coverage of the Vietnamese situation" and for a more "relaxed attitude on the part of US officials to the reports and assessments of the US press. This would do much to reduce the somewhat 'Alice in Wonderland' miasma that surrounds the Vietnamese press situation, and it would help to build a degree of mutual confidence and mutual credibility between American authorities and American correspondents covering Vietnam." This was a courageous report, for it clearly was pointed at, among others, the President. Although helpful, it did not deal with the basic issue, the intervention itself, for all the skilled press relations in the world could not obscure the fact of a deepening involvement in an insupportable war. Nonetheless, when Henry Cabot Lodge went to Saigon, he made a deliberate effort to get along with the American press corps. However, Kennedy himself, although accepting the substance of the Manning report, still attempted to get David Halberstam removed from Vietnam. In any case, Kennedy's death came too soon after the Manning report to know how much long-term effect the report would have had on the administration. One suspects not much, for the circumstances of the Vietnam war heightened the essential adversary relationship between the press and United States officials in Washington and Saigon.

Needless to say, the Washington press corps seized on the story of the self-immolations and on July 17 at a press conference Kennedy was asked "whether the difficulties between the Buddhist population there and the South Vietnamese Government had been an impediment to the effectiveness of American aid in the war against the Viet Cong?"

> Yes, I think it had. I think it is unfortunate that this dispute has arisen at the very time when the military situation has been going better than it has been going for many months. I would hope that some solution could be reached for this dispute, which certainly began as a religious dispute, and because we have invested a tremendous amount of effort and it is going quite well. . . . I would hope this would be settled, because we want to see a stable government there, carrying on a struggle to maintain its national independence.
>
> We believe strongly in that. We are not going to withdraw from that effort. In my opinion, for us to withdraw from that effort would mean a collapse not only of South Vietnam, but Southeast Asia. So we are going to stay there. . . .[27]

This illustrates the President's dilemma. He wanted to indicate United States displeasure with Diem's handling of the Buddhist problem, yet he didn't want to go too far in his criticism. At the same time, by asserting that the United States was going to stay, he removed the lever that most effectively could have been used to influence Diem. Incidentally, it should be noticed that this was one of the several times that Kennedy explicitly endorsed Eisenhower's "domino theory."

As the situation grew worse, several of Kennedy's advisers became increasingly ready to change the United States approach to Diem, among them Averell Harriman, who had always been more realistic than most of his colleagues, and Roger Hilsman, then Assistant Secretary of State for the Far East, a highly sophisticated hawk. This feeling that a change was necessary was reinforced not only by the continuing self-immolations but by stories out of Saigon that the war was going badly, that the situation was deteriorating.

In early July the Kennedy administration began to consider, apparently for the first time, the possibility of getting rid of Diem and his brother. But Kennedy and his top-level advisers concluded "that it would not be possible to get rid of the Nhus," that any attempt at a coup would "most likely" result in a civil war within a civil war and handicap the struggle against the Viet Cong. Yet even while Washington was finally coming to face the fact that things were going badly in Vietnam, as journalists were reporting, the Saigon Embassy kept up its flood of good news.[28]

In August a State Department specialist on Vietnam, Paul H. Kattenburg, suggested to the National Security Council that the United States should "make the decision to get out honorably. He went on to say that, having been acquainted with Diem for ten years, he was deeply disappointed in him, saying that he will not separate from his brother. It was Kattenburg's view that Diem will get little support from the military and, as time goes on, he will get less and less support and the country will go steadily downhill." In response to a question from General Maxwell Taylor, Chairman of the Joint Chiefs of Staff, "Kattenburg replied that in from six months to a year, as people see we are losing the war, they will gradually go to the other side and we will be obliged to leave." [28]

Frederick Nolting, who had just left Saigon to be replaced by Lodge, disagreed, arguing that "we have done a tremendous job toward winning the Vietnam war, working with the same imperfect, annoying government." Rusk, who chaired the meeting in Kennedy's absence, disagreed with Kattenburg's view, as did Defense Secretary McNamara. And Vice President Johnson declared that "from both a practical and political viewpoint, it would be a disaster to pull out; that we should stop playing cops and robbers and get back to talking straight to the GVN [Saigon government] and that we should once again go about winning the war." [28]

As the Pentagon Papers point out, Kattenburg saw the impossibility of winning the war, but his prophetic view was quickly dismissed by the top level of the Kennedy administration. With a presidential election campaign less than a year away, they did not want to be responsible for "losing" Vietnam as the Republicans had accused Harry Truman of "losing" China.

Lodge was too experienced a politician not to recognize the political motivation of his appointment to Saigon and too experienced a diplomat not to be unaware of how unpromising the situation was. Yet he took the job out of a sense of public service and, no doubt, because he thought he was entirely up to such a challenge. However, he was not available until toward the end of August, so poor Nolting was sent back to Saigon to hold the fort for a month. He still believed that wholehearted support of Diem was the only possible course. Nonetheless, before he left Saigon he got Diem to promise that he would make no more attacks on the Buddhists. This pledge was received with satisfaction in Washington, yet on August 20 and 21, the very eve of Lodge's arrival, Diem's Special Forces attacked pagodas in Saigon, Hue, and elsewhere. This was a deliberate affront to the new Ambassador and to Washington. It triggered new large-scale demonstrations joined by thousands of Vietnamese students.

When Lodge arrived on August 22, he demanded facts of the Embassy and got a terribly pessimistic report. He also heard rumors that Ngo Dinh Nhu, who seemed to be growing even more powerful, was ready to make a deal with Ho Chi Minh. Both Nhu and his wife "publicly castigated the United States for its efforts to broaden the government and get back to the war." [29] Lodge instantly departed from Nolting's tactics. He visited the monks who had taken refuge from government police in an American compound, and made clear that the Embassy was receptive to approaches by South Vietnamese generals who wanted to know very quickly—and very quietly—what the United States response would be if they felt they had to move against Nhu and the regime. Lodge cabled for instructions. The Diem regime was coming apart, and the war waited.

But Lodge, like Kennedy, was an activist. He pressed for action. By now many of Kennedy's advisers agreed that the United States had to take a stand against Diem. Thus, on August 24, just a couple of days after his arrival, a now-famous cable was sent to Lodge:

> U.S. government cannot tolerate situation in which power lies in Nhu's hands. Diem must be given chance to rid himself of Nhu and his coterie and replace them with best military and political personalities available.
> If in spite of all your efforts, Diem remains obdurate and refuses,

then we must face possibility that Diem himself cannot be preserved.

. . . You may also tell appropriate military commanders we will
give them direct support in any interim period of breakdown central
government mechanism. . . .

Concurrently with above, ambassador and country team should
urgently examine all possible alternative leadership and make detailed plans as to how we might bring Diem's replacement if this
should become necessary. . . .

Needless to say, we have held knowledge of this telegram to minimum essential people and assume you will take similar precautions
to prevent premature leaks.[30]

Lodge entirely endorsed this strong position and wanted to go
further, not even bothering to make a final approach to Diem. He
cabled back to Washington:

Believe that chances of Diem meeting our demands are virtually
nil. At the same time by making them, we give Nhu chance to forestall or block action by military. Risk, we believe, is not worth taking, with Nhu in control combat forces Saigon. Therefore, we propose to go straight to generals with our demands, without informing
Diem. Would tell them we prepared to have Diem without Nhu but
it is, in effect, up to them whether to keep him.[30]

The Washington cable was nothing less than an invitation to the
generals to overthrow Diem. But nothing about Vietnam was conclusive. The cable had been drafted over a weekend when Rusk,
McNamara, and John McCone of the CIA were out of town.
Rusk, who was in New York, cleared the cable through the facilities of the United States Mission to the United Nations, but it was
decided not to disturb the vacations of McNamara and McCone.
Kennedy, who was on Cape Cod, evidently thought that all his top
advisers had approved of this crucial cable. When he returned to
Washington, he found out that McNamara and McCone would
have opposed the cable had they seen it. So the United States
quickly began to back away from this tough line, thus weakening
whatever resolve the rebellious generals might have had.

Although the United States was still backing Diem, it was
trying to separate him from his brother, but, as Nolting had
warned, that was impossible. Yet all the top advisers, in Saigon as
well as Washington, agreed that the war could not be won if the

situation continued. In short, the Kennedy administration simply did not know what to do. It was in a box of its own devising. Kennedy had chosen to intervene militarily in Vietnam and had chosen to give unqualified support to Diem. He still wanted the former but he did not know how to disengage himself from the latter. No one who writes about Vietnam can do so with certitude; about the only thing of which one can be sure is that things are usually even worse than they look. In this situation there seemed to be another bad factor. The choice for the Kennedy administration was not only one of whether to continue the war with Diem or without him—if either was possible. There was also the possibility that Diem and Nhu, if pressed too hard by Washington, might attempt to exploit the neutralist sentiment that had always existed in South Vietnam and try to make a deal with Ho Chi Minh. This would obviously both end the war and increase communist influence, perhaps decisively so, inside South Vietnam. It is understandable that President Kennedy was finding it difficult to make up his mind. But something had to be done. Congress was getting restive; so was public opinion. The foreign-aid bill had just suffered the worst cut in history, and Kennedy "felt it was largely due to the sense of disillusionment about the whole effort in Vietnam." [31]

Finally, Kennedy decided to prod Diem publicly. He began on September 2 during a CBS television interview with Walter Cronkite.

> I don't think that unless a greater effort is made by the Government [of South Vietnam] to win popular support that the war can be won out there. In the final analysis, it is their war. They are the ones who have to win it or lose it. We can help them, we can give them equipment, we can send our men out there as advisers, but they have to win it, the people of Vietnam, against the communists.
>
> We are prepared to continue to assist them, but I don't think that the war can be won unless the people support the effort and, in my opinion, in the last two months, the government has gotten out of touch with the people.
>
> The repressions against the Buddhists, we felt, were very unwise. Now all we can do is to make it very clear that we don't think this is the way to win. It is my hope that this will become increasingly obvious to the government, that they will take steps to try to bring back the popular support for this very essential struggle. [32]

The President told Cronkite that he thought Diem could still gain the support of the people with "changes in policy and perhaps with personnel." This latter was presumably directed at Nhu. "If [he] doesn't make those changes, I would think that the chances of winning . . . would not be very good." But then Kennedy said,

> I don't agree with those who say we should withdraw. That would be a great mistake. I know people don't like Americans to be engaged in this kind of effort. Forty-seven Americans have been killed in combat with the enemy, but this is a very important struggle even though it is far away.
>
> We took all this—made this effort to defend Europe. Now Europe is quite secure. We also have to participate—we may not like it—in the defense of Asia.

These are crucial words in any estimate of John Kennedy. He made it clear that he did not intend, just weeks before his death, to withdraw from Vietnam. Further he again demonstrated a failure to distinguish between the experience with Soviet communism in Europe and "wars of national liberation." President of a country born in revolution, he did not understand revolution. He could not recognize that although the American Revolution gave meaning to its imperishable documents of revolution, the Revolution itself was far different in its circumstances from almost all those that took inspiration from it. The American Revolution was not a class revolution, the uprising of the masses against their masters, but the revolt of equals who demanded equal treatment even if they had to tear themselves away from the Crown to get it.

As John Kennedy was trying to make the terrible decision whether or not to discard Diem, whom he had so long admired, his brother Robert, the Attorney General, was beginning to show the differences he would later have with the Kennedy–Johnson Vietnam policy. At a National Security Council meeting on September 6, he raised the question whether any government in Saigon, under Diem or anyone else, could successfully resist a communist takeover. If not, now was the time to get out of Vietnam entirely, he thought. His colleagues could not give him a definite affirmative reply but were convinced that it was necessary to try to resist the Viet Cong with another government. As the Pentagon Papers reported, Robert "Kennedy's trenchant analysis, however, did not guarantee a searching reappraisal of US policy." [33]

Kennedy continued his public pressure on Diem in an appearance on NBC's Huntley–Brinkley Report on September 9. But more important, he stated publicly what had long been clear: that Washington's major preoccupation was not with Vietnam but with China. He was asked if he doubted the "domino theory."

> No, I believe it. I believe it. I think that the struggle is close enough. China is so large, looms so high just beyond the frontiers, that if South Vietnam went, it would not only give them an improved geographic position for a guerrilla assault on Malaya, but would give the impression that the wave of the future in Southeast Asia was China and the communists. So I believe it. . . .
>
> The fact of the matter is that with the assistance of the United States, SEATO, Southeast Asia and indeed all of Asia had been maintained independent against a powerful force, the Chinese communists. What I am concerned about is that Americans will get impatient and say because they don't like events in Southeast Asia or they don't like the government in Saigon, that we should withdraw. That only makes it easy for the communists. I think we should stay. We should use our influence in as effective a way as we can, but we should not withdraw.[34]

Again, his words are important. He was making the same judgment of China in the nineteen-sixties that his predecessors made of Russia from the mid-forties on. Even if one accepts the earlier assumptions about the Soviet Union—and there are good reasons not to—the situation in Asia was very different. Russia and the countries of Europe were not colonial possessions just establishing national identities in a revolutionary situation but countries with histories as modern, independent states. China, to a real degree, and the other Asian countries with few exceptions were just awakening from generations of colonial rule and chaotic pre-modern jurisdictions. And powerful as China was (potentially more than actually), its army, unlike Russia's, did not squat on the territory of its neighbors. Yet Kennedy did not make that distinction. Communism was communism and it must be opposed wherever it might be, even at the cost of American blood and treasure. He had learned, as evidenced by his American University speech, that a nuclear confrontation with the Soviet Union was too dangerous, but he had yet to learn of the terrible cost of intervention in revolution. He still saw a communist monolith that never existed beyond the sway of the Russian army. He sometimes spoke as if he understood, but seldom acted as if he did.

One more thing is evident from John Kennedy's final statements on Vietnam. Despite the rhetoric about self-determination and helping a beleaguered little nation, the Kennedy administration was not primarily interested in Vietnam and its people, but in the anti-communist war. Under Kennedy, as under Johnson and Nixon, Indochinese, with few exceptions, suffered, died, and were dispossessed not in pursuit of their own goals but as expendable counters to be shoved across the maps of a Washington elite. Theodore Sorensen was a little less blunt:

> But sometimes the national security required this country to aid dictators, particularly in the newer nations unprepared for true democracy. He knew that we were dangerously dependent on one man, but there was no simple way to force a broadening of that man's government or the development of more representative leaders without endangering the entire war effort.[35]

The President himself was admirably direct in a press conference on September 12: "What helps to win the war, we support; what interferes with the war effort, we oppose." [36]

It is difficult not to be bitter when contemplating the fact that three successive American Presidents, beginning with Kennedy, have sat in Washington, surrounded by their realistic advisers, and made decisions, however well intentioned, that have cost the lives of thousands upon thousands of people who wanted to be left alone. One thinks of the leaders and generals of the First World War, who sent thousands to useless deaths in the front lines, but at least they sacrificed their own countrymen. Whatever humane feelings Kennedy and Johnson and Nixon had about the people of Indochina—and it would be unfair and untrue to say they had none—the sad fact is that they saw Indochina primarily as a gameboard and its people primarily as pawns. This is a terrible, but inescapable indictment.

In late September, Kennedy sent McNamara, for the third time, and Taylor to Saigon. McNamara for the first time heard dissenting voices from within the Embassy. Somehow, despite the flood of press reports that had so enraged the administration, he and the President had never tried to get beneath the Embassy's surface unanimity. They should have known, from the constant disagreements within the administration in Washington, that there must be disagreements in Saigon. They might have probed beneath the surface and exposed the self-deception, but perhaps McNamara and Kennedy were unable to resist the human temptation to listen to good news even when there is reason to doubt its truth.

Yet even though Lodge convinced McNamara that the political situation was desperate, General Harkins convinced him that it had not yet materially affected the military situation. Thus, when McNamara returned to Washington, the White House announced on October 2 that a thousand men could be withdrawn by the end of the year and that the major part of the American military task would be over by the end of 1965. But McNamara's optimism did not convince all his colleagues, and "Kennedy's advisers were more deeply divided on the internal situation in Saigon than on any previous issue." [37]

Out of this conflict came the decision that Lodge would be coolly correct to Diem but avoid him as much as possible, in the hope that Diem would approach him for a substantive discussion. If so, Lodge would make three basic points: "the need for drastic improvement in the Vietnamese military effort; the crisis of confidence among the Vietnamese people caused by Diem's policy of repression and police-state methods; and the crisis of confidence among the American people and government." [38] And although no public announcement of American pressure would be made, so Diem could come around without losing face, the United States would stop payments for certain public-works projects and for Colonel Le Quang Tung's Special Forces until they were used to fight the Viet Cong. (Diem was like Chiang Kai-shek during the Second World War. He insisted on keeping his most loyal troops around him to protect him from internal enemies, rather than committing them to battle against the external foe. Like Chiang, Diem preferred to let the Americans do as much of the fighting as possible.)

The events of the last weeks of Diem's regime are so confused as to defy recapitulation. The accounts published thus far, even by insiders, are far from consistent with one another. One of the reasons for the confusion in Saigon was the confusion within the administration in Washington. The President himself was torn in two directions, on one hand "increasingly doubtful that the war could ever be won with Diem," and on the other retaining "great personal admiration" for Diem and accepting "the fact that the United States must not bring him down and would have to make the best of his staying. His hope was to change Diem's policies and personnel, not remove him." [39]

While Kennedy did not, according to his biographers, want to overthrow Diem, the American tactics to put pressure on the South Vietnamese regime undercut Diem's capacity for survival. Not only were funds cut off, but the administration, with Lodge's concurrence, removed the CIA station chief, John Richardson, a stanch defender of the Ngo brothers. The brothers correctly interpreted this as a sign that Washington meant business, but so, inevitably, did the generals who a month before had hinted a coup was in the works. Rumors of a coup began to spread, and Nhu said publicly just a few days before his death that the Vietnamese generals "haven't got a chance." [40]

The United States turned the screws a little tighter on October 21, when it announced publicly in Saigon what it had already told the Diem government privately: that Colonel Tung's Special Forces would no longer receive United States funds unless they fought the Viet Cong. All during these last weeks the Diem regime was further undercut by continuing demonstrations and several more self-immolations. Things were coming to a head. One of the generals who had approached the United States Embassy some weeks earlier approached an American official and told him that a decision had been made, but he would give no details.

> He said that the generals wanted the United States government to know that they were counting on what the United States had said in the past about such matters being a Vietnamese decision and counting on the United States neither to betray them nor to try to thwart their move when it was made. There was no date set, but they said they would give ample warning.[41]

Kennedy's indecision was reflected in the cables to Saigon. He wanted Diem to go, but he wasn't quite prepared to push him. After a National Security Council meeting in mid-September, the White House cabled Lodge:

We see no good opportunity for action to remove present government in immediate future; therefore, as your most recent message suggests, we must, for the present, apply such pressures as are available to secure whatever modest improvements on the scene as may be possible. . . . Such a course, moreover, is consistent with more drastic effort as and when means become available.[42]

The White House was still cautious in a cable sent in the first days of October:

. . . President today approved recommendations that no initiative should now be taken to given any active, covert encouragement to a coup. There should, however, be urgent covert effort with closest security under broad guidance of ambassador to identify and build contacts with possible alternative leadership as and when it appears.[42]

The differences in Washington continued to be fully mirrored in Saigon. While Lodge was trying to encourage a coup, General Harkins was using his influence among the Vietnamese generals to discourage one. Lodge began reporting to Washington his differences with Harkins. And he cabled that he did not have "the power to delay or discourage a coup." Since the United States has always had enormous influence in Saigon, this statement may well have reflected his own hopes for a coup. On October 30, on the very eve of the coup, McGeorge Bundy cabled from the White House: "Once a coup under responsible leadership has begun . . . it is in the interest of the US government that it should succeed." [42]

These last weeks of October were the time of decision for Washington but Kennedy did not know what decision to make. Diem could have been warned, and the warning could have been the ultimate pressure on him to make drastic changes or else. On the other hand, a warning could have caused Diem and Nhu to take violent action against any generals they did not trust, thus paralyzing the war effort which, as we have seen, was the overriding consideration. Washington decided to hold off and try to learn more about what was going on. But things were moving too swiftly. On October 30, Colonel Tung moved his forces, which were, in effect, the Diem–Nhu palace guard, out of Saigon. The

circumstances of this move are not clear, but the effect was to reduce greatly the security of the Ngo brothers. On November 1,
Admiral Harry D. Felt, United States Pacific Commander, was in
Saigon on a short inspection tour. Accompanied by Lodge, he
paid a brief courtesy call on Diem. As they were leaving, Diem
signaled to Lodge that he should stay for a moment, and said
something about one of these days discussing whatever it was the
United States wanted. Evidently the American pressure was making itself felt, but it was too late. That afternoon large numbers of
troops were seen moving through Saigon. Then, at exactly 1:45
p.m. Saigon time, General Joseph Stilwell, Jr., Harkins' deputy,
got a phone call from one of the Vietnamese generals saying that
the conspirators were all together at headquarters and that the
coup was under way.

Troops went efficiently to all the strategic places, and then the
coup took a curious turn. For the next several hours its fate depended on the telephone. The generals called Diem and Nhu peri-
odically, offering them safe conduct out of the country if they
would surrender. The Ngo brothers, for their part, were frantically
calling command posts all over the area, trying, without success,
to get help. Diem even called Lodge, who expressed polite and no
doubt genuine concern over the brothers' physical safety.

According to the Pentagon Papers, this was the conversation:

DIEM: Some units have made a rebellion and I want to know
what is the attitude of the US.

LODGE: I do not feel well enough informed to be able to tell you.
I have heard the shooting, but I am not acquainted with all the
facts. Also it is 4:30 a.m. in Washington and the US Government
cannot possibly have a view.

DIEM: But you must have some general ideas. After all, I am a
chief of state. I have tried to do my duty. I want to do now what
duty and good sense require. I believe in duty above all.

LODGE: You have certainly done your duty. As I told you only
this morning, I admire your courage and your great contributions
to your country. No one can take away from you the credit for all
you have done. Now I am worried about your physical safety. I
have a report that those in charge of the current activity offer you
and your brother safe conduct out of the country. Had you heard
this?

DIEM: No. (*And then after a pause*): You have my telephone number.

LODGE: Yes. If I can do anything for your physical safety, please call me.

DIEM: I am trying to re-establish order.[43]

Lodge was certainly less than candid, but no one can be sure whether candor on his part would have caused Diem and Nhu to abandon their attempts to regain power. And although there has not thus far been any concrete evidence that the United States took any positive steps to ensure their safety, there is every reason to believe that the Americans expected them to be given safe conduct. That may even have been the intention of the generals leading the coup. Perhaps if Diem and Nhu had surrendered, their lives would have been spared. Or perhaps the generals had decided, whatever they told the United States Embassy, to kill Diem and his brother, for alive, even in exile, they would have always been a threat.

At 4:45 p.m. the generals put Colonel Tung on the phone to inform Diem that the Special Forces had surrendered. The brothers still refused to surrender, and Tung was taken outside and shot. At 5:15 the senior general, Duong Van "Big" Minh, called and offered the brothers a last chance to surrender before the palace was bombed. Diem hung up.

The attack began at 3:30 a.m. November 2. The palace defenders soon surrendered, but the Ngo brothers had fled earlier through a tunnel. They took refuge in the home of a rich Chinese friend in Cholon, Saigon's twin city, which had long before been prepared as a communications center for such an eventuality. Soon, however, that hideout was discovered and Diem and Nhu fled to a nearby Catholic church. There they were captured, put into an armored personnel carrier, and, on the way to armed-forces headquarters, shot and killed. Whatever else they were, they were brave. They turned down safe conduct out of the country in a vain effort to regain control.

The news was flashed to Washington. Schlesinger writes movingly of President Kennedy's reaction.

I saw the President soon after he heard [the news]. I had not seen him so depressed since the Bay of Pigs. No doubt he realized

that Vietnam was his great failure in foreign policy, and that he had
never really given it his full attention. . . . By 1961 choice had already been fatally narrowed; but still, if Vietnam had been handled
as a political rather than a military problem, if Washington had not
listened to General Harkins for so long, if Diem had been subjected
to tactful pressure rather than uncritical respect, if Lodge had gone
to Saigon in 1961 instead of a Nolting, if, if, if—and now it was all
past, and Diem miserably dead. The Saigon generals were claiming
that he had killed himself; but the President, shaking his head,
doubted that, as a Catholic, he would have taken this way out. He
said that Diem had fought for his country for twenty years and that
it should not have ended like this.[44]

What Schlesinger does not write is that Kennedy must have
been thinking that he could have prevented the coup or taken
steps to attempt to guarantee Diem's safety in the event of a coup.
There is no attempt at judgment here. That would be grossly presumptuous, for Diem and Nhu were cruel and repressive men and,
perhaps, if any men deserve to die, they did. Yet there is no escaping the fact that Kennedy's policies, first in not exerting firm
pressure on Diem to reform, second in withdrawing support from
the Diem regime, made the coup possible, indeed inevitable.

Diem's death was followed only three weeks later by Kennedy's
—assassination upon assassination, the politics of the postwar
world. One can only speculate as to Kennedy's response to the
death of Diem. His admirers like to think that he would not have
let American intervention go as disastrously far as did Lyndon
Johnson. Perhaps that is so; perhaps his skepticism would have
prevailed over the advice of his senior colleagues. But there is
scanty evidence for that speculation. Kennedy had always reposed
great trust in McNamara, Taylor, Bundy, Rusk, Rostow, *et al.,*
and under President Johnson they continued to counsel that just a
little more pressure would break the resistance of "the other side."
Theirs was, to use Norman Mailer's term, "the logic of the next
step." Each step in itself did not seem so drastic, but all the steps
together have added up to a ten-year war. Further, Kennedy himself said time and again that the United States should not withdraw from Vietnam. On November 14 he expressed his hope for
"an increased effort in the war." [45] There is little reason to believe
that he would have changed his mind quickly, particularly with a

presidential election just around the corner. It would have taken extraordinary political courage—Kennedy might have regarded it as political idiocy—for him to face the inevitable Republican charges that he had "lost" Vietnam as Truman had "lost" China.

What he might have done is speculation. All we can be sure of is what he did. When Kennedy took office there were only about 600 advisers in Vietnam. At the time of his death there were some 25,000 Americans there, many of them actively engaged in combat, about 50 already dead. There is a great difference, qualitative as well as quantitative, between a few hundred and 25,000, particularly since the momentum was toward greater numbers and greater involvement in combat.[46] It is true that Kennedy had inherited a very bad situation from President Eisenhower, but it is inconceivable that any short-term divisiveness caused by a realistic policy of disengagement from Vietnam in 1961 and 1962 could have approached that caused by seeking a military victory. More important, all that human suffering could have been avoided. There is no escaping the fact that, whatever the subsequent responsibility of Lyndon Johnson or Richard Nixon, Kennedy began the Vietnam war. It has been his most enduring legacy.

Yet he had accomplished so much: the new hope for peace
on earth, the elimination of nuclear testing in the atmosphere,
and abolition of nuclear diplomacy, the new policies toward
Latin America and the Third World, the reordering of American defense. . . . The energies he released, the standards he
set, the purposes he inspired, the goals he established would
guide the land he loved for years to come. Above all he gave
the world for an imperishable moment the vision of a leader
who greatly understood the terror and the hope, the diversity
and the possibility, of life on this planet and who made people
look beyond nation and race to the future of humanity. So the
people of the world grieved as if they had terribly lost their
own leader, friend, brother.[1]

—ARTHUR SCHLESINGER

CHAPTER TEN

The Kennedy Years

The preceding chapters have concentrated on the most important
foreign-policy issues of the Kennedy years. But the President, unlike an author, cannot divide his problems into tidy piles and deal
with them one at a time. The President is more like a juggler, already juggling too many eggs, who, often at the most anxious moments, is forever having more eggs tossed at him. No writer, no
presidential adviser, perhaps not even the President himself can be
fully aware of the size and complexity of the job. It is too big for
one man, yet only one man can fill it. It is too big not only because no mortal man can do it, but because, particularly in foreign
and military matters, it lifts the President almost beyond the reach
of Congress and, between elections, the people. Not only is all the
enormous power of the executive branch concentrated in one man,
but that man has the initiative. Although the Senate has the power
of confirmation and the Congress has the power of the purse, these
powers are diffused among parties, personalities, and committees,

allowing the President ample scope for maneuver. Although Congress can frustrate the President, it cannot often effectively compete with him, and in matters of foreign policy and national security it has usually been content—eager, even—to surrender what powers it does have. Kennedy, although constantly frustrated by Congress on domestic matters, had pretty much his own way on foreign and military matters. He preferred foreign affairs anyway, and his tendency to emphasize them was thus reinforced. While understandable, this tendency has had serious long-term consequences. Kennedy spent so much time on foreign affairs, often dealing with crises of his own making, that he devoted insufficient time to domestic matters. In fact he, like his predecessors, seemed largely unaware of the enormous problems festering just beneath the surface of American life. If he had devoted adequate time, energy, and resources to domestic problems, some of them might not have erupted after his death in such virulent form. His neglect of them was a major failing.

As we saw earlier, immediately upon taking office he grappled with the complexities of Laos, moved toward the Bay of Pigs, began the big military buildup, learned of the seriousness of the situation in Vietnam, authorized Stevenson to take a pro-African stand on the Angola question at the United Nations, and began to cope, with remarkable success, with the Congo. Few questions since the end of World War II have been as difficult at the Congo. Belgium, suddenly and with wholly inadequate preparation, gave the Congo its independence in mid-1960. Immediately the country began to disintegrate. Belgium had provided absolutely no structure capable of holding the vast, potentially rich nation together —perhaps cynically, as many thought, so Belgium itself would be invited back to pick up the pieces. But the Congolese turned instead to the United Nations, which bravely attempted to put Humpty-Dumpty together again. It eventually succeeded, although its uncertain, halting, often self-contradictory actions brought the United Nations itself to the brink of bankruptcy and, in 1964 and 1965, to a year-long state of paralysis that very nearly amounted to self-destruction. The story of the Congo is much too complex to discuss in detail here, but the key to the survival of the Congo was to preserve its territorial integrity by preventing the secession of the mineral-rich province of Katanga. Most of the African members of the United Nations, with varying degrees of militancy, wanted the United Nations to hold the Congo together with armed force if necessary. The communist bloc went along with the Africans, Russia taking advantage of the chaos to try to get a firm foothold in central Africa. Many of the neutral and Latin American nations supported the Africans, but Britain and France, both of which had enormous investments in Katanga, were dead set against vigorous United Nations action. Dag Hammarskjöld, who died when his plane crashed on a flight to the Congo, and his successor, U Thant, both advocated an active United Nations role.

The big question mark was the United States. There was considerable division, not only in the country as a whole but within the administration. The right-wingers in Congress and the nation pictured Moïse Tshombe, the Katangan leader, as a stanch anticommunist deserving of American support. He was, however, as the African nations recognized immediately, an instrument of European financial interests, although himself a bold, stubborn, and skilled exploiter of the chaotic conditions. Within the American administration, the pro-NATO, pro-European officials (both career and appointed) were for going slow in support of the United Nations. The pro-African, pro-United Nations people, again career and appointed, were for backing the United Nations all the way. The breakdown was far from exact, but, roughly speaking, those who were "hawks" on Indochina were "doves" on the Congo, and vice versa. (It is an interesting commentary that the "realists" in Washington have often been willing to intervene on behalf of right-wing governments but seldom otherwise, even when the government—if it can be so dignified—in Léopoldville was substantially pro-Western.)

Kennedy decided to back the United Nations. He was a genuine supporter of the United Nations, although in that American way of seeing the United Nations and the United States as substantially synonymous. In those days, to a large extent, they were. Kennedy recognized—as did the outraged Russians—that the United Nations could be used to keep the communist nations out of the Congo. In this his view was more perceptive than that of the right-wingers and even the pro-NATO officials in the government. It was because of their recognition of this that the Russians demanded the resignation of Hammarskjöld and the establishment of a "troika," a three-headed Secretary-Generalship, one to represent the West, one the communist bloc, and one the neutralists, with unanimity required for action. The neutralists immediately saw that extending the right of veto from the Security Council to the Secretariat would paralyze the only international instrument of substantial value to them.

Despite the hue and cry from the right, led by Senator Thomas Dodd of Connecticut and handsomely financed by European mining interests, Kennedy stuck with the United Nations, not only for the reasons cited above but because he had great sympathy for Africa and this was what the Africans wanted. For whatever reason, he did not put Africa into the context of the Cold War so firmly as he did the rest of the underdeveloped world. Perhaps it was his service on the African subcommittee of the Senate Foreign Relations Committee that gave him a more sophisticated viewpoint. Perhaps the reason was that Africa had not, for geographic or historical reasons, been involved in classical Cold War situations; there was little communist element in the African nationalist movements. In any case Kennedy was able to maintain a cool perspective on Africa, and he was steadfast in his support of the United Nations, despite the pressure, despite the often discouraging lack of progress. During his term the United States provided not only political support but substantial support in money and matériel, including the purchase on a matching basis of up to $100 million in United Nations bonds to meet the heavy expenses of the United Nations force in the Congo manned by troops from neutral nations. When the Katanga secession eventually collapsed at the end of 1962, much of the credit was due to John Kennedy. This was one of his most substantial achievements.

One of Kennedy's best appointments was of G. Mennen (Soapy) Williams, who had many times been elected Governor of Michigan, as Assistant Secretary of State for African Affairs. The indefatigable Williams and his aggressive African Bureau were forever challenging—with some success—the long-established primacy of the Europeanists in the State Department. And Williams seemed always to be on a trip to Africa, wading earnestly, campaign-style, through rivers and swamps, shaking hands with bewildered but pleased villagers. On his very first trip he caused something of a furor among Europeans in Africa by proclaiming "Africa for the

Africans." The President, at a press conference, immediately supported Williams. "The statement 'Africa for the Africans' does
not seem to me to be a very unreasonable statement. He made it
clear that he was talking about all those who felt that they were
Africans, whatever their color might be, whatever their race might
be. I do not know who else Africa should be for." 2

For a proud and sensitive people, long used to being treated as
inferiors by Europeans (a term that means whites, regardless of
their origin) the warm treatment afforded by Kennedy, Williams,
Adlai Stevenson at the United Nations, and the entire administration was gratefully received. African leaders, not only presidents
and prime ministers but lesser officials as well, were forever being
invited to the White House for long, friendly talks, not the pro
forma brush-offs that had been customary. Even on the late afternoon of October 22, 1962, just before Kennedy made his historic
Cuban-missile-crisis speech, the President talked for nearly an
hour with Milton Obote, as if he had nothing but the problems of
Uganda and Africa on his mind. And Kwame Nkrumah, the vain
and mercurial President of Ghana, was totally captivated by the
President and his wife during a March 1961 visit.

Kennedy's handling of Nkrumah demonstrated how far he had
moved from the Dulles neutrality-is-immoral concept. Nkrumah
wanted the United States to contribute a substantial sum to a con-
sortium that would build a lasting monument to him, a hydroelec-
tric-aluminum project on the Volta River. Kennedy agreed, only
to have Nkrumah, the self-professed neutralist, rush off to a number of communist capitals, Peking included, for a series of communiqués that did not sound very nonaligned. There was considerable pressure on Kennedy, even from liberals within the
administration, and more from Congress and the public, to withdraw the American support. Kennedy, however, got assurances
from technical people that the project was valid. Fearing that to
withdraw the $40-million American loan would trigger in Africa
a response similar to that evoked when Dulles suddenly canceled
American participation in Gamal Abdel Nasser's Aswan High
Dam, Kennedy decided to go ahead. He wanted Africans to understand that the United States did not demand political fealty in
return for large-scale assistance.

Such a loan would never have been possible during the

Eisenhower–Dulles years; Eisenhower's administration demanded a quid pro quo for assistance on that scale. Kennedy admirers cite this case to demonstrate how deep was his sympathy for the emerging nations. There is absolutely no doubt of that, yet this sympathy, real as it was, received tangible expression only in those countries where there was no significant communist participation in the government. He did not mind if a government had political or economic relations with Russia or China, so long as that country was resolutely non-communist at home. It did not seem to occur to Kennedy or his advisers that there might be circumstances when a people, through revolution, might validly choose communism as offering the best path to economic and social development. Freedom of choice or diversity—Kennedy's admirers constantly cite his devotion to diversity—did not extend that far.

The case of the Dominican Republic is instructive. On May 30, 1961, four Dominican army officers, acting as much for personal reasons as out of principle, shot down Rafael Trujillo, who had maintained his cruel, repressive, and corrupt dictatorship for three decades. When Kennedy returned from his European visits with De Gaulle and Khrushchev, the Dominican regime was headed by Joaquin Balaguer, the nominal president under Trujillo, although the armed forces were controlled by Trujillo's playboy son, Ramfis. Kennedy examined the situation, to use Schlesinger's term, "realistically."

> "There are three possibilities in descending order of preference: a decent democratic regime, a continuation of the Trujillo regime or a Castro regime. We ought to aim at the first, but we really can't renounce the second until we are sure that we can avoid the third." [3]

This demonstrates still again Kennedy's misunderstanding of revolution: he was prepared to see a continuation of the despicable Trujillo regime rather than permit the Dominican people to choose a leftist or communist government. One can only wonder what gave Kennedy the right to make such a decision for the people of another country. It points up the reason the United States so often in the postwar years has found itself on the side not of the people but of a repressive government. It is difficult to think of a single revolution from the left directed against a decent government. Despite Kennedy's genuine sympathy for the peoples of the Third World, his definition of progress and self-determination was limited to regimes found acceptable by Washington—almost always not on the basis of their service to their own people but on the basis of their anti-communism. Thus the Bay of Pigs, thus Vietnam, thus British Guiana, and thus, after Kennedy's death, the unforgivable intervention in the Dominican Republic.

Kennedy decided to back Balaguer largely because there was no immediate alternative. For a time, in the fall of 1961, it seemed as if Ramfis Trujillo and his two uncles might attempt a military takeover, but Kennedy instructed Rusk to issue a statement that the United States would not remain indifferent if the Trujillos attempted to "reassert dictatorial domination." The President backed up his administration's words by ordering eight American warships, with 1800 Marines aboard, to steam ostentatiously just outside the three-mile limit at Santo Domingo. It was made plain that the Marines would land if Balaguer requested them.

American gunboat diplomacy had long been hated in Latin America, but, as Schlesinger wrote proudly, "it would be, for once, Yankee intervention to sustain a democratic movement rather than to destroy it, and the President was prepared to take his chance." [4] Soon the good news came. The Dominican military establishment, given this clear signal from Washington, decided to back Balaguer, and the Trujillos fled. Schlesinger reports that the people danced in the streets, for once cheering rather than cursing the *norteamericano* fleet. Latin America cheered, and only Fidel Castro objected. "The incident proved striking evidence of the change in Latin American attitudes Kennedy had wrought in the seven months since the Bay of Pigs."

Thus far Kennedy was prepared to go to implement his belief that "Balaguer is our only tool. The anti-communist liberals aren't strong enough. We must use our influence to take Balaguer along the road to democracy." [5] Kennedy had not learned, nor did he ever, history's lesson that the United States had never, beginning with the Truman Doctrine in Greece, succeeded in moving a right-wing government toward democracy. Whether in Greece or South Vietnam or Latin America, these governments soon learned that the Americans, under whatever President, were more interested in anti-communism than in the welfare of the people. In the case at hand, Kennedy was for democratic government—up to a point. The entire American apparatus descended on Santo Domingo—AID, USIA, CIA, etc.—and in December 1962 elections were held, the first democratic elections in more than three decades.

Elected was Juan Bosch, a long-time exiled foe of the Trujillo regime, a writer and a progressive democrat. Bosch immediately ran into difficulties. He may not have been the most effective leader possible, but then perhaps no one could have successfully coped with the legacy of thirty years of tyranny and exploitation. Further, Bosch, who believed in democracy, did not curb the communists as the Dominican right wing and Washington would have liked him to. By the end of the summer of 1963 it became apparent that the right-wing militarists would soon attempt to overthrow him, and as the crisis came to a head, Bosch asked for the same kind of support Kennedy had given Balaguer. An urgent cable was sent to Washington by John Bartlow Martin, a journalist and an intimate of Stevenson's, whom Kennedy had appointed as Ambassador to the Dominican Republic. He asked that an aircraft carrier be sent to the waters off Santo Domingo. The reply, Martin has written,

> said that the Department could do little more to save Bosch in view of his past performance despite all my efforts to persuade him to govern effectively. The forces arrayed against him were largely of his own creation. Now he must save himself. The Department did not oppose the moves I had already recommended to him but warned me not to tie such moves to any commitment by the United States. It suggested that perhaps he also should take some "positive" steps. (I wondered how.) As for the aircraft carrier, the Department refused to intervene militarily unless a communist takeover were threatened. A show of force we were not prepared to back up would be only a meaningless gesture, ineffective in a situation which had gone so far.[6]

Kennedy had sent an American fleet to preserve the regime of one of Trujillo's henchmen but was not prepared to send such help to preserve the *elected* government of a democratic progressive. Democratic government had been given a trial of less than seven months, but now there would be no "Yankee intervention to sustain a democratic movement rather than destroy it. . . ." Rather bleakly Schlesinger records that "the road to democracy remained hard. On September 25, 1963, the Dominican military overthrew Juan Bosch in the Dominican Republic." [7] End of discussion.

This was the origin of another Kennedy legacy—the April 1965 intervention in the Dominican Republic, not so important a legacy to the American people as Vietnam, perhaps, but important enough for the people of the Dominican Republic.

President Kennedy demonstrated his consistency, although not his candor, in the matter of British Guiana, now the independent nation of Guyana. Cheddi Jagan, the leading figure in British Guiana, proclaimed his Marxism openly, based his political program on socialist theories, and named his party the People's Progressive Party. He never tried to deceive anyone on these points, at home or abroad. Elected Prime Minister after his PPP won parliamentary elections in 1953, 1957, and 1961, running on a platform of socialism and early independence from Britain, he was clearly the most popular leader in British Guiana. But both London and Washington saw him as a communist. He was constantly harassed, and sometimes jailed, by the British. These methods were, in a way, understandable, for jailing national leaders was for decades the traditional British way of training colonial subjects for independence. Understandable too was Washington's interest. British Guiana was, after all, in the Western Hemisphere, and Washington had often exercised the power, if not the right, of veto in the hemisphere. So from the early 1950s the CIA, working primarily through Serafino Romualdi of the AFL-CIO, involved itself in Guiana's labor movement and politics. [8]

In October 1961, after his electoral victory, Jagan came to Washington. "He made his American debut, like so many other visiting statesmen, on *Meet the Press,* where he resolutely declined to say anything critical of the Soviet Union and left an impression of either wooliness or fellow-traveling." [9] The President saw part of the television program and ordered that no commitments be made to Jagan until he had seen him personally. Kennedy and Jagan met on October 25. Jagan, according to Schlesinger, who was at the meeting, made clear that he thought socialism was the only answer to his country's economic problems. Kennedy replied that the United States was not engaged in a crusade for the free-enterprise system, that it did not care with whom Jagan traded after independence, as long as the result was not economic dependence.[10] The President avoided any concrete discussion of aid funds. Jagan had asked for $40 million, a large sum for a nation of only 600,000, particularly since larger countries with closer ties to the United States were also seeking substantial sums. But Kennedy only agreed to examine specific projects on their merits. This distressed Jagan, who asked to see Kennedy again. Kennedy and his advisers denied this request, but the President decided, in view of Britain's great concern that Jagan not be sent home empty-handed, that Schlesinger should meet with Jagan and attempt to work something out. After complicated negotiations, Jagan and the United States agreed on a statement that the United States would send a mission to British Guiana to determine what assistance it could offer. In return, Jagan committed himself "to uphold the political freedoms and defend the parliamentary democracy which is his country's fundamental heritage."

Washington did not know what to do. The estimate was that with United States aid there was a 50-per-cent chance that an independent Guiana would go communist and that without it the chances would be 90 per cent. At first the thought was to give aid a try, but early in 1962 Dean Rusk reversed this position, presumably with Kennedy's approval. Kennedy was growing increasingly distrustful, despite the British contention that Jagan was preferable to Forbes Burnham, the black leader of the People's National Congress. When Burnham visited Washington, he struck the administration as an "intelligent, self-possessed, reasonable man, insisting quite firmly on his 'socialism' and 'neutralism' but stoutly anti-communist." [11] Burnham also convinced the administration of his awareness that Guiana would have an unhappy future unless its leaders overcame the racial conflicts that had led to bitter race riots in early 1962, causing Prime Minister Jagan to call in British troops, hardly a welcome sight to him, to re-establish order. Thus, the administration decided to back Burnham against Jagan.

On August 20, 1963, Kennedy was asked a three-part question. "Do you feel that Cheddi Jagan, Prime Minister of British Guiana, is a communist? And what do you think of the possibilities of British Guiana becoming another Cuba should the British leave very soon? And is the United States exerting any—trying to exert any influence on the British to stay in British Guiana, or to suspend the Guiana constitution?"

Well, I don't think it would be useful to respond, really, to any of those questions. With regard to Mr. Jagan's political philosophy, I think he has made it clear himself, and his associates have made it clear. The British still exercise a responsibility in the matter. I think we should leave it to them to exercise that in a responsible manner.

As to what might happen under hypothetical conditions in the future, quite obviously the United States Government is concerned about what happens in this hemisphere and observes matters in this hemisphere closely. But I think it is very important that we point out that this is primarily a British matter and we should leave the judgment to them.[12]

This statement was less than candid. Far from leaving the matter to the British, Washington exerted constant pressure on London to postpone British Guiana's independence so it would not come while Cheddi Jagan was in power. And the CIA, functioning through a number of labor groups, was hard at work. British Guiana was fertile ground. The population was about 50 per cent East Indian and 35 per cent African; the rest was divided among indigenous Indians, Europeans, Chinese, and various mixtures. The East Indians were largely rural and almost entirely supported Jagan. The blacks were clustered in the towns and largely supported Burnham. There was also, on the far right, a party called the United Force.

In February 1963 pro-Burnham forces rioted against a Jagan-proposed labor bill. By April a general strike had developed. A number of CIA-financed labor leaders were involved in the planning of the strike, and CIA money through several conduits kept the strike alive, allowing the leaders to make new demands as Jagan compromised on earlier ones. As cited in Ronald Radosh's essential *American Labor and United States Foreign Policy,* the London *Times,* in a detailed series, wrote that the overthrow of Jagan's government "was engineered largely by the CIA."[13] The cover was "a London-based international trades union secretariat, the Public Services International." As coups go, the *Times* reported, "it was not expensive: over five years the CIA paid out something over 250,000 pounds. . . . For the colony . . . the result was about 170 dead, untold hundreds wounded, roughly ten million pounds' worth of damage to the economy and a legacy of racial bitterness."

The British government used the riots and the strike as proof that Jagan could not govern, and suspended the constitution, providing eventually a new one along lines that Washington approved. The new constitution provided for proportional representation in Parliament, which later permitted Burnham's People's National Congress and the right-wing United Force to form a coalition government. Although the Kennedy administration pushed for proportional representation, it is an electoral form that has seldom been used in the United States. The conclusion is obvious; it was a device to remove Jagan from power.

The point is not that Jagan was better qualified to be prime minister than Burnham; that was, and is, a question for the people of Guyana to decide. The point is that the United States again intervened in the domestic affairs of a state, not out of concern for the welfare of the people of that state but to serve Washington's selfish and essentially counterrevolutionary purposes.

John Kennedy's preoccupation with Latin America took various forms. They ranged from interventionism to the Alliance for Progress, reflecting his ambivalence; even the Alliance itself reflected it. There is no reason to doubt that Kennedy wanted to help the people of Latin America, most of whom seemed doomed to lives of poverty, disease, and despair, that melancholy trinity that has been invoked so often that it has lost its concrete meaning. Although months of reading Kennedy's speeches leads one to wonder how much of their soaring rhetoric was born of conviction and how much from a desire to bedazzle contemporary and future chroniclers, the idea of the Alliance was good, and, if it has failed, there were still certain specific achievements in health and education, housing and economic development that might never have been registered without it. It is a complex and difficult subject, requiring a book to itself.[14] But there can be little doubt, as was recognized even during the Kennedy years, that "reality did not match the rhetoric which flowed about the Alliance on both sides of the Rio Grande." [15]

The Alliance certainly had a hopeful beginning. Less than two months after he took office, Kennedy invited all the Latin American ambassadors to the White House to announce the birth of "a new Alliance for Progress . . . a vast, cooperative effort, unparalleled in magnitude and nobility of purpose, to satisfy the basic needs of the American people for homes, work and land, health and schools . . . a plan to transform the 1960s into a historic decade of democratic progress." [16] The speech was broadcast across the hemisphere by the Voice of America, and enthusiastic Latinos proclaimed that not since Franklin D. Roosevelt had such words by an American President been heard.

The appropriate ministers of the members of the Organization of American States met in August 1961 at Punta del Este, Uruguay, to give shape to the Alianza. They heard Secretary of the Treasury C. Douglas Dillon declare that the United States would devote $20 billion over the next ten years to those American nations that would commit themselves to economic and social reform. There was enormous enthusiasm and optimism. Two years later President Kennedy, at a news conference, made this candid and cheerless statement:

Well, I am always depressed, to an extent, by the size of the problems that we face in Latin America, with the population increases, the drop in commodity prices, and all the rest. We sometimes feel that we are not going ahead. In addition, in nearly every country there are serious domestic problems.

On the other hand, there have been some changes in Latin America which I think are encouraging. I think there has been a common recognition that there is the necessity for revolution in Latin America, and it is either going to be peaceful or bloody. But there must be progress, there must be a revolution. In my opinion, it can be peaceful. In my opinion, given time and concentrated effort on behalf of all of us, in Latin America, and in this country, we can bring about success.

So I think the Alliance for Progress should be pursued, its efforts should be intensified. Wherever it has failed, if it has failed, and it has failed, of course, to some degree, because the problems are almost insuperable, and for years the United States ignored them, and for years so did some of the groups in Latin America themselves, but now we are attempting, we have a program, I think we should pursue it. I think we should do more about it. I am not sure that we are giving still enough attention to Latin America.

What I find to be almost incomprehensible are those who speak about Cuba all the time, and yet are not willing to give the kind of assistance and the kind of support to assist other countries of Latin

America to develop themselves in a peaceful way. So I say on the second anniversary, we have a long, long way to go, and in fact in some ways the road seems longer than it was when the journey started. But I think we ought to keep at it.[17]

What went wrong with the Alliance? It can hardly be blamed entirely on John Kennedy. Part of the problem was that in most of the Latin American nations neither the will nor the people necessary for change of such dimension could be found at the top levels of government. The instruments of change were largely nonexistent. But it took Kennedy a while to comprehend that the United States, with all its resources, with all its self-confidence, with all its intelligence and energy, cannot remake the world. The job is too big even for America. Further, Kennedy learned that the machinery of his own government was painfully, infuriatingly slow to respond to reality.

Yet even if one concedes that the problems were bigger than Kennedy recognized, that he overreached himself, even if one concedes that his rhetoric raised hopes unrealistically high, the Alianza could have done better than it did. Its major failing was again Kennedy's misunderstanding of the revolutionary situation. In his fine book *Pax Americana,* Ronald Steel argues that the Alliance "has almost totally failed as an instrument of social reform because it was never able to project a mystique to galvanize the Latin Americans. Yet without the mystique and without the social change, the Alianza is nothing more than another foreign-aid program, better than some, worse than others—depending on which Latin American country one considers." [18]

Arthur Schlesinger, who was one of Kennedy's foremost advisers on Latin America, saw it in somewhat similar terms.

> One sometimes felt that the communists, operating on a shoestring in city universities or back-country villages, were reaching the people who mattered for the future—the students, the intellectuals, the labor leaders, the nationalist militants—while our billions were bringing us into contact only with governments of doubtful good faith and questionable life expectancy. Latin American democratic leaders themselves began to express increasing concern about the "degeneration" of the Alliance into a bilateral and technical program without political drive or continental vision.[19]

The Alianza could have had this "continental vision," this "mystique," probably did have it in the first hopeful months. No American President since Roosevelt had such capacity to invest a program with these elusive but essential qualities, but Kennedy could not sustain it. He wanted change, but he wanted stanch anti-communism as well, and leaders who could provide both were rare indeed.

> The Alianza was also hobbled by its preoccupation with communism. When the chips were down, the oligarchies and the generals who backed them up knew that Washington's fear of communism was even greater than its desire for reform. If reform could be connected with communism and social stability made to seem a bulwark against communist penetration, the structural reforms could be quietly dropped by the wayside. The lesson was easily drawn and, in the wake of the Bay of Pigs, it was soon applied. Encouraged by Washington's fear of communism and by its preference for verbally anti-communist regimes, would-be *caudillos*—usually trained and equipped by the United States—moved in to depose a number of legally elected governments. Within the first four years after the Alianza was launched at Punta del Este, civilian governments were toppled by the military in no less than seven countries: the Dominican Republic (twice), Guatemala, Ecuador, Bolivia, Argentina, Peru and Brazil.[20]

Obviously the kind of Latin American government that provides a welcome climate for the investment of American corporations is not likely to be reform-minded. Nor when Kennedy needed votes to exclude Cuba from the OAS or to impose economic and political sanctions was he likely to get them from reform governments. Thus Kennedy could hardly promote a "continental vision" of reform while wooing right-wing dictators. He could not have it both ways.

There is a terrible irony here: Castro no doubt was largely responsible for the birth of the Alianza, yet the attempt to use it against him was largely responsible for its failure. It succeeded neither in seriously weakening Castro nor in substantially furthering the cause of social and economic reform in Latin America. Students of irony might want to add that Cuba did better economically in the early 1960s than most of the Alliance members.

Kennedy was the father not only of the Alliance for Progress but of the United Nations Development Decade as well. In his first speech at the United Nations, in September 1961, he suggested that the General Assembly proclaim the 1960s as the Decade of Development, with the rich nations and the poor working together to raise the standard of living in the developing countries. This proposal too was adopted enthusiastically, and it too was a failure. Again, the problems were enormous, and again the nations involved often had neither sufficient will nor sufficient numbers of trained people to do what was necessary. There were the now customary bureaucratic problems, in both the United Nations and the host countries, and the haggling over which nations were to get what. No minor factor was the failure of the richer nations to make adequate contributions to the United Nations development funds. And the United States lagged well behind the level of contributions it itself had suggested as the goal: 1 per cent of the gross national product. So too did the Soviet Union.

President Kennedy wanted to spend more money on foreign aid, not only because he believed in it for its own sake but because he saw it as an essential counter to communism. But foreign aid during the Kennedy years was cut as never before. For fiscal 1963, for instance, he asked Congress for $4.9 billion. By the time Congress got through with his request—despite an intensive campaign in its behalf—it was slashed to $3.2 billion, the largest cut in the history of foreign aid. It is hard to say why. Perhaps Congress, which had always had to be bludgeoned into large foreign-aid appropriations, had finally tired of spending huge sums that seemed to profit the United States little. Perhaps it had wearied of the argument, pushed again by Kennedy, that foreign aid was a bulwark against communism. Certainly it had never been much impressed by the argument that it was the obligation of the United States to help the poorer nations. Nor was it even persuaded by the argument that it was in the national interest not to let the gap between the rich and poor nations grow. Probably a sense of disillusion over Vietnam contributed. Whatever the reason, this was a bitter defeat for Kennedy, yet its impact on development was not so great as it might seem. As Kennedy pointed out in one of his desperate attempts to forestall the ax, "Over half of it is directly tied to arms assistance, which means that it represents an additional appropriation, in a sense, for the Pentagon." [21] What has been labeled as foreign aid has often been more than half military aid. This not only more deeply involved the United States with governments that were usually right-wing, but almost always hurt the economy of the recipient nation. Although these governments were eager to get planes, tanks, etc., often because they helped them stay in power, they had to raise substantial sums for recurring expenses—pay, quarters, food, etc.—that could better have been used for economic development.

The Food for Peace program was also born under Kennedy. It was a good idea—using American surplus food products to help poor nations in their economic development—and unquestionably the program did a great deal of good, but it has been learned recently that in past years some recipient nations sold the food to raise money for military purposes, a direct contradiction of what was intended. It is not yet clear how much of this maneuvering, if any, took place during the Kennedy years. Perhaps none, but successive administrations have become so skilled at using tax money in devious military ways that one remains skeptical.

Although Kennedy's ventures into the Third World were motivated by his anti-communist impulse as well as by his humanitarian concern, that concern was real. It manifested itself in his genuine affection for Africa and its people, his understanding of nonalignment, his generous feelings toward the poor and the despairing. This concern led to one of Kennedy's most lasting accomplishments: the establishment of the Peace Corps, one of the few original and creative programs devised since the end of World War II. Unlike most other Kennedy programs in the foreign field, it was entirely an expression of American idealism. Developed from an idea of Hubert Humphrey's, it might have been John Kennedy's most enduring contribution had not another legacy, the Vietnam war and the foreign policy it came to symbolize, lessened the appeal of the Peace Corps. Not only foreign countries but many young Americans became suspicious of the Peace Corps, and many Americans became reluctant to serve, even in such a useful and imaginative way, a government they had come to distrust. The language President Kennedy used in establishing the Peace Corps was less rhetorical than was customary for him on such occasions but—or perhaps thus—more eloquent.

The initial reactions to the Peace Corps proposal are convincing proof that we have, in this country, an immense reservoir of such men and women—anxious to sacrifice their energies and time and toil to the cause of world peace and human progress. . . .

Life in the Peace Corps will not be easy. There will be no salary and allowances will be at a level sufficient only to maintain health and meet basic needs. Men and women will be expected to work and live alongside the nationals of the country in which they are stationed—doing the same work, eating the same food, talking the same language.

But if the life will not be easy, it will be rich and satisfying. For every young American who participates in the Peace Corps—who works in a foreign land—will know that he or she is sharing in the great common task of bringing to man that decent way of life which is the foundation of freedom and a condition of peace.[22]

What a different world it would have been if the John Kennedy who sent idealistic young volunteers to the villages of Africa, Asia, and Latin America had prevailed over the John Kennedy who sent young soldiers to the jungles of South Vietnam. By the end of Kennedy's first year he had met his goal of 500 Peace Corps volunteers overseas. By March 1963 the number had swelled to 5000, and in another year, 10,000, about half the number of troops in Vietnam.

Although Kennedy did not share the obsession of the Eisenhower–Dulles years that NATO was central to all America's foreign concerns, his thinking on the question was wholly conventional. "NATO has kept the peace of Europe and the Atlantic through twelve dangerous years. . . ."[23] This has long been an article of faith in Washington, and the proof offered has been simplicity itself: NATO has existed, and so has peace between the Soviet bloc and the West; ergo, NATO is responsible for the peace. It is impossible to resist quoting from a letter to *The New York Times* by Charles Sheldon of Amherst, Massachusetts, dated February 23, 1971:

. . . Consider the similarity of this reasoning to the story about the man who travels over the hills of New England ringing a bell. His purpose, so he says, is to keep the elephants away. When someone —seeing the absurdity of this argument—points out that there are no elephants in New England, the man with the bell beams. "Pretty effective method, isn't it?"

Although a discussion of NATO merits fuller treatment than this, a respectable argument can be made that Russia never intended a military adventure into Western Europe, that there was simply no need for NATO, and that its existence did more to increase tensions than to preserve the peace.

Nonetheless, although Kennedy was determined to do whatever he could to maintain and increase the strength of NATO, his view was sophisticated. He understood that a decrease in East–West tensions and the passage of time would inevitably diminish the sense of urgency that had brought NATO into being. He understood also that as the strength of Western Europe grew, its dependence on the United States would wane and so would its willingness to be dominated by Washington. He understood that to oppose such inevitable trends would be futile and harmful to what he saw as an Atlantic partnership. Thus the President encouraged unity within Western Europe and did all he could to influence the Common Market to admit Great Britain. He made his view plain in a speech at NATO headquarters in Naples on July 2, 1963:

> It is increasingly clear that the United States and Western Europe are tightly bound by shared goals and mutual respect. On both sides of the Atlantic, trade barriers are being reduced, military cooperation is increasing, and the cause of Atlantic unity is being promoted. There will always be honest differences among friends; and they should be freely and frankly discussed. But these are differences of means, not ends. They are differences of approach, not spirit. Our efforts and techniques of consultation must be improved. We must strengthen our efforts in such fields as monetary payments, foreign assistance, and agriculture. But, recognizing these and other problems, I return to the United States more firmly convinced than ever that common ideals have given us all a common destiny—that together we can serve our own people and all humanity—and that the Atlantic partnership is a growing reality.[24]

This is a view that many Americans have shared, particularly that enormously influential group of moderates and moderate-liberals often called the East Coast Establishment. The goal of Kennedy and this group—a genuine, deeply felt goal—was "Atlantic partnership," with the United States as senior partner. What they did not understand was that the Russians inevitably saw efforts at formalization of these natural Western ties as Washington's attempt to recruit Western Europe into an anti-Soviet compact, giving further dimension to the military pact that already existed in NATO. Russia saw this "Atlantic partnership" as the latest installment of the old Washington story, "peace through strength." It would have been better if Kennedy had just relaxed on this matter, in the confidence that the natural course of events would keep Western Europe close to the United States.

On this question, however, Kennedy's chief adversary was not Khrushchev but De Gaulle, who had a different vision from Kennedy's. He saw Western Europe, eventually all Europe, as a powerful Third Force, independent of both the United States and the Soviet Union, capable of mediating between them. France, needless to say, would be the leading influence in this new Europe. An Atlantic partnership, as De Gaulle saw it, would mean perpetual European subordination to *"les Anglo-Saxons."* This was his basic reason for keeping Britain out of the Common Market; he saw Britain, with its "special relationship" to the United States, as a means of preserving American dominance within the Atlantic Community. There was some basis for De Gaulle's concern. Part of it was vanity; he did not want Paris subordinate to Washington. But there was more to it than that. History has demonstrated that a divided Europe contributes more to tension than to peace. If peace, rather than the absence of war, is to come to Europe, barriers between East and West will have to be reduced. The enlistment of Western Europe in the American camp can only preserve barriers, not reduce them. Unity through division is a contradiction of terms—a lesson, however, that should be learned in Moscow as well as in Washington.

De Gaulle's concerns had a military dimension too. That is why he drastically lessened French participation in NATO, and that is why he developed his own nuclear deterrent, the *force de frappe.* The development of his own nuclear force was no doubt vain, in both senses of the word. But was De Gaulle as absurd as many Americans have contended, during the Kennedy years and after, in questioning whether the United States would always, under any circumstances, expose itself to nuclear destruction to protect Western Europe? The answer, of course, is no. It is entirely true that in the past quarter-century any attack on Western Europe would have been countered by an American military response, including, if necessary, nuclear weapons. But can any country depend indefinitely on another for its physical defense? De Gaulle, for example, rallied loyally to Kennedy's side during the Cuban missile crisis, but did not that crisis confirm his long-term doubts about America's reliability? It could very easily have escalated into nuclear war—indeed, that danger was only a matter of hours or, at most, days away—yet though the United States had embarked on a course that very likely could have involved Western Europe in nuclear warfare, these countries were not consulted.

It was to answer such concerns and to try to persuade West Germany not to develop its own nuclear capability that Kennedy pursued one of the most futile goals of his administration: the multilateral force (MLF). It is hard to say exactly what began this attempt to square the circle, a plan that would give the European allies more say in the nuclear deterrent. Arthur Schlesinger was also unable to find a source. The best he could offer was: "These suggestions were evidently responsive to sentiment of some sort in Europe; but the nature of this sentiment remained hard to define. Clearly there was no popular pressure for the [nuclear] weapons. But a discontent with the American monopoly was rising in top military and government circles." [25]

In brief, the problem was this. Kennedy had no intention, and rightly so, of allowing any other nation access to the nuclear button. Either the United States would share that terrible responsibility or it wouldn't. The multilateral force, which sent high-ranking Kennedy officials flying off to European capitals and flying back with solemn statements for the press, was an attempt to disguise the fact that Washington, and Washington alone, would decide whether or not to use nuclear weapons. There were some fairly ingenious disguises, such as naval forces with mixed crews, but the only people to be fooled—although it is hard to take their protests seriously—were the Russians. Since of the Allies only the West Germans showed any real interest in the plan (the others expressed only polite interest), the Russians, always suspicious, however unlikely their suspicions, could proclaim that MLF was a nefarious scheme to allow the "revanchist" Germans to get their hands near the nuclear button. The Russians refused to believe, publicly at least, that just the opposite was intended, for there were few Allied leaders, even a generation after the war, keen on allowing the Germans to have nuclear weapons, their own or NATO's. The project eventually faded away, the victim of self-contradictions that should have been obvious from the beginning. Further, the idea of a nuclear submarine, or even a surface ship, manned by a mixed crew of Americans, British, Italians, Germans, French, etc., could lend comfort only to the enemy and/or cartoonists.

It is quite understandable that Kennedy and De Gaulle should find themselves at odds, for they held mutually exclusive views of Europe. It is less understandable that Kennedy and Macmillan should find themselves for a moment at the point of a public break, for they held each other in the highest regard personally and shared similar views on most issues. But the break almost happened in late 1962 as the brief but gaudy Skybolt flap shook London and Washington.

Eisenhower had agreed that the United States would undertake all the costs of research and development for the Skybolt, an airborne ballistic missile, allowing the British to buy it for only the production cost. Thus Britain, for reasons of national pride, would be able to maintain an independent deterrent, the mark in the postwar world of great-power status. In the early months of 1962, Defense Secretary McNamara concluded that Skybolt was costing too much and was not sufficiently reliable—another of the awesomely expensive weapons systems upon which billions were spent before its usefulness was demonstrated. He recommended to Kennedy that it be canceled. Kennedy agreed but, recognizing that the British government had a great political stake in Skybolt, ordered that the British be informed in plenty of time before the decision to cancel was announced. The British were promptly informed, Ambassador David Ormsby-Gore predicting, accurately, that this would be "political dynamite" in London. Then, after some preliminary talks, each capital sat around waiting for the other to make alternate proposals. Neither did, and eventually the decision to cancel leaked out. The British press was eager to leap on the charges by some of Macmillan's associates that this was an attempt by Washington to force Britain to surrender its independent deterrent; it was widely known that many within the Kennedy administration believed it was silly for Britain to maintain a deterrent that was not only inadequate but gave Washington problems with other allies who wanted to be in the nuclear club.

All this developed in the autumn of 1962, when Kennedy was preoccupied with the missile crisis and its aftermath. Finally, when the situation had come to full boil and the Anglo–American alliance was in disarray, Kennedy and Macmillan met at Nassau just before Christmas. Kennedy first offered to patch up the Skybolt proposal, but Macmillan turned that down because by now its technical shortcomings were public knowledge—"the lady had been violated in public." Macmillan now wanted Polaris missiles and he wanted them as an independent force, not as part of MLF. Kennedy, of course, was willing to give Polaris, but as part of MLF to avoid aggravating his problems with the French and the Germans. Macmillan insisted, implying that he would put the Tories on an anti-American course if Kennedy deprived Britain of the independent nuclear role its great history demanded. Kennedy agreed, and the President and the Prime Minister turned the problem over to the masters of ambiguity on their staffs, who drew up an agreement suitably imprecise, so that Britain got what it wanted without flaunting it in the faces of the French and the Germans. This story is instructive not for its inherent significance but as an illustration of how even two closely allied nations in daily and intimate contact can stumble into a public controversy that could easily have been avoided.[26]

By now it is hardly a secret that one of the fundamental theses of this book is that John Kennedy was an entirely conventional Cold Warrior. Nowhere is this more apparent than in his dealings with mainland China. Although there is comparatively little on the public record about China, most of what there is is unrelentingly hostile. This opposition, of course, was the standard Washington position of the previous two administrations, but Kennedy, like those before and after him, did not seem to recognize that Peking's hostility toward Washington was based on Washington's long and continuing hostility toward Peking, which found expression not only in words but in a series of specific acts, political, economic, and military.

In an interview, Dean Rusk told me that Kennedy was much harder on China, less willing to consider a more flexible approach, than Lyndon Johnson. Kennedy's approach was no different from Dulles's: be firm, and eventually, once the Chinese find that there are no rewards for aggression, they'll fall in line. Roger Hilsman put it this way:

> Although it was certainly true that United States policy needed to be more flexible than in the past, what everyone had to understand was that before increased flexibility would work there probably also had to be more firmness. So long as the Chinese felt that aggression and their policy of hardline intransigence were successful, they would hardly turn to "peaceful coexistence." Basically, it was this policy that combined firmness with flexibility that had not only checked the expansionism of the Soviet Union but had done so without war.[27]

The President did not waste time in making his views known. Though his new administration could have raised matters of substance with the Chinese, such as mutual steps to improve Chinese–American relations, he announced on February 1, in his second news conference, that he had "asked for a delay in the meetings which take place in Warsaw, between the United States representative and that of the Chinese communists, from February to March because they have become merely a matter of form and nothing of substance happened." [28] And in that same press conference he asserted that growing communist Chinese strength was a reason for studying whether the United States had sufficient military nuclear and conventional strength.

On March 3, 1961, following a meeting with Prime Minister Keith Holyoake of New Zealand, a joint statement was issued that contained this paragraph: "President Kennedy and Prime Minister Holyoake noted with deep concern the hostile and aggressive attitude of the Chinese communist regime and the particular menace it poses to the peace of Asia, Africa, and Latin America." [29]

Again, it was an indictment with no bill of particulars as to *how* China threatened the peace. And on August 2, after a meeting with Vice President Chen Cheng of Nationalist China, the White House issued a statement saying that the United States would again oppose the seating of mainland China in the United

Nations. In the statement Kennedy hailed the improvement in the standard of living on Taiwan and went so far as to assert that "in contrast to the disregard for human rights manifested by the Chinese communist regime, this record was accomplished without violence to the great traditions and human values which have been cherished throughout history by the Chinese people." [30] Kennedy presumably knew that the Chiang Kai-shek government was a police state imposed on an unwilling Taiwanese people.

According to Schlesinger, Kennedy "considered the state of our relations with communist China as irrational" and "did not exclude the possibility of doing something to change them in the course of his administration." [31] But there is little in the public record to substantiate that view. He instructed Adlai Stevenson to keep China out of the United Nations during the 1961 General Assembly, clearly because he did not want to raise a domestic political fuss. He repeated these instructions in 1962 and 1963. In October 1961, Kennedy had a chance to move toward an improvement in Chinese–American relations, when Foreign Minister Chen Yi said China would be willing to talk at the foreign-minister level, provided the United States took the initiative. (This was a bit of face-saving, for Chen Yi's statement was in fact the initiative.) Yet Kennedy turned him down flat. "We have not seen any evidence as yet that the Chinese communists wish to live in comity with us, and our desire is to live in friendship with all people. But we have not seen that attitude manifested. In fact, just a few days ago there was a statement about Berlin that was quite bellicose." [32] It was a rather weak rejoinder from the President who had declared in his inaugural address that "we would never fear to negotiate."

On November 29, Kennedy made a statement that put him, to a degree at least, with those who in 1949 had charged Harry Truman with "losing" China.

> But my—I've always felt, and I think history will record, that the change of China from being a country friendly to us to a country which is unremittingly hostile affected very strongly the balance of power in the world. And while there were—there still is, of course, room for argument as to whether any United States actions would have changed the course of events there, I think a greater effort would have been wiser. I said it in '49, so it isn't totally hindsight.[33]

The events of twelve years seemed only to have reinforced I. tendency to think in Cold War clichés. He also subscribed to another cliché, that the Chinese were indifferent to human life. "These Chinese are tough. It isn't just what they say about us but what they say about the Russians. They are in the Stalinist phase, believe in class war and the use of force, and seem prepared to sacrifice 300 million people if necessary to dominate Asia." [34]

In 1962 the hard-liners in the Kennedy administration supported Chiang Kai-shek's proposal that he be allowed to invade the mainland. This proposal, which seems even more absurd than the Bay of Pigs, had some supporters who argued that China was ready for a revolt that could be sparked by an invasion and that the Sino–Soviet rivalry made it less likely that Russia would help China. Fortunately, Kennedy scotched that plan and had his representative at Warsaw tell the Chinese representative that the United States would not support a Nationalist invasion. But to make sure that no one could accuse him of protecting the communists, Kennedy covered up this sensible move by calling attention to a Chinese buildup on the mainland opposite the Nationalist-held islands of Quemoy and Matsu. He declared that the United States would take any action necessary to defend Taiwan, and he ostentatiously reinforced the Seventh Fleet offshore. The President did not feel it necessary to speculate that perhaps the Chinese buildup was in response to Chiang Kai-shek's threat to invade the mainland.

When in the fall of 1962 mainland China initiated a series of border clashes along the Indian frontier, Kennedy moved instinctively to help India. Not only was he sympathetic to India but he was convinced that India and China were waging a titanic struggle to develop themselves, which would have vast influence all over Asia. He thought that if China succeeded and India failed, the interests of the West and of democracy would be severely affected. This is a variation of the domino theory, but it is not so certain that the Asian nations see things in such simplistic, symbolic terms. Each will, no doubt, learn something from the successes and failures of its neighbors, but each will probably be most responsive to local conditions, if outside forces leave it alone.

But Kennedy had more immediate reasons for helping India. Any foe of China was a friend of the United States—Russia not cessarily excepted. Also, helping India might cause it to use its influence—given a higher estimate in New Delhi and Washington than elsewhere—in a friendlier way than it had in the past. Whatever the proportion of various reasons, Kennedy moved to exploit the border conflict as proof of Chinese aggressive expansionism. He could hardly be expected to point out that communist China's territorial claims were exactly those of Nationalist China, and that China did not go beyond those claims even when India's army had demonstrated its helplessness. Nor, apparently, did he examine the evidence suggesting that perhaps India had provoked the attacks. No doubt China's resort to force had the effect desired by Kennedy, but it may have had another effect as well: to demonstrate China's power.

China was about to succeed Russia as Kennedy's adversary, another result of the Cuban missile crisis. "By 1963," as Schlesinger wrote, "Kennedy and Macmillan were reaching the conclusion that China presented the long-term danger to the peace." [35] This could be termed proof by repetition. Again, no bill of particulars. Chinese troops had left Chinese soil twice in thirteen years—once for Korea, after China had explicitly warned the United States not to cross the 38th parallel and after Douglas MacArthur's forces had pushed right up to the Chinese border. The other time was in the Indian–Chinese border region, but there the Chinese moved only as far as the limits of the territory China had claimed for generations. It is true, of course, that such border disputes should be settled by negotiation, but the same could be said of India, which in December 1961 seized the Portuguese enclave of Goa by force. Despite these two instances, if deeds and not words are to be the criterion, China's foreign policy through the end of 1963 —and since—has been far more cautious than the United States'.

Although some have suggested that in a second term Kennedy would have sought an improvement in relations with China, there is little in the public record to sustain such a belief. As late as eight days before his death, Kennedy made this statement.

> We are not planning to trade with Red China in view of the policy that Red China pursues. When the Red Chinese indicate a desire to live at peace with the United States, with other countries surrounding it, then quite obviously the United States would reappraise its policies. We are not wedded to a policy of hostility to Red

China. It seems to me Red China's policies are what create the tension between not only the United States and Red China but between Red China and India, between Red China and her immediate neighbors to the south, and even between Red China and other communist countries.[36]

No doubt the hard line followed by Kennedy—and those who preceded and followed him—has hurt the People's Republic, but who can any longer doubt that it, as well as being wrong, has hurt the United States and the non-Chinese people of Asia even more. Yet again John Kennedy demonstrated his lack of understanding of the postwar world.

Before closing, I must say a few words about President Kennedy's foreign-policy advisers—only a few, for this book is based on the premise that a President is responsible for all that takes place in his administration. Yet much about a man can be learned from those he chooses to be close to him. Obviously there were individual differences, but something of a group profile can be attempted. They were youngish but wedded to the old Cold War visions. They were intellectuals but understood the new world no better than the old businessmen of the Eisenhower years. They were liberal—by self-definition—but prosecuted the Cold War more vigorously than had the Eisenhower conservatives. They were realists, they thought, but their advice, during Kennedy's term and after, led to a series of disasters, each of which confirmed them in their wisdom. They had an enormous appetite for work, an insatiable thirst for facts, an impregnable self-confidence, and, above all, a passion for the exercise of power. They were a tough, hard-nosed (such terms were regarded as complimentary) elite, awesomely articulate, the finest products, in their view, of social Darwinism. They would remake the world in their image, and the world would be grateful. They sought peace, but it was to be America's kind of peace at America's terms.

They spoke, and seemed to think, in a higher jargon: Free World, commitment, graduated response, firm but flexible, fruits of aggression, credibility, deterrence, national interest—portentous terms that disguised the poverty of their perception. Of all those who so spoke, foremost was the President. No one in postwar political life was more skilled at investing such code words with a somber significance that did not permit of further discussion. These and similar terms, evoking as they did patriotism, honor, courage, resolution, became the semantic screen behind which the Kennedy administration executed an unimaginative, often dangerous foreign policy. Rhetoric gave a semantic disguise to militarism.

There were few mavericks among them. Stevenson, scorned by many of them for his "fuzzy idealism," was consigned to the outer circle, at the United Nations, where he was, nonetheless, the best United Nations Ambassador the United States has had. Chester Bowles was exiled, and the most maverick of the bunch, Robert Kennedy, was still in the developing stage. The bureaucratic infighting of resourceful, ambitious, and determined men is fascinating, particularly when the struggle is at the very pinnacle of world power. But that, if anyone is still interested, is a story for someone else. However, the smaller story of Kennedy's treatment of Chester Bowles reveals a great deal about Kennedy the man and President. Bowles was one of Kennedy's earliest and most loyal supporters for the Presidency, and a leading adviser on foreign affairs. After the election, Kennedy named him as Dean Rusk's first deputy in the State Department. He was instrumental in recruiting superior men for ambassadorships and in stimulating some new thinking in the department. For both these efforts he aroused the enmity of the old foreign-service officers who resented the New Frontier. Bowles was right on the Bay of Pigs, and in the fall of 1961, when the administration was moving toward its first big decisions to intervene in Vietnam, he suggested that the entire area be neutralized. Roger Hilsman writes: "As far as I know, President Kennedy did not make any specific comment on this suggestion, but my sense of his attitude is that he accepted the concept as a far-seeing expression of the ultimate goal for Southeast Asia toward which we should work, but that its time had not yet come." [37] Since neutralism was just what the National Liberation Front was calling for in South Vietnam, a Kennedy decision to explore this possibility could well have meant avoidance of the entire Vietnam tragedy.

Although a good case can be made that Bowles was a most valuable man in the State Department, Kennedy soon decided that he had to go. He liked Bowles, admired his thoughtful and im native suggestions, but saw no other way to shake up a departme whose lack of responsiveness had distressed him. To remove Rusk would, as Schlesinger put it, "constitute too severe a comment on his original judgment." [38] The conclusion was that Bowles had not succeeded in running the department, although he had not been given the authority to do so. Yet Bowles—as a successful businessman, as director of the Office of Price Administration in World War II, and as Governor of Connecticut—had more executive experience than anyone else there.

One gets the feeling that Bowles's chief offense was that he was not in the New Frontier style. When with the President, he could not depart from his normal spacious, discursive discussion of a question in favor of the crisp, decisive response preferred by Kennedy. He was seen as a bit too sentimental, a bit too fuzzy, much like Stevenson. They were not the bright young men that Kennedy admired, but the fact is that they were often right when the bright young New Frontiersmen were wrong. In banishing Bowles from the inner circle and making him a special roving Ambassador— the banishment was postponed until November 1961 after a newspaper furor in July gave him a temporary reprieve—and in seldom seeking Stevenson's counsel, Kennedy made himself a prisoner of those advisers, the majority, who sought military solutions to political problems. Both Bowles and Stevenson saw the dangers, and the futility, of sending soldiers to do diplomats' work. The question is not the injustice to Bowles, although the episode is less than edifying, but the disservice to the nation. It is a nice irony that these public servants of an older generation were much more imaginative and innovative in their thinking than their brisk juniors, who were the subject of such awed respect from journalists, who themselves—it is an occupational hazard—often value brevity and crispness above substance. Bowles and Stevenson, who were not academicians, valued thoughtfulness and nuance more than those who were.

One is reluctant to make a final judgment of John Kennedy, but he does not lack his eloquent advocates. Probably he will live most vividly through history in the pages of Arthur Schlesinger's book. It is an appealing picture, vital, intelligent, humorous, and

ɔic, and since I draw so different a conclusion, it is only fair in
ɛse final pages to quote again those words that began this chap-
er.

> Yet he had accomplished so much: the new hope for peace on
> earth, the elimination of nuclear testing in the atmosphere, and abo-
> lition of nuclear diplomacy, the new policies toward Latin America
> and the Third World, the reordering of American defense. . . . The
> energies he released, the standards he set, the purposes he inspired,
> the goals he established would guide the land he loved for years to
> come. Above all he gave the world for an imperishable moment the
> vision of a leader who greatly understood the terror and the hope,
> the diversity and the possibility, of life on this planet and who made
> people look beyond nation and race to the future of humanity. So
> the people of the world grieved as if they had terribly lost their own
> leader, friend, brother.

Arthur Schlesinger wrote those words not as the gifted historian
he is but as grieving friend and colleague. That is proper, for seldom should anything be put before friendship and loyalty, but, as
Schlesinger knows better than most of us, one man's truth, no matter how deeply and genuinely felt, is not necessarily another's. It
would be presumptuous for me to say that my truth is nearer *the*
truth, that my separation from John Kennedy in time and space
and attitude more than compensates for the intimate knowledge
that Arthur Schlesinger, Theodore Sorensen, Pierre Salinger,
Roger Hilsman had of the man. Yet I must believe it to be so. I
am no enemy, although some may think otherwise, of John Kennedy. And it seems cruel to judge a man who died such a death so
young, who had so little time in office. But if ever a man demands
judgment it is he who offers himself for and is elected to the most
powerful position on earth. John Kennedy's time was short, but
much happened in those "thousand days" and we live still with
their legacy. Others may dispute my judgment, may think it too
harsh. They may be right, but it was the only judgment I could
make, based on a study of the public record, of John Kennedy's
own words, and of the tributes written to him. Indeed, virtually all
my research has been based on John Kennedy's own words and
deeds and on the words of his friends, certainly not hostile testimony. From the same evidence I have drawn a different conclusion.

There can be no doubt that the impact of John Kennedy's death was, the world over, extraordinary beyond description, in turns numbing and hysterical. No doubt, too, this impact resulted from more even than the circumstances of his death. John Kennedy was a symbol of youth, of hope, of change in a world that desperately needed change. He was a symbol of enormous value in a dreary world, but a symbol cannot endure unless it is based on substance. My conviction is that the symbolism of John F. Kennedy, shining and universal as it was at the hour of his death and for months afterward, was based not on achievement but on personality. All those things that have so often been written about—his physical appeal, his grace, his style, his wit, his physical courage, his family—made John Kennedy the first television-star President, recognized in all but the most remote corners of the earth. But beneath all this radiance—and even now, eight years after his death, one can feel it—was an entirely conventional politician.

As Congressman and Senator, Kennedy was never a liberal, and as President he prosecuted the Cold War more vigorously, and thus more dangerously, than did Eisenhower and Dulles. It is true that five months before his death he publicly recognized, in the American University speech, that nuclear diplomacy was unacceptably dangerous, but only after he had taken the world to the brink of nuclear war. It is to his lasting credit that he urged the American people to re-examine its attitudes toward the Cold War, but he himself did not understand it and confused the entirely normal competition between the United States and the Soviet Union with the inevitable revolutionary struggle in Asia and Latin America. Thus, perhaps unknowingly, John Kennedy, with his Green Berets and his counterinsurgency programs and his swift and massive military buildup, became the great counterrevolutionary of the postwar world. What an irony. The great colonial powers had to surrender their colonies because, after World War II, they were no longer capable of controlling them. Whereas the United States, traditionally an anti-colonial power, assumed the counterrevolutionary struggle and, under John Kennedy, pressed it in Cuba and Vietnam and even in insignificant British Guiana. What a tragedy that the anti-communist impulse in Kennedy prevailed over his idealism, his genuine sympathy for the poor peoples of the world. One final irony: although neither could say so, both Robert and Edward Kennedy have campaigned against the foreign policies of their brother John.

Perhaps if he had not been in such a rush to get to the White House, John Kennedy would have served America better. Elected when he was, he did not change the course of American history but pushed to its logical, tragic conclusion in Vietnam the course begun by Harry Truman and carried on by Dwight Eisenhower. For Kennedy was not one to attempt to change America's sentiment; rather he was one to respond to its mood and exploit it. He moved back, not ahead as he had promised. A few years later, when the mood of the nation was changing, he might have successfully guided us through the difficult transition period, for his political gifts were unequaled. But that possibility, like what he might have done given another five years in office, is speculation.

There is tragedy enough in the Kennedy story, but if his admirers are correct, if he would have learned from the first years in Vietnam and changed the nation's course away from escalation, then the greatest tragedy of all is that Lyndon Johnson, with Kennedy's advisers at his side, carried on, at increasing and terrible cost, a policy that Kennedy himself would have abandoned as indefensible. But that, too, is speculation. All we are left with are those three short years. The record seems clear. Whatever his achievements in less significant areas, whatever he might have done later, John F. Kennedy as President was Cold Warrior and counterrevolutionary. Cuba, Berlin, Vietnam—those are his monuments.

Notes

Chapter One: *The Beginning*

1. Theodore C. Sorensen, *Kennedy* (New York, 1965), p. 758.
2. Harold Macmillan, quoted in Arthur M. Schlesinger, Jr., *A Thousand Days* (Boston, 1965), p. 1028.
3. Sorensen, op. cit., p. 509.
4. Roger Hilsman, *To Move a Nation* (New York, 1967), p. 53.
5. John F. Kennedy, *Public Papers of the President 1961–1963* (Washington, 1962–1964), 1961, p. 3.
6. Pierre Salinger, *With Kennedy* (New York, 1966), p. 138.
7. Kennedy, op. cit., 1961, pp. 19, 22 ff.
8. Schlesinger, op. cit., p. 301.
9. United States Senate, Commerce Committee (Senate, 87:1). *Senate Report 994, Part I: The Speeches, Remarks, Press Conferences, and Statements of John F. Kennedy, September 13, 1961; Part III: The Joint Appearance of Senator John F. Kennedy and Vice President Richard M. Nixon and Other Campaign Presentations, December 11, 1961,* Part I, p. 44.
10. *Senate Report 994,* Part I, pp. 297 ff.
11. Ibid., Part I, p. 347.
12. Sorensen, op. cit., p. 26.
13. Schlesinger, op. cit., p. 904.

Chapter Two: *The First Crisis*

1. Schlesinger, op. cit., p. 206.
2. Sorensen, op. cit., p. 640.
3. Bernard B. Fall, *Anatomy of a Crisis* (New York, 1969). Although good accounts of the Laos situation appear in Sorensen, Schlesinger, and Hilsman, this is fuller, more objective, and firsthand. I have relied heavily upon it.
4. From a review of the Fall book by the author, appearing in *The Nation,* May 19, 1969, p. 639.
5. United States House of Representatives, 86th Congress, Committee on Government Operations, *United States Aid Operations in Laos* (Washington, June 15, 1959), p. 8.
6. Fall, op. cit., p. 182.
7. Cited in Fall, op. cit., p. 186.

8. Cited in Fall, op. cit., p. 193.
9. Fall, op. cit., p. 198.
10. Schlesinger, op. cit., p. 329.
11. Cited in Schlesinger, op. cit., p. 332.
12. Hilsman, op. cit., p. 91.
13. Cited in Schlesinger, op. cit., p. 334.
14. Ibid., p. 337.
15. Hilsman, op. cit., p. 136.
16. Fall, op. cit., p. 229.
17. A good account of this period is given by Hilsman, who was intimately involved.
18. Hilsman, op. cit., p. 141.
19. Ibid., p. 152.
20. Associated Press dispatch, dated June 7, 1970, appearing in *The New York Times* of June 8.
21. Schlesinger, op. cit., p. 340. Hilsman, op. cit., pp. 154, 155.

Chapter Three: *The Bay of Pigs*

1. Hugh Sidey, *John F. Kennedy, President* (New York, 1965), p. 124.
2. John F. Kennedy, *The Strategy of Peace* (New York, 1961), pp. 172, 173.
3. Ibid., p. 168.
4. This and following campaign statements are from *Senate Report 994*, op. cit.
5. Schlesinger, op. cit., p. 220.
6. Ibid., p. 240.
7. Cited ibid., p. 251.
8. Ibid., p. 259.
9. Dean Acheson, Oral History interview, Kennedy Library.
10. Salinger, op. cit., p. 146.
11. The full story of the press and the Bay of Pigs has been told by Victor Bernstein and Jesse Gordon of *The Nation* in the Fall 1967 issue of the Columbia University *Forum*. The larger story of *The Press and the Cold War* is told in a book of that name by James Aronson (New York, 1970).
12. Robert A. Hurwitch, Oral History interview, Kennedy Library, pp. 12, 33.
13. Senator George Smathers, Oral History interview, Kennedy Library, p. 68.
14. Kennedy, *Public Papers, 1961*, p. 286.
15. Ibid., pp. 304 ff.
16. Sorensen, op. cit., p. 297.
17. Schlesinger, op. cit., p. 287.
18. Kennedy, *Public Papers, 1961*, pp. 334 ff.
19. Hilsman, op. cit., p. 30.
20. Sorensen, op. cit., p. 308.
21. Schlesinger, op. cit., p. 297.

Chapter Four: *The Military Buildup*

1. Sorensen, op. cit., p. 608.
2. Adam Yarmolinsky, *The Military Establishment* (New York, 1971).
3. A good study of this question is in David Horowitz, *The Free World Colossus* (New York, 1965), pp. 342 ff.
4. Cited ibid., p. 345.
5. A roundup of these data is provided in Horowitz, op. cit.
6. A good account of this incident is given by I. F. Stone in an article in the November 7, 1968, issue of *The New York Review of Books*.
7. Robert F. Kennedy, *Thirteen Days* (New York, 1969), p. 120.
8. Aida DiPace Donald, ed., *John F. Kennedy and the New Frontier* (New York, 1966), p. 132. Reprinted from *The American Review*, Winter 1963.
9. Seymour Melman, *Pentagon Capitalism* (New York, 1970), p. 6.

Chapter Five: *Vienna and Berlin*

1. Sorensen, op. cit., p. 584.
2. Schlesinger, op. cit., p. 404.
3. Christopher Lasch, article in *The Nation*, September 11, 1967.
4. Kennedy, *Strategy*, p. 255.
5. Cited in Schlesinger, op. cit., p. 381.
6. Sorensen, op. cit., p. 544.
7. Schlesinger, op. cit., p. 374.
8. Sorensen, op. cit., p. 550.
9. See Schlesinger, op. cit., p. 365.
10. Ibid., p. 348.
11. Kennedy, *Public Papers*, 1961, pp. 442, 444.
12. The Soviet *aide-mémoire* of June 4, 1961, handed by Khrushchev to Kennedy is moderate in tone and specific and reasonable in content. Department of State *Bulletin*, XLV, No. 1154 (August 7, 1961), 231–33.
13. Schlesinger, op. cit., p. 384.
14. Sorensen, op. cit., p. 588.
15. Schlesinger, op. cit., p. 391.
16. Kennedy, *Public Papers*, 1961, pp. 476, 477.
17. Schlesinger, op. cit., p. 385.
18. Ibid., pp. 397, 398.
19. Kennedy, *Public Papers*, 1961, pp. 533 ff.
20. Schlesinger, op. cit., p. 392.
21. Ibid., p. 395.
22. Sidey, op. cit., p. 202.
23. Ibid., p. 229.
24. See Schlesinger, op. cit., p. 852.
25. Ibid., p. 400.
26. Ibid.

Chapter Six: *Nuclear Testing*

1. Sorensen, op. cit., p. 26.
2. Kennedy, *Strategy*, p. 45.
3. Sorensen, op. cit., p. 618.
4. Schlesinger, op. cit., p. 454.
5. Kennedy, *Public Papers*, 1961, p. 693.
6. Horowitz, op. cit., p. 371.
7. Schlesinger, op. cit., p. 488.
8. Ibid., p. 496.
9. Ibid., p. 497.
10. Kennedy, *Public Papers*, 1962, p. 591.
11. Ibid., p. 644.
12. Ibid., p. 649.

Chapter Seven: *The Cuban Missile Crisis*

1. Sorensen, op. cit., p. 717.
2. Schlesinger, op. cit., p. 840.
3. David L. Larson, ed., *The Cuban Crisis of 1962* (Boston, 1963), p. 299. This contains a valuable collection of documents and a useful chronology.
4. Kennedy, *Public Papers*, 1961, p. 304.
5. For this account I am indebted to the Larson chronology.
6. See Schlesinger, op. cit., p. 783.
7. Elie Abel, *The Missile Crisis* (New York, 1966), p. 18.
8. Kennedy, *Public Papers*, 1962, p. 652.
9. Abel, op. cit., p. 19.
10. See Henry Pachter, *Collision Course* (New York, 1963). Abel's and Pachter's are very informative studies of the missile crisis. I have relied on both.
11. Department of State *Bulletin*, XLVII, No. 1213 (September 24, 1962), 450.
12. *The New York Times*, September 8, 1962, p. 2.
13. Kennedy, *Public Papers*, 1962, p. 665.
14. *The New York Times*, September 12, 1962, p. 16.
15. Department of State *Bulletin*, XLVII, No. 1220 (November 12, 1962), 734. Roger Hilsman mentions the passage quoted by Stevenson but does not discuss its significance.
16. Larson, op. cit., pp. 83, 103.
17. Department of State *Bulletin*, XLVII, No. 1219 (November 5, 1962), 706–708.
18. Schlesinger, op. cit., p. 391.
19. There are numerous accounts of those tense thirteen days and, since they substantially agree, there is little reason to doubt their essential accuracy. My account of the events—as distinguished from interpretation and conclusion—is based upon them. See Schlesinger, Sorensen, Salinger, Hilsman, Abel, Pachter, Horowitz, and most interestingly, Robert Kennedy.

20. Sorensen, op. cit., p. 696.
21. *The New York Times Book Review*, January 24, 1971, p. 28.
22. Yarmolinsky, op. cit.
23. Stevenson's role in both the Kennedy and Johnson administrations is the subject of my book *The Remnants of Power*.
24. Hilsman, op. cit., p. 198.
25. Sorensen, op. cit., p. 676.
26. Ibid., p. 678.
27. *The New York Times*, November 12, 1962.
28. Kennedy, *Public Papers*, 1962, p. 898.
29. Hilsman, op. cit., p. 199.
30. Schlesinger, op. cit., p. 803.
31. Sorensen, op. cit., p. 684.
32. Kennedy, *Public Papers*, 1962, pp. 806–809.
33. Robert Kennedy, op. cit., p. 62.
34. Ibid., p. 80.
35. The United Nations aspect of the crisis is covered in detail in my book *The Remnants of Power*.
36. United Nations Document S/PV 1025.
37. A. G. Mezerik, *Cuba and the United States* (New York, 1963), p. 143. This and other International Review Service publications contain invaluable chronologies and documents on international affairs.
38. Kennedy, *Public Papers*, 1962, p. 811.
39. Cited in Schlesinger, op. cit., p. 817.
40. Cited in Abel, op. cit., p. 144.
41. United Nations Press Release SG/1357, October 26, 1962, pp. 1–2.
42. United Nations Press Release SG/1358, October 26, 1962, pp. 1–2.
43. United Nations Press Release SG/1357, October 26, 1962, pp. 2–3.
44. United Nations Press Release SG/1358, October 26, 1962, pp. 2–3.
45. Robert Kennedy, op. cit., p. 86.
46. The direct quotations are from ibid. A larger proportion of the Khrushchev letter is carried in paraphrase in Abel, op. cit., pp. 180–86.
47. Robert Kennedy, op. cit., p. 94.
48. Ibid.
49. Kennedy, *Public Papers*, 1962, p. 813.
50. Robert Kennedy, op. cit., p. 108.
51. Ibid., p. 98.
52. Ibid., p. 109.
53. Ibid.
54. Hilsman, op. cit., p. 221.
55. See Mezerik, op. cit., p. 149.
56. Kennedy, *Public Papers*, 1963, p. 462.

Chapter Eight: *Détente*

1. Sorensen, op. cit., p. 745.
2. Ibid., p. 727.

3. Cited in Schlesinger, op. cit., p. 895.
4. Ibid.
5. Ibid., p. 897.
6. Ibid.
7. Kennedy, *Public Papers,* 1963, p. 104.
8. Ibid., p. 237.
9. Sorensen, op. cit., p. 730.
10. Kennedy, *Public Papers,* 1963, pp. 459–64.
11. Cited in Schlesinger, op. cit., p. 904.
12. Kennedy, *Public Papers,* 1963, p. 449.
13. Ibid., p. 524.
14. Schlesinger, op. cit., p. 904.
15. Kennedy, *Public Papers,* 1963, p. 606.
16. This skeptical view is not unique to I. F. Stone, but not one has presented it more brilliantly than he in his essential essay in the May 7, 1970, issue of *The New York Review of Books,* pp. 14–22. Anyone interested in the ABM, MIRV, SALT, and other alphabetical aspects of the largely futile attempts to end the nuclear arms race will find this essay invaluable. This does not mean there is no room for disagreement with some of Stone's theses.
17. See Schlesinger, op. cit., p. 912.
18. *United States Senate Hearings, August 22–27, 1963,* p. 105.
19. Schlesinger, op. cit., p. 912.
20. *Senate Hearings,* op. cit., pp. 274–75.
21. George McGovern, *A Time of War, a Time of Peace* (New York, 1968), p. 40. The speech was delivered September 16, 1963.
22. *Senate Hearings,* op. cit., pp. 404–405.
23. I. F. Stone, article in *The New York Review of Books,* May 7, 1970, p. 21.
24. Kennedy, *Public Papers,* 1963, p. 694.
25. United Nations General Assembly Resolution 1884 (XVIII), October 17, 1963.
26. Kennedy, *Public Papers,* 1963, p. 797.
27. Ibid., p. 861.

Chapter Nine: *Vietnam*

1. Kennedy, *Public Papers,* 1963, p. 652.
2. Kennedy, *Strategy,* p. 86.
3. Ibid., p. 89.
4. Hilsman, op. cit., p. 12.
5. Ibid., p. 426.
6. *The New York Times,* July 1, 1971.
7. Material from the *Chicago Sun-Times,* reprinted in the *New York Post,* June 24, 1971.
8. Schlesinger, op. cit., p. 542.
9. *The New York Times,* October 8, 1970. Quoted from *The Renewal,* the first volume of de Gaulle's three-volume *Memoirs of Hope.* It is a curious footnote to the Kennedy–De Gaulle meetings

that both Schlesinger and Sorensen skip lightly past this, the most significant part of the talks.

10. Jean Lacouture, *Vietnam: Between Two Truces* (New York, 1966), p. 89.
11. Hilsman, op. cit., p. 426.
12. Cited in Sidey, op. cit., p. 231.
13. Sorensen, op. cit., p. 632.
14. Cited in Sidey, op. cit., p. 212.
15. Cited in Schlesinger, op. cit., p. 544.
16. Cited in Schlesinger, op. cit., p. 547.
17. Sorensen, op. cit., p. 655.
18. *The New York Times,* July 1, 1971.
19. Sorensen, op. cit., p. 656.
20. A splendid discussion of this point and detailed quotations from the relevant NLF documents are provided by George McTurnan Kahin and John W. Lewis in their essential *The United States in Vietnam* (New York, 1967), pp. 132–37.
21. David Halberstam, *The Making of a Quagmire* (New York, 1964), p. 69.
22. This question is fully discussed in ibid., pp. 266–76. Salinger, op. cit., also provides a useful discussion, pp. 320–29.
23. Schlesinger, op. cit., p. 550.
24. Lacouture, op. cit., p. 78.
25. Ibid., p. 91.
26. Cited in Salinger, op. cit., p. 328.
27. Kennedy, *Public Papers,* 1963, p. 569.
28. Material from the *Los Angeles Times,* reprinted in the *New York Post,* June 24, 1971.
29. Sorensen, op. cit., p. 657.
30. *Los Angeles Times,* loc. cit.
31. Hilsman, op. cit., p. 496.
32. Kennedy, *Public Papers,* 1963, p. 652.
33. *Los Angeles Times,* loc. cit.
34. Kennedy, *Public Papers,* 1963, p. 660.
35. Sorensen, op. cit., p. 657.
36. Kennedy, *Public Papers,* 1963, p. 673.
37. Sorensen, op. cit., p. 659.
38. Hilsman, op. cit., p. 511.
39. Sorensen, op. cit., p. 659.
40. Lacouture, op. cit., p. 84.
41. Hilsman, op. cit., p. 518.
42. *Los Angeles Times,* loc. cit.
43. *Chicago Sun-Times,* loc. cit.
44. Schlesinger, op. cit., p. 998.
45. Kennedy, *Public Papers,* 1963, p. 846.
46. Although the figure customarily used is 16,000, Kennedy himself on September 12 and 25 said 25,000. Kennedy, *Public Papers,* 1963, pp. 673, 724.

Chapter Ten: *The Kennedy Years*

1. Schlesinger, op. cit., p. 1030.
2. Kennedy, *Public Papers,* 1961, p. 139.
3. Schlesinger, op. cit., p. 769.
4. Ibid., p. 771.
5. Ibid., p. 770.
6. John Bartlow Martin, *Overtaken by Events* (New York, 1966), p. 570.
7. Schlesinger, op. cit., p. 1001.
8. Ronald Radosh, *American Labor and United States Foreign Policy* (New York, 1970), pp. 393–405. This book is essential to an understanding of how the AFL-CIO was an eager tool of the CIA, not only in Latin America but throughout the world.
9. Schlesinger, op. cit., p. 775.
10. Ibid.
11. Ibid., p. 778.
12. Kennedy, *Public Papers,* 1963, p. 633.
13. Radosh, op. cit., p. 402.
14. Just such a book has recently been published: Jerome Levinson and Juan DeOnis, *The Alliance That Lost Its Way* (Chicago, 1970).
15. Sorensen, op. cit., p. 537.
16. Kennedy, *Public Papers,* 1961, p. 172.
17. Ibid., 1963, p. 617.
18. Ronald Steel, *Pax Americana* (New York, 1968), p. 218.
19. Schlesinger, op. cit., p. 792.
20. Steel, op. cit., p. 218.
21. Kennedy, *Public Papers,* 1962, p. 226.
22. Ibid., 1961, p. 134.
23. Ibid., p. 256.
24. Ibid., 1963, p. 552.
25. Schlesinger, op. cit., p. 850.
26. This is studied in detail in Richard E. Neustadt's *Alliance Politics* (New York, 1970).
27. Hilsman, op. cit., p. 346.
28. Kennedy, *Public Papers,* 1961, p. 38.
29. Ibid., p. 149.
30. Ibid., p. 546.
31. Schlesinger, op. cit., p. 479.
32. Kennedy, *Public Papers,* 1961, p. 658.
33. Ibid., p. 764.
34. Sorensen, op. cit., p. 665.
35. Schlesinger, op. cit., p. 904.
36. Kennedy, *Public Papers,* 1963, p. 846.
37. Hilsman, op. cit., p. 423.
38. Schlesinger, op. cit., p. 436.

Bibliography

Abel, Elie. *The Missile Crisis.* New York: Lippincott, 1966.

Aronson, James. *The Press and the Cold War.* New York: Bobbs-Merrill, 1971.

Barnet, Richard J. *Intervention and Revolution.* Cleveland: World, 1968.

Chase, Harold W., and Lerman, Allen H., eds. *Kennedy and the Press.* New York: Crowell, 1965.

Crankshaw, Edward. *Khrushchev: A Career.* New York: Viking, 1966.

Crown, James Tracy, and Penty, George P. *Kennedy in Power.* New York: Ballantine, 1961.

Donald, Aida DiPace, ed. *John F. Kennedy and the New Frontier.* New York: Hill & Wang, 1966.

Fall, Bernard B. *Anatomy of a Crisis.* Garden City, N.Y.: Doubleday, 1969.

Gettleman, Marvin E. and Susan, and Kaplan, Lawrence and Carol. *Conflict in Indochina.* New York: Random House, 1970.

Halberstam, David. *The Making of a Quagmire.* New York: Random House, 1964.

Halle, Louis J. *The Cold War as History.* New York: Harper & Row, 1967.

Hilsman, Roger. *To Move a Nation.* Garden City, N.Y.: Doubleday, 1967.

Horowitz, David. *The Free World Colossus.* New York: Hill & Wang, 1965.

Johnson, Haynes. *The Bay of Pigs.* New York: Norton, 1964.

Kahin, George McTurnan, and Lewis, John W. *The United States in Vietnam.* New York: Dial, 1967.

Kennedy, John F. *Public Papers of the President 1961–1963.* Washington: United States Government Printing Office, 1962, 1963, 1964.

————. *The Strategy of Peace.* New York: Harper, 1960.

Kennedy, Robert F. *Thirteen Days.* New York: Norton, 1969.

Lacouture, Jean. *Vietnam: Between Two Truces.* New York: Random House, 1966.

Larson, David L., ed. *The "Cuban Crisis" of 1962.* Boston: Houghton-Mifflin, 1963.

243

Levinson, Jerome, and DeOnis, Juan. *The Alliance That Lost Its Way.* Chicago: Quadrangle, 1971.

Martin, John Bartlow. *Overtaken by Events.* Garden City, N.Y.: Doubleday, 1966.

McNamara, Robert S. *The Essence of Security.* New York: Harper & Row, 1968.

Mecklin, John. *Mission in Torment.* Garden City, N.Y.: Doubleday, 1965.

Melman, Seymour. *Pentagon Capitalism.* New York: McGraw-Hill, 1970.

Mezerik, A. G. *Cuba and the United States.* New York: International Review Service, 1963.

Neustadt, Richard E. *Alliance Politics.* New York: Columbia University Press, 1970.

Pachter, Henry M. *Collision Course.* New York: Praeger, 1963.

Radosh, Ronald. *American Labor and United States Foreign Policy.* New York: Random House, 1970.

Salinger, Pierre. *With Kennedy.* Garden City, N.Y.: Doubleday, 1966.

Schlesinger, Arthur M., Jr. *A Thousand Days.* Boston: Houghton-Mifflin, 1965.

Sidey, Hugh. *John F. Kennedy, President.* New York: Atheneum, 1964.

Sorensen, Theodore C. *Decision-Making in the White House.* New York: Columbia University Press, 1964.

———. *Kennedy.* New York: Harper & Row, 1965.

———. *The Kennedy Legacy.* New York: Macmillan, 1969.

Steel, Ronald. *Pax Americana.* New York: Viking, 1968.

Thomas, Hugh. *Cuba: The Pursuit of Freedom.* New York: Harper & Row, 1971.

Ulam, Adam B. *Expansion and Coexistence: The History of Soviet Foreign Policy 1917–1967.* New York: Praeger, 1968.

United States Senate. Commerce Committee. (Senate, 87:1) *Senate Report 994, Part I. The Speeches, Remarks, Press Conferences and Statements of John F. Kennedy. September 13, 1961; Part III. The Joint Appearances of Senator John F. Kennedy and Vice President Richard M. Nixon and Other Campaign Presentations. December 11, 1961.*

Walton, Richard J. *The Remnants of Power: The Tragic Last Years of Adlai Stevenson.* New York: Coward-McCann, 1968.

Wicker, Tom. *JFK and LBJ.* New York: Morrow, 1968.

———. *Kennedy without Tears.* New York: Morrow, 1964.

White, Theodore H. *The Making of the President 1960.* New York: Atheneum, 1961.

Index

Abel, Elie, 132
Abraham, Richard, 88
Abramov, Alexander, 17
Acheson, Dean, 44, 53, 115, 119; and Berlin crisis, 77-78, 84-85, 86, 89, 92, 115
Africa, and U.S., 205-206, 218; see also Angola, Congo, Third World
Agency for International Development (AID), 31, 209
Alliance for Progress, 11, 71, 213-16
Alsop, Joseph, 25, 77
Alsop, Stewart, 119
American Revolution, 192
Anderson, Maj. Rudolf, Jr., 136, 138
Angola, 11, 203
anti-communism, see communism and anti-communism
arms race, 7, 8, 9, 61, 62, 63, 67, 68, 78, 83, 93, 102, 137, 145, 150, 153, 159; see also military buildup
Arnett, Peter, 183
Atomic Energy Commission, 157

Balaguer, Joaquin, 207, 208
Bartlett, Charles, 119
Batista, Fulgencio, 35, 37, 38
Bay of Pigs, see Cuba, Bay of Pigs
Belgium, and the Congo, 203
Berlin, 121, 123, 152; blockade (1948), 80, 90; crisis (1958-59), 83; crisis (1961), 27, 51, 58, 71, 74-93 passim, 95, 96, 97, 100, 104, 113, 115, 116, 141, 158, 164, 180, 234
Berlin Wall, 89, 90, 93
Bethe, Hans, 98
Bigart, Homer, 183
Bohlen, Charles, 82

Bosch, Juan, 209, 210
Boun Oum, 27
Bowles, Chester, 8, 43, 71, 230-31
Brezhnev, Leonid, 5, 86, 113, 159
British Guiana (Guyana), 33, 166, 208, 210-13, 233
Browne, Malcolm, 183, 184
Bundy, McGeorge, 58, 71, 117, 166, 197, 200
Burma, 11
Burnham, Forbes, 211, 212, 213

Cambodia, 172, 181; see also Indochina
Capehart, Homer, 108-109
Castro, Fidel, 35-48 passim, 54, 104-109 passim, 113, 132, 140, 163, 165, 166, 208
Castro, Raúl, 107
Central Intelligence Agency (CIA), 61, 108, 209; and British Guiana, 210, 212; and Cuba, 38, 40, 41, 43, 46, 47; and Laos, 13, 18, 30, 31; and Vietnam, 168, 173, 196
Central Treaty Organization (CENTO), 111, 160
Chen Chang, 225
Chen Yi, 226
Chiang Kai-shek, 11, 195, 226, 227
China, communist, 157, 163, 164, 188, 193, 201, 227-28; and Cuba, 36, 105, 106; and Laos, 12, 13, 15, 19, 28; and U.S.S.R., 105, 106, 153, 227; and U.S., 6, 9, 25, 30, 34, 121, 193, 224-29
China, Nationalist, 11, 225-26, 227
CIA, see Central Intelligence Agency
Clay, Gen. Lucius, 90